I0132297

Sustaining Employment and Wage Gains in Brazil

DIRECTIONS IN DEVELOPMENT
Human Development

Sustaining Employment and Wage Gains in Brazil

A Skills and Jobs Agenda

Joana Silva, Rita Almeida, and Victoria Strokova

WORLD BANK GROUP

© 2015 International Bank for Reconstruction and Development / The World Bank
1818 H Street NW, Washington DC 20433
Telephone: 202-473-1000; Internet: www.worldbank.org

Some rights reserved

1 2 3 4 18 17 16 15

This work is a product of the staff of The World Bank with external contributions. The findings, interpreta-tions, and conclusions expressed in this work do not necessarily reflect the views of The World Bank, its Board of Executive Directors, or the governments they represent. The World Bank does not guarantee the accuracy of the data included in this work. The boundaries, colors, denominations, and other information shown on any map in this work do not imply any judgment on the part of The World Bank concerning the legal status of any territory or the endorsement or acceptance of such boundaries.

Nothing herein shall constitute or be considered to be a limitation upon or waiver of the privileges and immunities of The World Bank, all of which are specifically reserved.

Rights and Permissions

This work is available under the Creative Commons Attribution 3.0 IGO license (CC BY 3.0 IGO) http://creativecommons.org/licenses/by/3.0/igo. Under the Creative Commons Attribution license, you are free to copy, distribute, transmit, and adapt this work, including for commercial purposes, under the following conditions:

Attribution—Please cite the work as follows: Silva, Joana, Rita Almeida, and Victoria Strokova. 2015. *Sustaining Employment and Wage Gains in Brazil: A Skills and Jobs Agenda.* Directions in Development. Washington, DC: World Bank. doi:10.1596/978-1-4648-0644-5. License: Creative Commons Attribution CC BY 3.0 IGO

Translations—If you create a translation of this work, please add the following disclaimer along with the attribution: *This translation was not created by The World Bank and should not be considered an official World Bank translation. The World Bank shall not be liable for any content or error in this translation.*

Adaptations—If you create an adaptation of this work, please add the following disclaimer along with the attribution: *This is an adaptation of an original work by The World Bank. Views and opinions expressed in the adaptation are the sole responsibility of the author or authors of the adaptation and are not endorsed by The World Bank.*

Third-party content—The World Bank does not necessarily own each component of the content con-tained within the work. The World Bank therefore does not warrant that the use of any third-party-owned individual component or part contained in the work will not infringe on the rights of those third parties. The risk of claims resulting from such infringement rests solely with you. If you wish to re-use a component of the work, it is your responsibility to determine whether permission is needed for that re-use and to obtain permission from the copyright owner. Examples of components can include, but are not limited to, tables, figures, or images.

All queries on rights and licenses should be addressed to the Publishing and Knowledge Division, The World Bank, 1818 H Street NW, Washington, DC 20433, USA; fax: 202-522-2625; e-mail: pubrights@worldbank.org.

ISBN (paper): 978-1-4648-0644-5
ISBN (electronic): 978-1-4648-0645-2
DOI: 10.1596/978-1-4648-0644-5

Cover photo: © Luis Alegre / ideiascompeso.pt. Used with permission. Further permission required for reuse.

Library of Congress Cataloging-in-Publication Data has been requested.

Contents

Boxes

Figures

Tables

Acknowledgments

This report is the product of a collaborative effort of a core team led by Joana Silva (Task Team Leader) with Rita Almeida (co-Task Team Leader) and Victoria Strokova (principal authors), and comprising Renata Gukovas, Rafael Prado Proença, and Nicole Amaral (data management and authors of background papers), with important contributions from Mary Hallward-Driemeier (on firm-level analysis); Ana Maria Oviedo (on labor regulations); Ulrich Hoerning (on labor programs); Maria Concepción Steta-Gándara (on social protection) and Maria de Fátima Amazonas (on productive inclusion); Chiara Monti (data analysis); and Lerick S. Kebeck, Marize Santos, Gabriel Barrientos, Renata Pereira De Mello, and Luiza Helena Guaraciaba (administrative support). The team worked under the guidance and is extremely grateful for the continuous support of Deborah Wetzel, Margaret Grosh, Magnus Lindelow, Reema Nayar, and Mansoora Rashid. We also thank our peer reviewers, Dena Ringold, Thomas Kenyon, Emanuela Di Gropello, and Carmen de Paula for their insightful comments, which substantially improved this volume.

Many colleagues provided useful inputs at different stages of this report, including Daniel Lederman, Omar Arias, Mark Dutz, Ronald Clark, Arvo Kuddo, Cristian Aedo, Diego Angel-Urdinola, Emmanuela Galasso, Claudia Baddini, Arup Banerji, David Evans, Barbara Bruns, Andre Loureiro, Rafael de Hoyos, Antonio Nucifora, Natalia Millan, and Reyes Aterido. The team is grateful to Mary A. Anderson for editing the manuscript and providing feedback on organization and content. Paola Scalabrin, Mark Ingebretsen, Andres Meneses, and Deborah Appel-Barker of the World Bank's Publishing and Knowledge Division coordinated book production including design, editing, typesetting, and printing. Candyce Da Cruz Rocha, Juliana Braga Machado, Mariana Kaipper Ceratti, Renata Pereira De Mello, Patricia da Camara, Marcela Sanchez-Bender, Mohamad Al-Arief, Gabriela Bastos, and Julia Pacheco assisted in communications and dissemination events.

This report builds on a series of background papers, further described in an annex to the Overview chapter. They include the following: "Employment Creation, Labor Productivity and Firms' Dynamics" by Aguinaldo Maciente, Joana Silva, and Renata Gukovas; "The Wage Returns and Employability of Vocational Training in Brazil: Evidence from Matched Provider-Employer Administrative Data" by Joana Silva, Luiz Caruso, and Renata Gukovas; "Earnings

Consequences of Labor Turnover: The Case of Brazil" by Eduardo Zylberstajn and Joana Silva; "Labor Market Institutions and Regulations in Brazil" by Ana Maria Oviedo; "Mapping of the Current Network of Active Labor Market Programs (ALMPs)" by Karla Marra, Jociany Luz, Joana Silva, and Renata Gukovas; "Mapping Institutions and Policies in Technical Education and Vocational Training (TVET) in Brazil" by Rita Almeida, Nicole Amaral, and Fabiana de Felicio; "Technical and Vocational Education and Training: Micro Evidence from Brazil" by Rita Almeida, Leandro Anazawa, Naércio Menezes-Filho, and Ligia Vasconcellos; "Impacts of the Bolsa Família Program on Education: A Regression Discontinuity Approach" by Joana Silva, Rafael Proença, and Flávio Cireno; "Insertion in Formal Employment among the Poor and Vulnerable" by Alexandre Leichsenring, Joana Silva, and Rafael Proença; and "Favela Pilot-Study on Productive Inclusion" by Francesco di Villarosa.

We are extremely grateful to several colleagues in Brazil in partnering institutions, who were critical in helping to build this report and the underlying analytical work. In particular, we are very thankful to our close partner—the Institute for Applied Economic Research (IPEA)—for ample support on the drafting of important sections of this report and background papers, as well as to the Ministry of Labor and Employment (MTE), the Ministry of Social Development and Fight against Hunger (MDS), the Ministry of Education (MEC), the National Confederation of Industry (CNI), and the University of São Paulo. We would especially like to thank Sergei Soares, Fernanda De Negri, Paulo Januzi, Aguinaldo Maciente, Paulo Nascimento, Flávio Cireno, Luiz Caruso, Renato da Fonseca, Luis Henrique Paiva, Marcelo Feres, Leticia Bartolo, Paula Montagner, Eduardo Zylberstajn, Naércio Menezes-Filho, Karla Marra, and Jociany Luz.

We would also like to thank colleagues from the World Bank for their insightful suggestions at various stages in developing the concept note and the drafts and presentations of the book. We are grateful to all of them, particularly Omar Arias, Emmanuela Galasso, Phillippe Leite, Michael Weber, Ciro Avitabile, Bob Rijkers, Stephanie Kuttner, Miriam Bruhn, John Giles, Jee-Peng Tan, Francisco Ferreira, Andreas Blom, Pablo Acosta, Roland Clark, and Aude-Sophie Rodella.

We also thank the participants of the many workshops, seminars, and consultations organized in Washington, DC; Brasilia; Rio de Janeiro; and São Paulo. In particular, we are extremely grateful to Sergei Soares, Fernanda De Negri, Aguinaldo Maciente, Paulo Nascimento, Divonzir Gusso, André Gambier Campos, Miguel Nathan Foguel, Carlos Henrique Corseuil, Renato da Fonseca, Luiz Caruzo, Jonas Bertucci, Ivanete Mendonca Araldi Maciente, Theresa Jones, Aléssio de Barros Trindade, Mariângela Abrahão, Karla Marra, Jociany Luz, Paula Montagner, Flávio Cireno, Daniel Ximenes, Leticia Bartolo, Luis-Henrique Paiva, Marconi Fernandes de Sousa, Janete Duarte, Rebeca Regina Regatieri, Leandro Anazawa, Naércio Menezes-Filho, and Ligia Vasconcellos. We would also like to thank all peer reviewers at the authors' workshops in Washington, DC, including Ronald Clark, Mark Dutz, Dena Ringold, Emanuela Di Gropello, Omar Arias,

Mary Hallward-Driemeier, Bob Rijkers, Ulrich Hoerning, Diego Angel-Urdinola, Miriam Bruhn, John Giles, Michael Weber, Emmanuela Galasso, Ciro Avitabile, Phillippe Leite, Claudia Baddini, Jee-Peng Tan, Andreas Blom, Pablo Acosta, and Eduardo Zylberstajn. We gratefully acknowledge the insightful comments and suggestions of these workshop participants.

About the Authors

Joana Silva is a senior economist in the World Bank's Office of the Chief Economist for Latin America and the Caribbean. Since joining the World Bank in 2007 in the Young Professionals Program, Ms. Silva has published several books and articles on a broad set of subjects including labor economics, international trade, education and skills, social safety nets, poverty, inequality, political economy of economic reforms, firm productivity and innovation policies, and the evaluation of social programs. Her research has been published in a variety of top general-interest and specialized journals, including the *Journal of International Economics, Economics Letters, Review of World Economics*, and *IZA Journal of Labor Policy*. Book titles authored or coauthored by Ms. Silva include *Inclusion and Resilience: The Way Forward for Social Safety Nets in the Middle East and North Africa*; and *Striving for Better Jobs: The Challenge of Informality in the Middle East and North Africa*. While at the Bank, she has led teams producing thematic flagship reports (such as the 2013 MENA Development Report); managed cross-sectoral lending projects (on labor, social protection, and private sector development); led policy dialogue on a wide range of countries; and authored analytical studies on the design and evaluation of social programs, labor market reforms, social welfare systems, the investment climate, and firm productivity. She holds a PhD in economics from the University of Nottingham. Before joining the World Bank, she also worked for the Globalization and Economic Policy Research Center at the University of Nottingham and for the Inter-American Development Bank.

Rita Almeida is a senior economist in the World Bank's Education Global Practice. Since joining the World Bank in 2002, Ms. Almeida has led policy dialogue on diverse economies, ranging from lower-income countries (such as Tunisia) to higher-income countries (such as Argentina, Brazil, Chile, Costa Rica, Panama, and Turkey). Her experience covers topics including labor market analysis, skills development policies, activation and graduation policies, labor market regulations, social protection for workers, firm productivity and innovation policies, and the evaluation of social programs. Ms. Almeida coauthored the book, *The Right Skills for the Job? Rethinking Training Policies for Workers*, which examines the effective design and implementation of skills development policies. Her work in the fields of development, labor economics, international economics, and industrial relations has been published in a variety of top general-interest and specialized journals, including *The Economic Journal, American Economic Journal: Applied Economics, Journal of International Economics, Labour Economics,* and *World Development.* Ms. Almeida holds a PhD in economics from Universitat Pompeu Fabra in Barcelona. She has been a fellow of the Institute for the Study of Labor (IZA) since 2003.

Victoria Strokova is an economist in the Jobs Cross-Cutting Solutions Area (CCSA) at the World Bank since September 2014, where she leads several jobs diagnostics and country engagements focused on identifying jobs challenges and solutions. Previously she worked in the Bank's Social Protection and Labor Units in the Latin America and the Caribbean Region, which she joined as a Young Professional in September 2013, and the Europe and Central Asia Region, where she worked as a consultant for three years. Her analytical and policy dialogue work has focused on social safety net spending and performance, activation policies and work incentives, and political economy of transfers and taxes. She has coauthored numerous country-specific research and policy papers and contributed to several poverty assessments, public expenditure reviews, and regional reports (including "Activation and Smart Safety Nets in the Western Balkans" and "Efficiency and Equity in Social Sector Spending in EU New Member States"). Ms. Strokova holds a master's degree in public policy from the University of Chicago, where she trained extensively in quantitative methods, including econometrics and program evaluation.

Abbreviations

ACP	academic and career plan of study
ALMP	active labor market program
BSM	Brasil Sem Miséria (Brazil without Extreme Poverty)
CAGED	General Register of Employed and Unemployed Individuals (Cadastro Geral de Empregados e Desempregados)
CDD	community-driven development
CLT	consolidation of the labor laws
CNI	National Confederation of Industry (Confederação Nacional da Indústria)
Enem	National High School Exam (Exame Nacional do Ensino Médio)
FGTS	Severance Indemnity Fund (Fundo de Garantia do Tempo e Serviço)
FIC	Initial and Continuing Training Programs (Formação Inicial e Continuada) [PRONATEC modality]
FIES	Financing of Higher Education Students (Fundo de Financiamento ao Estudante do Ensino Superior)
GDP	gross domestic product
GNI	gross national income
IAPs	individual action plans
INSS	National Institute of Social Security
IPEA	Institute for Applied Economic Research (Instituto de Pesquisa Econômica Aplicada)
LTU	long-term unemployment
M&E	monitoring and evaluation
MDS	Ministry of Social Development and Fight against Hunger (Ministério do Desenvolvimento Social e Combate à Fome)
MEC	Ministry of Education (Ministério da Educação)
MEI	Single Microentrepreneur Program (Microempreendedor Individual)

MTE	Ministry of Labor and Employment (Ministério do Trabalho e Emprego)
OECD	Organisation for Economic Co-operation and Development
PAA	Food Acquisition Program (Programa de Aquisição de Alimentos)
PES	public employment service(s)
PISA	Program for International Student Assessment
PME	Monthly Employment Survey (Pesquisa Mensal de Emprego)
PNAD	National Sample Survey of Households (Pesquisa Nacional por Amostra de Domicílios)
PNMPO	National Program for Targeted Productive Microcredit (Programa Nacional do Microcrédito Produtivo Orientado)
PROGER	Employment and Income Generation Program (Programa de Geração de Renda)
PRONATEC	National Program for Access to Technical Education and Employment (Programa Nacional de Acesso ao Ensino Técnico e Emprego)
PROUNI	University for All Program (Programa Universidade para Todos)
RAIS	Annual Social Information Report (Relaçao Anual de Informaçoes Sociai)
SEBRAE	Brazilian Micro and Small Business Support Service (Serviço Brasileiro de Apoio às Micro e Pequenas Empresas)
SENAC	National Commercial Training Service (Serviço Nacional de Aprendizagem Comercial)
SENAI	National Service for Industrial Education (Serviço Nacional de Aprendizagem Industrial)
SENAR	National Rural Training Service (Serviço Nacional de Aprendizagem Rural)
SINE	National Employment System (Sistema Nacional de Emprego)
SISTEC	National System of Vocational Education and Information Technology (Sistema Nacional de Informações da Educação Profissional e Tecnológica)
STEM	science, technology, engineering, and math
SUAS	Central Social Assistance System (Sistema Único de Assistência Social)
TEC	technical education [PRONATEC modality]
TVET	technical vocational education and training
UI	unemployment insurance

Overview

Summary of Findings and Discussion of Possible Reforms

Brazilian Labor Markets Have Performed Remarkably Well in the Past 15 Years

In the past 15 years, employment, labor market participation, and labor earnings have grown significantly in Brazil. Brazilian labor markets expanded greatly since 2002. Unemployment has declined (from 12.9 percent in 2002 to 4.9 percent in 2014), while employment and labor force participation have grown. Labor income grew by an average of 2.5 percent in real terms per year from 2002 to 2014 (IBGE 2014). In contrast with earlier periods, formal employment expanded greatly, exceeding informal employment since 2007.

Improved labor market outcomes have been the main driver of reductions in poverty and inequality. Not only did average labor market outcomes improve, but they improved the most among the poor. Real earnings also grew at a higher rate among the poor (Maciente, Silva, and Gukovas 2015). And so did formal labor market insertion, with gains among the poor driven by a particular group of workers: young workers who completed high school (Leichsenring, Silva, and Proença 2015). These pro-poor labor markets were the main driver of reduction in inequality and poverty.

Labor Productivity Growth Is Needed to Sustain Continued Wage Growth

Continued progress in employment and labor earnings will depend on achieving a first critical goal: *raising labor productivity*. Although wages have been growing, labor productivity growth (using aggregate and firm-level data) has been low (below both the Latin American and Caribbean regional average and the Organisation for Economic Co-operation and Development [OECD] average) and stagnant (with an average annual growth since 1995 of 1 percent) over the past 15 years.[1] Faster growth in wages than in labor productivity since 2004 generated an increasing gap between these two aggregates—in stark contrast to trends in the Group of Twenty (G20) advanced countries (ILO, OECD, and World Bank Group 2014). This implies rising unit labor costs, which erode the competitiveness of the tradable sector.

Today job creation is already slowing in Brazil. Net job creation has been in a downward trend since December 2012. Both the nonemployment (the working-age population who are out of work and not seeking jobs) and unemployment rates declined in parallel until December 2012 (Zylberstajn and Silva 2015). Since then, however, the nonemployment rate has been increasing. Looking ahead, labor productivity growth is key to sustain future wage increases and high employment.

To Sustain Poverty and Inequality Reduction, Brazil Must Focus on Improving Further the Job Prospects of the Poor

Continued improvements in the livelihoods of the poor will depend on achieving a second critical goal: *connecting the poor to better, more productive jobs*. In the current context of slower growth and stagnant labor productivity, sustaining the pro-poor earnings growth of the past 15 years is a challenge for four main reasons:

- Earnings increases at the bottom of the wage distribution were highly influenced by a minimum-wage policy that links its annual change to gross domestic product (GDP) growth.[2] In the current context of lower growth, high earnings increases through this channel might be more difficult.

- Brazil remains an unequal country, and the poor lag behind the nonpoor in terms of educational endowments and access to and ownership of capital and land. For example, the overwhelming majority of adults (18 and older) in the bottom income quintile have below-primary education (62.5 percent) compared with 40.4 percent nationally. Only 14.2 percent in the bottom quintile have completed secondary education, compared with 26.1 percent nationally. Finally, only 1.0 percent of those in the bottom quintile have completed tertiary education, compared with 10.1 percent nationally (based on IBGE 2002, 2013). These educational disadvantages take a long time to reverse[3] and make the mobility of poor workers across jobs as well as their access to and retention of high-productivity jobs harder, particularly in tighter labor markets.

- Converting higher skills into "sustainable" incomes is harder for the poor because they face a number of mutually reinforcing barriers to employability beyond a lack of technical skills. For example, most Brazilians (80 percent) rely on informal networks to find jobs (DIEESE 2011), and the poor are less likely than the rich to have networks that include well-connected, high-earning people. Another important factor that potentially limits labor force participation among the poor is lower access to child care: in 2013, only 15 percent of poor families (in the bottom two income quintiles) with children below 3 years old had access to child care, but 40 percent of rich families did (based on IBGE 2013).[4]

- The poor are most likely to work in sectors with bleaker prospects, such as agriculture and construction. Out of all rural jobs, 65 percent are in agriculture, and this share is even higher (82.4 percent) among the poor (based on IBGE 2013). Moreover, between 2008 and 2011 the poor increased their share of formal employment the most in the manufacturing and construction sectors, which are also declining (Leichsenring, Silva, and Proença 2015).

A Three-Layered Policy Approach Can Raise Labor Productivity and Connect the Poor to Better, More Productive Jobs

Achieving the two critical goals—*raising labor productivity* and *connecting the poor to better, more productive jobs*—requires a three-layered policy approach. The needed policies encompass sound economic growth policies, incremental reforms to skills development and labor policies, and revitalized productive inclusion policies for the urban and rural poor (figure O.1).

Sound policy fundamentals are key for economic growth and job creation. Policies conducive to growth are a necessary precondition for job creation, encompassing macroeconomic stability; an enabling business environment; a strong human capital base; firms that are innovative, adopt new technologies, and enter new markets; and a sound national infrastructure (World Bank 2013). A range of World Bank and IPEA work has shed light on many of these issues (for instance, Bruns, Evans, and Luque 2012; Evans and Kosec 2012; Gill 2002; de Negri and Cavalcante 2014), and an ongoing study is analyzing how reforms in different dimensions of the Brazilian business environment, including technology and innovation policies, can promote competitiveness (Dutz, forthcoming).

Figure O.1 A Three-Layered Policy Approach to Sustain Wage Growth and Poverty and Inequality Reductions in Brazil

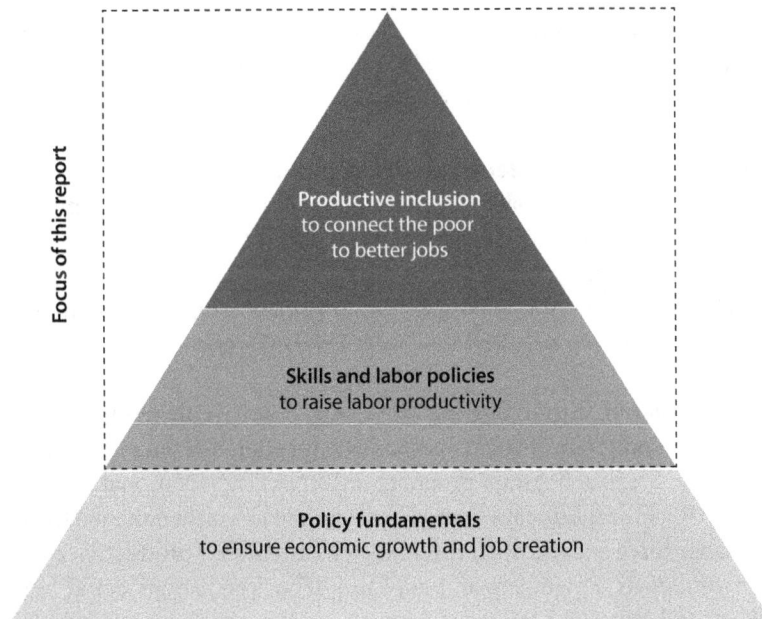

Source: Based on World Bank 2012.

The government implemented several recent reforms in these areas to reduce the cost of doing business, such as the reduction of electricity prices and certain tax exemptions for exporters. Recent policy also has focused on public-private partnerships to revamp ports and airports, recognizing the need to upgrade the country's infrastructure. Other sector-specific measures have been put in place to support domestic production and exports, some of them involving tax relief or credit expansion to specific sectors. This report argues that all these government channels for improving competitiveness and total factor productivity are relevant and still in need of policy reflection. However, they are not the main focus of the report.

Skills development and labor policies (including active labor market programs [ALMPs] and labor market regulations)[5] can help to raise labor productivity (Goal 1). Because growth alone might not be enough to sustain wage growth and reductions in poverty and inequality, it is essential to also focus on *jobs* (which can translate labor productivity gains into improved living standards) and *skills* (which can enhance employment opportunities and labor productivity).

The productive inclusion agenda is an important complement because it can help connect the poor to better, more productive jobs—requiring focused action and adaptation of skill and labor policies to the needs of the poor (Goal 2). *Inclusive* labor productivity growth is also critical to sustain both wage growth and reductions in poverty and inequality. For wage growth to be *sustained*, it must be accompanied by increased labor productivity and include areas where incomes have traditionally been low. For wage growth to be *pro-poor*, it must most benefit those with lower earnings and be accompanied by opportunities for the poor and disadvantaged to upgrade their own productivity and convert skill gains into sustainable incomes. Because the poor have specific challenges, the tasks of coordinating the existing (skills and jobs) services and tailoring them to the poor present their own sets of challenges and priorities.

Incremental Reforms Are Needed, Not New Frontiers

Achieving the two critical goals requires adjustments of design and implementation to existing skills and jobs policies. Brazil's rich set of skills and jobs programs covers many needs and groups. Consequently, the next-level challenges can be met on familiar terrain, not by forging new frontiers. This report contends that incremental changes are required in four key policy areas:

- *Skills development.* Strengthening the design and implementation of skills development programs linked to technical education and vocational training—particularly Brazil's flagship program, PRONATEC (National Program for Access to Technical Education and Employment)—could enhance the quality of the labor force and, through this channel, foster labor productivity (Goal 1).
- *Labor regulations.* Reviewing and adjusting labor regulations could help shift workers' and firms' incentives to encourage longer tenures, more hiring, and ultimately higher labor productivity (Goal 1).

- *Labor programs.* Strengthening the design, management, and monitoring and evaluation (M&E) systems of Brazil's National Employment System (SINE) and other ALMPs will improve job matches and better equip youth for jobs—ultimately reducing frictional unemployment for a given level of aggregate demand while also increasing the labor productivity and yield of small businesses (Goal 1).
- *Productive inclusion.* This policy area refers to programs that promote employability or income-earning opportunities for the poorest segments of the population in both urban and rural areas. Brazil's approach has been to make existing skills development, labor, agricultural, and rural programs more inclusive (and better connected to each other). Rather than creating new programs, the coverage of existing ones has been expanded to the poor, using the national registry of the poor and vulnerable (Cadastro Único) to target new beneficiaries.[6] The available programs range from training to support of self-employment, entrepreneurship, and family agriculture. Adapting the existing programs to the needs of the poor, diversifying the program supply, and strengthening the programs' M&E systems could better help the poor to connect to more productive jobs (Goal 2).

While the proposed reforms of *skills development, labor regulations,* and *labor programs* focus on enhancing these policies' contribution to raising labor productivity (Goal 1), the proposed *productive inclusion* reforms are geared toward making these policies more pro-poor (Goal 2).

Skills Development Programs to Help Workers Become More Employable and Productive

Brazil can continue to build upon the progress achieved in educational coverage and quality over recent decades not only to prepare a high-quality workforce but also to extend opportunities to the most vulnerable, who may lack relevant qualifications for an increasingly competitive labor market. Brazil's progress in expanding education coverage and quality has been extensively discussed and documented (Bruns, Evans, and Luque 2012). However, many challenges remain. For example, average schooling is only 8.4 years (completion of only lower-secondary education) and the educational quality is low, and 18.7 percent of 18- to 24-year-olds are neither in school nor at work (de Hoyos, Halsey, and Popova 2015). Within this context, technical vocational education and training (TVET), and in particular technical education, provides options for learning an applied vocation and for keeping at-risk and unmotivated youth in school through the upper-secondary level, while vocational training provides opportunities to adapt a low-qualified or unqualified labor force, update obsolete skills, and prepare workers for new opportunities in new or fast-growing sectors. Interestingly, the share of students enrolled in technical education at the upper-secondary level is low by international standards (13.5 percent of total upper-secondary enrollment, which is substantially below the 46 percent OECD average in 2011) (OECD 2012).

Since 2011, Brazil has invested significantly in TVET through the flagship program, PRONATEC. Government spending on skills development increased significantly with the creation and expansion of PRONATEC, the federal technical education and vocational training program.[7] The program offered 8.8 million training slots between 2011 and 2014, including both the secondary students enrolled in TVET and 5 million new slots for vocational training of the existing workforce. Importantly, PRONATEC has focused on reaching the poor and disadvantaged populations, with around 40 percent of the slots filled by Cadastro Único registrants (Brazil, Ministry of Social Development and Fight against Hunger 2013). PRONATEC changed the traditional panorama of TVET in Brazil, whereby technical education had primarily reached students of high socioeconomic backgrounds and vocational training was geared toward the needs of larger firms. For instance, since PRONATEC's creation in 2011, at the upper-secondary level alone, enrollments in technical education have grown by around 60 percent (based on IBGE 2010, 2013). PRONATEC has greatly expanded opportunities in Brazil not only for technical education but also for lifelong skills development, with short-duration courses representing most of the new slots created.[8] In addition to PRONATEC, postsecondary technical education has also grown significantly with recent support from the federal PROUNI[9] and FIES[10] programs.

Even though persistent weaknesses in the general education system may be hampering the TVET system's effectiveness, TVET in Brazil has several strong and well-designed features. Positive features of the TVET system include (a) a strong articulation of general and technical skills across tracks at the secondary level (Almeida et al. 2015; Almeida, Amaral, and Felicio 2015; Schwartzman and Moura Castro 2013); and (b) a well-coordinated set of diverse, short-duration courses that often yield good employability and productivity results (Silva, Gukovas, and Caruso 2015). But, as the general education system still faces multiple quality challenges (Bruns, Evans, and Luque 2012), the effectiveness of TVET programs may be limited by weak foundations of the general education system and limited opportunities for second-chance education programs.

Brazil could fine-tune the design and implementation of its TVET system, including PRONATEC, to enhance its efficiency and sustainability in producing a more productive workforce. The TVET system faces important challenges, including (for several providers) little coordination with the private sector in technical education (Almeida, Amaral, and Felicio 2015). Moreover, while Brazil has good administrative datasets and strong monitoring of technical education and vocational training programs through the National System of Vocational Education and Information Technology (SISTEC), these are not regularly used to track employability and inform policy. Anticipating a period of fiscal consolidation, PRONATEC's efficiency and labor market results are even more critical. Moreover, most PRONATEC expansion happened through the Sistema S (S System) network of course providers, whose trainings have high quality and returns (Silva, Gukovas, and Caruso 2015).[11] This expansion was anchored on the gratuity agreement between Sistema S and the government, establishing that

60 percent of total revenues from taxes directed at Sistema S be used to provide subsidized training. However, this allocation is now being met. Looking forward, the expansion will likely rely on a more diverse set of training providers, which will inevitably bring new challenges, including quality certification and accreditation issues (Almeida, Amaral, and Felicio 2015).

Selected design and implementation challenges provide concrete opportunities for incremental changes to ultimately strengthen the delivery of TVET and its focus on the skills needed for the labor market. Even though there is no "one-size-fits-all" solution to Brazil's complex TVET delivery challenges, key strategic priorities for PRONATEC and the general delivery of TVET in Brazil include the following:

- *Strengthening Monitoring and Evaluation (M&E) systems* (building on the country's strong administrative data) to measure results by tracking learning and labor market outcomes (employability and earnings increases) of trainees, systematically using that information to inform program expansion, and making it also available to students and trainees so they can make more informed decisions
- *Improving partnerships with the private sector and access to apprenticeships*, thus better aligning training offerings and content with employers' needs
- *Guaranteeing the quality and relevance of program content*, including through more innovative curricula and pedagogies, a strong attention, and articulation to, core foundational skills (cognitive, and socio-emotional); and stronger technical preparation for teachers and trainers, including greater linkage with sector experience
- *Making career guidance available* to support students' school-to-work transition and older trainees' sector or job redeployment

Although all of these reforms are important, promoting evidence-based policy making through better M&E systems is an essential first step to begin adjusting resources and program content depending on labor market needs. While the existing M&E systems (for example, SISTEC) represent an important first step, they do not focus on trainees' employability or earnings increases upon training completion. Without strong M&E systems that trace the impacts of TVET on trainees' labor market outcomes and knowledge acquired—and without using this information to inform policy making—PRONATEC will lack a solid mechanism for ensuring internal efficiency and of aligning course content with actual labor market needs.

Labor Regulations Reform to Support Firm Productivity While Also Protecting Workers

Brazil has a rich set of labor market regulations and institutions. Consolidated by the 1988 Constitution, current labor regulations and institutions are well established in Brazil and are based on the principles of universality, nondiscrimination, and workers' rights. The latter include worker protection against dismissals and the provision of income support in case of dismissal without just cause (through unemployment insurance [UI] and severance pay [FGTS]). Labor market regulations also include the minimum wage and its automatic adjustment rule that each year's increase must equal the GDP growth rate of two years prior. In addition, the constitution defined a set of mandated nonlabor costs (such as contributions to social insurance and labor-related taxes) that are applicable to formal workers, defined as "workers with carteira" (Oviedo 2015).[12]

Strengthening UI work and job-search incentives, reviewing nonwage labor costs, and improving efficiency in labor disputes resolution could help to shift workers' and firms' incentives to encourage longer tenures, more hiring, and ultimately higher labor productivity. Some areas of labor regulations in Brazil have been linked to distortions that are detrimental to labor market outcomes:

- *UI eligibility.* Job turnover in Brazil is high by international standards, and low job duration can decrease firms' incentives to invest in training. High turnover is a feature of both formal and informal labor markets (where workers are not entitled to UI) and in most cases (57 percent in 2013) is motivated by workers' reallocation to higher-paying jobs (Zylberstajn and Silva 2015). Still, separations in formal jobs are influenced by the design of UI, as they are more likely to happen around the thresholds of the minimum time required for UI eligibility and that exogenous increases in UI maximum benefit duration in Brazil led to falls in formal-sector reemployment rates due to offsetting rises in informal employment (Gerard and Gonzaga 2012).[13] In addition, UI has important fiscal implications, given that total UI spending tripled in the 2000s despite record low unemployment.
- *Mandated nonwage labor costs.* Brazil is also an outlier when it comes to nonwage labor costs such as social insurance expenditures and labor-related taxes. These expenditures represent 33 percent of labor costs in the formal sector versus the OECD average of about 20 percent (ILO 2014). Importantly, several additional mandated costs specific to Brazil make labor expenditures on formal employment soar even higher.[14] High nonwage labor costs may constrain formalization, firm growth, and ultimately labor productivity.
- *Labor dispute litigation.* Finally, the increasingly high number of labor court cases (more than 3 million in 2013) can hinder expedited decision making, ultimately reducing firms' incentives to hire new workers.

An important question moving forward is, how can labor regulations more effectively support firm productivity while best balancing protections and incentives for individuals? Labor regulation is one of the more difficult social policy areas, offering perhaps the fewest clear answers, and yet it is an issue of growing importance. As part of a broader social contract between the state and its citizens, labor regulations and institutions occupy a policy area where reforms must preserve protections and incentives for individuals. However, the agenda of labor productivity growth calls for efficient, agile workforce reallocations among skills and firms. This report highlights some agenda items based on their potential impact in moving workers' and firms' incentives toward longer tenures, more hiring, and ultimately higher labor productivity:

- *Integrating job-search requirements into UI eligibility* to encourage the unemployed to seek work more actively
- *Analyzing mandated nonwage nonlabor costs* to understand the effects of each (social security contributions, unemployment funds, labor-related taxes) and considering whether selected fine-tuning could more effectively support the desired social contract of worker protections and growth of formal sector employment and wages—part of a broader discussion on the adequacy and sustainability of the social security (pension) system
- *Reducing incentives for unnecessary labor disputes* while streamlining dispute resolution by creating automatic mechanisms for some types of labor disputes, revising and strengthening the mediation and negotiation mechanisms, and simplifying labor codes to reduce the scope for ambiguity and therefore litigation.

In addition to these reforms, it is important to recognize that although labor productivity affects the *path* of the minimum wage through the annual adjustment formula, that path also affects labor productivity. Brazil's minimum wage has almost doubled in real terms since 2002, which has helped to reduce poverty and inequality. This growth has been faster than in most Latin American and Caribbean countries, but its current level (as measured by the share of gross national income per worker) is in line with international comparators. The minimum-wage automatic adjustment rule in Brazil establishes that each year's increase be equal to the GDP growth rate of two years prior, which maintains a link to labor productivity. In view of slower GDP growth and tighter labor markets, achieving simultaneous minimum-wage expansion, high employment of low-skilled workers, and strong firm performance and competitiveness will require a focus on rising labor productivity (Goal 1).

Labor Market Programs to Strengthen the Workforce and Raise Business Productivity

Brazil has an opportunity to leverage its labor market programs and policies to promote more effective job matches, address skill gaps, and support entrepreneurship. Brazil, like most other middle-income countries, has a range of ALMPs that aim to facilitate job searching and matching, improve employability, and connect people to more productive employment, as well as several financial and nonfinancial programs and services to promote self-employment and growth of micro and small enterprises.[15] In addition to PRONATEC's vocational training courses, Brazil's primary ALMPs include its labor intermediation services through the National Employment System (SINE), programs that specifically support unemployed and vulnerable youth, and other training programs such as professional training for unemployment benefit recipients (Bolsa Formação). Finally, Brazil has been a pioneer in promoting the "solidarity economy" (Economía Solidaria). In all of these areas, Brazil has invested in programs and policies that address the key challenges identified in this report (see Marra et al. 2015).

However, improvements to several areas could help to achieve better outcomes. Several OECD and Latin American countries implemented major reforms to public employment services to focus them more on the job placement rates of their clients. Such a reform could improve SINE's results in Brazil. Similarly, youth programs could be further strengthened by adding "soft skills" (personal skills) and on-the-job components (in the workplace) to training. Entrepreneurship programs, in turn, could be better coordinated to avoid fragmentation and better linked to programs and complementary services to maximize their impact. Overall, given the wealth of available information and the innovative nature of active labor market policies (including Economía Solidaria programs that support urban and rural cooperatives), strengthening of monitoring and evaluation systems for regular follow-up on uptake and results of the various programs could be a powerful tool for their improvement.

To further foster labor productivity, it is necessary to adapt and refocus ALMPs and entrepreneurship support policies around their key objectives and to strengthen their M&E systems. Specifically, *more-efficient public employment services* could support better, faster job searches and produce better job matches. *Higher-quality youth programs and policies* could better equip unemployed youth for jobs and provide firms with better-prepared workers. *More-coordinated, more-effective entrepreneurship programs* could promote earnings growth and increase small-business productivity, thus increasing microentrepreneurs' earnings. Strengthening the design, management, and M&E systems of SINE and the ALMPs could improve job matches, better equip youth for jobs, and increase the productivity of small businesses—ultimately promoting firms' and workers' overall productivity. Achieving these goals will require commitment to several key priorities:

- *Adopting a placement-focused management approach in SINE* by (a) introducing client profiling and placement-focused case management; (b) strengthening services for businesses that seek low-skilled workers; (c) outsourcing of certain SINE functions to private sector providers; and (d) using results-based reimbursements
- *Adding both on-the-job and "soft-skills" components to youth-targeted ALMPs* to better equip unemployed youth for jobs, including links between training and apprenticeships (for example, by redesigning the "Apprentice Law," under which firms have hired only 23 percent of the number mandated)
- *Improving the coordination among various entrepreneurship support programs* by (a) establishing more effective links between financial and nonfinancial support programs, as well as links with other labor market program services, to

promote small-business productivity; and (b) by reviewing and consolidating fragmented programs to improve efficiency

- *Ensuring that M&E systems provide adequate data* on SINE's placement rates, youth programs' results on beneficiaries' earnings and employability, and entrepreneurship support on business survival, for evidence-based program expansion and design adjustment.

Although all these reforms are critical, reform of SINE emerges as a top priority to improve overall ALMP system performance. A reformed SINE can play an integrative role across different programs and services. International experience shows that public employment services are the lowest-cost ALMP intervention and can be particularly effective in increasing placements among the poor. They can also refer the poor to other needed services (not just training). In Brazil, SINE can significantly improve the overall system's efficiency by adopting the approach that the service it provides is *placement*, referring a person to training only if not placed in a job. Countries such as Australia, Mexico, and the United Kingdom have faced similar design challenges and, as this report describes in detail, have achieved important results with this type of reform. Brazil has rich administrative data from the Annual Social Information Report (RAIS) and resources such as the "More Employment portal" (Portal Mais Emprego) for job search, and could use them to better help beneficiaries of labor market programs access jobs and track their employment outcomes and further contribute to this important reform.

Productive Inclusion Policies to Better Connect the Poor with More Productive Jobs

To expand the opportunities and earnings of the poor, the government launched "productive inclusion" policies and programs in 2011 as a next step of its social assistance policy. Since the 2000s, social assistance in Brazil has focused on finding the poor, reaching them, and helping their children. This effort included, for example, setting up the flagship conditional cash transfer program Bolsa Família (the biggest in the world) and a strong network of social assistance centers. As a next step in 2011, the policies also started to focus on connecting the poor to jobs. In this spirit, the government launched the (rural and urban) "productive inclusion" axis of the "Brazil without Extreme Poverty" (Brasil Sem Miséria, BSM) Plan in 2011 (Brazil, Ministry of Social Development and Fight against Hunger 2013).[16] This axis fosters the participation and inclusion of the poor in the economic arena (employment or other income-generating activities). It thereby helps the poor to improve their own productivity and convert it into sustainable incomes. Brazil's approach in this policy area has been to make existing skills, labor, agricultural, and rural development programs more inclusive and better connected to each other. The main focus, as opposed to creating new programs for the poor, has been on expanding the coverage of existing ones, using the national registry of the poor and vulnerable (Cadastro Único) to select new beneficiaries. The Bolsa Família programs and operating systems were instrumental in launching and linking complementary social assistance policies under the BSM umbrella framework. Similarly, expanding the network of social assistance centers further promoted the integration of social policy actions and expanded the services and support available.

Urban and rural areas require specific productive inclusion approaches based on the differing nature of their economic activities. In urban areas, the approaches focus on training (through 40 percent of the PRONATEC slots allocated to the poor) and support to microentrepreneurs (through incentives to formalization and microcredit programs). In rural areas, the approaches focus on providing integrated interventions to support family agriculture. Rural productive inclusion focuses on family agriculture and includes the provision of three types of support: (a) microcredit and matching grants to improve agriculture production, (b) technical assistance, and (c) improved access to market through public procurement and private productive alliances.

Promoting employability and earnings opportunities for the poor brings new challenges but also encouraging results. Compared with the Brasil Sem Miséria income support axis (through Bolsa Família), the productive inclusion axis involves a greater range of programs that require coordination across a wider range of agencies and whose results depend not only on more-complex household behaviors but also on the broader economic context. Despite these challenges, new evidence in this report shows that incorporating productive inclusion into Brazil's overall skills and jobs agenda holds great promise. For example, in spite of lower socioeconomic backgrounds, subsidized PRONATEC graduates who complete vocational training and find formal jobs have the same or better returns than nonsubsidized students (Silva, Gukovas, and Caruso 2015). However, results also show that a smaller share of PRONATEC graduates than non-PRONATEC graduates find formal jobs within three or six months, calling for better coordination of training with SINE, and with SEBRAE[17] and technical assistance support to entrepreneurship.

Brazil has been a pioneer in this area, innovating in ways that have inspired many other countries. Rather than redesigning its flagship income support program (Bolsa Família), Brazil complemented it through the productive inclusion axis of Brasil Sem Miséria, which made existing educational, agricultural, and rural development programs more inclusive. Existing social assistance targeting and management tools (such as Cadastro Único) were used to identify beneficiaries and target the complementary support. In addition, it promoted integration and coordination of policies, programs, and actions between the different sectors and across the federal, state, and municipal levels. Brazil's innovation—linking social assistance with skills (through PRONATEC) and with agricultural and rural development (through microcredit and matching grants, technical assistance, and public procurement)—is closely watched by countries facing similar challenges, such as Mexico and Peru.

In urban areas, improving productive inclusion involves strengthening and diversifying programs beyond training and better linking social assistance with ALMPs such as SINE's intermediation services, entrepreneurship support, and

start-up incentives. Because the poor face diverse employability challenges, more effective productive inclusion will involve not only traditional skills development but also a comprehensive integration of those programs with (a) added "soft skills" training (including communication, perseverance, and conflict resolution skills); (b) apprenticeships and other hands-on training components; and (c) placement services that better serve their needs. In short, the goal is to better link social assistance not only to training (such as through PRONATEC) but also to Brazil's several ALMPs, including SINE's intermediation services as well as entrepreneurship support and start-up incentives provided by SEBRAE (Brazilian Micro and Small Business Support Service) and others.

In addition, a more complete set of programs and intersectoral coordination will allow social assistance workers to increasingly refer beneficiaries to labor programs, follow up with them to avoid dropout, and address gaps in services to the poor that affect their employability. Given the diverse profiles and needs of social assistance beneficiaries, the availability of a more complete set of interventions beyond PRONATEC could strengthen social workers' role, thus better leveraging their presence on the ground, and their knowledge and relationship with those in need, in the productive inclusion agenda. Beyond the link of social assistance with labor programs, addressing gaps in other types of social services is also key. For example, despite advances in the universalization of child care for children ages four years and older, gaps remain in poor households' access to child care (for younger children), other social services, or psychosocial support—gaps that significantly hamper the employability of the poor. Brazil has programs in all these areas, but it is worth considering whether they are present in the right balance and quality, and importantly, whether they are adequately integrated and sequenced for each client.

Brazil's programs that promote employability or income-earning opportunities for the poorest segments of the urban population lack M&E systems that can regularly and systematically trace the results and performance of the full range of programs. Given the multifaceted set of employability challenges facing the poor, fostering their inclusion in more productive jobs requires data on the programs' skills acquisition and employment outcomes, including the trainees' or beneficiaries' increased employability, wages, and job quality. Government efforts to cross administrative information from the Ministry of Education's SISTEC (on PRONATEC) and registries of Single Microentrepreneur (MEI) and Crescer program beneficiaries with Cadastro Único have been key to understanding the reach of individual programs among the poor. A new poverty panel and module on the National Sample Survey of Households (PNAD) are also important steps forward. But strong M&E systems that can track the impact of individual programs and the performance of the overall urban productive inclusion system are lacking.

Refocusing this broader portfolio of urban productive inclusion programs around the objective of labor market insertion and increased earnings could improve the whole system's efficiency. This report argues that the path forward on productive inclusion will be to address next-level challenges on familiar terrain, not new frontiers. Toward the goal of diversifying support and making existing programs more efficient and sustainable, key strategic areas include the following:

- *Adapt public employment services (SINE) and other ALMPs to better serve the poor*, such as through better alignment of services with beneficiary profiles and local labor markets, *and diversify urban productive inclusion beyond PRONATEC* through synergies with these adapted programs
- *Expand support to address employment barriers beyond technical skills* by adding soft-skills and more hands-on components to PRONATEC while increasing students' or trainees' accessibility to child and elder care, transportation subsidies, night courses, and other support for the poor
- *Strengthen M&E systems* to provide adequate data on the job placement rates of trainees who completed the courses and on earnings or wage increases associated with program participation, as well as business survival and expansion linked with entrepreneurship support, thus enabling evidence-based program expansion and design adjustment

In *rural areas*, improving productive inclusion involves increasing the quality and efficiency of the current assistance model of expanding the coverage of existing agricultural and other rural development programs for the poor. Workers in family agriculture are a diverse group in terms of their experience (varying types of agricultural activities), and the impact of assistance is likely to depend on these aspects. However, although support of employment and productivity in family agriculture will increase incomes for many, for others upward mobility will mean moving to the nonagriculture sector. In this context, training and entrepreneurship programs adapted to their skills and experience will increase the returns to their assets, supporting them in moving to better jobs while improved educational foundations can give the extra push. Furthermore, although the existing rural productive inclusion model is comprehensive, it lacks M&E systems to trace its success. The lack of data on programs' impact on the earnings and business survival of beneficiaries poses an important constraint on their expansion and quality because such information could play a key role in enhancing the cost-effectiveness and impact of these interventions. This is particularly important in this area where Brazil has pioneered many of the interventions and information on the type of service that is most effective for the targeted population (for example, benchmarking technical assistance versus other types of interventions). In the overall context of rural productive inclusion, key strategic areas include the following:

- *Establish M&E systems* to measure programs' results on beneficiaries' earnings and business survival and use this information to adapt management approaches and institute results-based reimbursements
- *Introduce profiling of family farmers* (including their experience in different types of agricultural activities) and use the results to decide how to best allocate benefits

- *Continue to encourage use of Cadastro Único to target expanded coverage of rural development and agriculture programs* among the poor
- *Diversify support aimed at enhancing access to markets* for the goods produced by poor farmers beyond the quotas for public procurement
- *Promote private sector partnerships,* including with the financial system, to improve access to credit and technology
- *Adapt and improve access to rural entrepreneurship (microenterprise) programs* and to hands-on, community-based training and skills certification to enhance people's productivity

Report Objectives

This report aims to meet two broad objectives: collect new evidence and propose incremental policy reforms. First, it assembles new evidence and data to inform and update policy makers, academics, and other stakeholders on Brazilian employment growth and skill use as well as the performance of existing education and labor policies. Second, it facilitates and informs the policy debate by advancing feasible policy options to increase employment and productive inclusion. To those ends, the report addresses the questions described in annex table OB.1. The report summarizes the findings of 10 background papers produced as part of this activity in partnership with Brazilian government and private agencies including the Institute for Applied Economic Research (IPEA),[18] the Ministry of Labor and Employment (MTE), the Ministry of Social Development and Fight against Hunger (MDS), the National Confederation of Industry (CNI) (listed with abstracts in the annex table OA.1) and puts them in the context of the broader labor literature.

Moreover, the report provides an international context for Brazil's skills and jobs challenges. It benchmarks Brazil against other countries while also compiling and summarizing the findings and discussion from the in-depth policy and technical papers prepared as background for this report. In addition to its original research, the report reviews and incorporates recent findings from other World Bank teams, IPEA researchers, and other think tanks and academic institutions in Brazil.

Report Structure

Chapter 1, "Main Achievements and Remaining Challenges," describes the main strides of labor markets in Brazil in the past 15 years and identifies the key challenges to prioritize: (a) stagnant labor productivity, and (b) limited access to and retention of better, more productive jobs among the poor.

Chapter 2, "Skills Development Programs to Help Workers Become More Employable and Productive," assesses the sustainability and effectiveness of Brazil's existing professional and technical education system. It benchmarks key indicators against those of other countries and identifies gaps and areas for improvement. It proposes an agenda for reform and illustrates how other countries have dealt with similar challenges.

Chapter 3, "Labor Regulations Reform to Support Firm Productivity While Also Protecting Workers" reviews current labor regulations and institutions in Brazil. Using examples from other countries, it proposes an agenda of incremental policy changes that could more effectively support firm productivity while maintaining worker protection.

Chapter 4, "Labor Market Programs to Strengthen the Workforce and Policies to Raise Small-Business Productivity," assesses an array of active labor market programs (ALMPs) in Brazil and discusses what adjustments may be needed to more effectively connect job seekers to jobs, promote youth employability, and raise the productivity of small businesses, following examples from best international practices.

Chapter 5, "Productive Inclusion Policies to Better Connect the Poor with More Productive Jobs," assesses existing productive inclusion policies and discusses ways of adjusting them to improve results for the urban and rural poor.

Annex OA, "Background Papers," includes a table that supplements the main text of this Overview chapter. Table OA.1, as mentioned earlier, lists and provides abstracts for the 10 background papers produced during the preparation of this report. *Annex OB, "Summary Skills and Jobs Agenda for Brazil, by Program Area,"* in its table OB.1, presents the main questions and answers that the report addresses in each chapter. As the table shows, while chapters 2, 3, and 4 focus on the goal of raising labor productivity, chapter 5 focuses on how the policies discussed in the preceding chapters could be adapted specifically to achieve the goal of connecting the poor to better, more productive jobs.

Annex OA: Background Papers List

Table OA.1 Background Papers List

Firms' Growth and Skill Use

Title: Employment Creation, Labor Productivity, and Firms' Dynamics [research paper]
Partner institution: IPEA
Authors: Aguinaldo Maciente (IPEA), Joana Silva (WB), and Renata Gukovas (WB)
Abstract: This paper describes the types of firms that registered the largest employment creation and their experience with changes in their workforce occupations and skills. It uses data from the Brazilian matched employer-employee social security records (RAIS) merged with customs and manufacturing census (PIA) data.

Title: The Wage Returns and Employability of Vocational Training in Brazil: Evidence from Matched Provider-Employer Administrative Data [research paper]
Partner institution: SENAI
Authors: Joana Silva (WB), Renata Gukovas (WB), and Luiz Caruso (SENAI)

table continues next page

Table OA.1 Background Papers List *(continued)*

Abstract: The paper investigates the impact of vocational training (SENAI) on wages of graduates and assesses heterogeneity across course modalities. It also evaluates whether beneficiaries of subsidized PRONATEC training have lower returns and insertion in formal jobs than other students. It uses data from RAIS merged with trainee-level SENAI records.

Labor Regulations

Title: Earnings Consequences of Labor Turnover: the Case of Brazil [research paper]

Partner institution: Fundação Instituto de Pesquisas Econômicas/Universidade de São Paulo (FIPE/USP)

Authors: Eduardo Zylberstajn (FIPE/USP) and Joana Silva (WB)

Abstract: Although unemployment reached its historical minimum, spending on unemployment insurance (UI) tripled in the 2000s and the labor turnover rate increased, reaching 55 percent among formal workers. This paper aims at reconciling both sides of this paradox, showing that UI expenditure growth is explained by the growth of formal employment and wages, job turnover is even higher in the formal sector (where UI is not an issue), and most turnover was in fact reallocation to higher-paying jobs, compatible with a heated labor market.

Title: Labor Market Institutions and Regulations in Brazil [policy paper]

Author: Ana Maria Oviedo (WB)

Abstract: This paper describes the main labor market institutions and regulations in Brazil, highlighting some key challenges going forward. It discusses a reform agenda to allow workers to make better, longer-lasting matches and to encourage unemployed workers to reenter employment faster.

Active Labor Market Programs: TVET and International Best Practices

Title: Mapping of the Current Network of Active Labor Market Programs (ALMPs) [policy report]

Partner institution: Ministry of Labor and Employment (MTE)

Authors: Karla Marra (MTE), Jociany Luz (MTE), Joana Silva (WB), and Renata Gukovas (WB)

Abstract: Active labor market programs (ALMPs) play an important role in leveraging opportunity in Brazil. This report systematically describes existing ALMP programs, detailing their objectives, key design and implementation features, main operational challenges, and how other countries have dealt with similar issues and options to enhance M&E.

Title: Mapping Institutions and Policies in Technical Education and Vocational Training (TVET) in Brazil [policy report]

table continues next page

Table OA.1 Background Papers List *(continued)*

Partner institution: METAS

Authors: Rita Almeida (WB), Nicole Amaral (WB), and Fabiana de Felicio (METAS)

Abstract: In Brazil since 2011 there was a significant expansion of TVET through the national flagship program, PRONATEC. This report describes the design and delivery of PRONATEC, taking a critical view of upcoming opportunities. It shares international best practices on selected operational issues identified as strategic bottlenecks.

Title: Technical and Vocational Education and Training: Micro Evidence from Brazil [research paper]

Partner institutions: Insper/USP and Itau-Social

Authors: Rita Almeida (WB), Leandro Anazawa (USP), Naercio Menezes-Filho (Insper/USP), and Ligia Vasconcellos (Itau-Social)

Abstract: This paper analyzes the wage returns of completing TVET courses compared with the general education track, for similar years of education. Exploring data from PNAD, it quantifies the wage gains associated with the different types of courses. This paper is complemented by a short note that profiles the students across the different modalities and returns.

Education and Labor Trajectories of the Poor

Title: Impacts of the Bolsa Família Program on Education: A Regression Discontinuity Approach [research paper]

Partner institution: Ministry of Social Development and Fight against Hunger (MDS)

Authors: Joana Silva (WB), Rafael Proença (WB), and Flávio Cireno (MDS)

Abstract: This paper investigates the impacts of the Bolsa Família program on the education trajectories and school performance of beneficiaries. It uses detailed administrative records from the program payment records and from the registry of the poor and vulnerable in Brazil (Cadastro Único), matched with the education census and national student test scores.

Title: Formal Employment Insertion among the Poor and Vulnerable [research paper]

Authors: Alexandre Leichsenring (consultant), Joana Silva (WB), and Rafael Proença (WB)

Abstract: This paper analyzes the inclusion of Bolsa Família beneficiaries in the formal labor market and compares it with the formal employment insertion of the nonpoor. It uses data from Ministry for Social Development and Fight against Hunger administrative records merged with administrative data from

table continues next page

Table OA.1 Background Papers List *(continued)*

the Ministry of Labor and Employment on formal employment in Brazil (RAIS) for the period of 2008–11.

Title: Favela Pilot-Study on Productive Inclusion [policy report]

Partner institution: Instituto Pereira Passos (IPP)

Author: Francesco di Villarosa (consultant)

Abstract: This report describes the results of the pilot study of productive inclusion programs in three favelas in Rio de Janeiro, using information collected during stakeholder consultations and field interviews of beneficiaries. It unveils key challenges and opportunities emerging from the operations of PRONATEC and other ALMPs in favelas.

Annex OB: Summary Skills and Jobs Agenda for Brazil, by Program Area

Table OB.1 Summary Skills and Jobs Agenda for Brazil, by Program Area

Overall question: How can Brazil sustain employment and wage gains? Which reforms in skills and labor policies could help?		
CHAPTER 1: Brazilian Labor Markets: Main Achievements and Remaining Challenges **What is the panorama of labor markets in Brazil and the challenges to prioritize?**		
Brazilian labor markets have performed remarkably well in the past 15 years, and improvements in labor market outcomes have been the main driver of reduction in poverty and inequality. Today, however, job creation is slowing, and continued progress in employment and labor earnings will depend on addressing two critical challenges: (1) low and stagnant labor productivity, and (2) limited access to and retention of better, more productive jobs among the poor.		
IN SEARCH OF RAISING LABOR PRODUCTIVITY (GOAL 1)		
CHAPTER 2: Skills Development Programs to Help Workers Become More Employable and Productive	**CHAPTER 4: Labor Market Programs to Strengthen the Workforce and Policies to Raise Small-Business Productivity**	**CHAPTER 3: Labor Regulation Reform to Support Firm Productivity While Also Protecting Workers**
Policy concern: Are the technical and vocational skills in which people are being educated or trained increasing workers' employability and productivity?	*Policy concern:* How can public employment services be more effective in connecting job seekers to jobs?	*Policy concern:* How can labor regulations more effectively support firm productivity while best balancing protections and incentives for individuals?
Analysis: In general, wage returns to TVET are large. However, there is substantial heterogeneity across contents and providers. There are also concerns about the share of graduates working outside their fields of study as well as about limited hands-on experience and the lack of soft skills in the curricula.	*Analysis:* SINE placement rates are relatively low by international standards (12% vs. 36% in Mexico) and only 23% of vacancies offered by firms were filled. Existing M&E systems and management model are not focused on placement rates as the key outcome.	*Analysis:* Three stylized facts are in need of attention. First, job turnover is high. This can decrease investment in training, therefore reducing labor productivity. UI spending has tripled since 2002 despite record low unemployment. Although there is no single solution to increase job attachment, increasing the minimum employment duration for UI eligibility can reduce spending, but coverage among the low-skilled will also decrease. Second, Brazil's high nonwage labor costs (second to Sweden in the OECD) can hurt firms' investment in innovation and training and promote firm exit, further hurting labor productivity. Third, there is an increasingly high number of disputes reaching labor courts every year (3 million cases in 2013). Reducing incentives for unnecessary labor disputes while streamlining dispute resolution can cut administrative costs and waiting times.
Recommendations: Policies need to focus on making PRONATEC more efficient and sustainable by • Strengthening M&E systems to trace outcomes and support program expansion; • Improving partnerships with the private sector and access to apprenticeships;	*Recommendations:* Policies need to focus on strengthening SINE to facilitate job searches and matches by adopting a management approach that is more focused on placements (including the introduction of client profiling, strengthened services for businesses that demand low-skilled workers, and use of results-based reimbursements).	
	Policy concern: Can the current design of the "Apprentice Law" and other youth-targeted programs be improved to increase their impact on equipping youth for jobs?	
	Analysis: The Apprentice Law establishes a minimum 5% apprentices-to-workforce ratio, but compliance is low (firms have filled only 23% of the mandated number of apprenticeship positions). A better understanding of business needs, the pool of candidates, and the benefits for youth is key. The impact of existing youth-targeted	

table continues next page

Table OB.1 Summary Skills and Jobs Agenda for Brazil, by Program Area *(continued)*

• Guaranteeing the quality and relevance of contents, including through innovative curricula and pedagogies and stronger technical preparation for teachers; and • Making career guidance available to support students' school-to-work transition and older trainees' sector or job redeployment.	programs can be improved if they are combined with on-the-job and "soft skills" training. Currently these programs tend to be small scale and focus on classroom training. *Recommendations:* For increasing impact, evaluating and redesigning the "Apprentice Law" by setting more realistic requirements could be valuable. Addressing the causes of low compliance, including introducing more flexibility across sectors or firm types and incentive packages, could give firms more incentive to recruit apprentices. In other youth-targeted ALMPs, including on-the-job and "soft skills" components as well as better links between training and apprenticeships could better equip unemployed youth for jobs. *Policy concern:* How can entrepreneurship and self-employment support more systematically promote the productivity of small businesses? *Analysis:* Brazil's rich set of entrepreneurship programs (both financial and nonfinancial support) are not always targeted at the micro and small businesses. Coordination among various programs could be improved and overlaps identified and reduced. *Recommendations:* Better coordination of entrepreneurship support programs would promote small-business productivity by (a) establishing more effective links between financial and nonfinancial support and with other labor market programs and services, and (b) reviewing and consolidating fragmented programs to improve efficiency. *Policy concern:* How to strengthen existing ALMP's M&E systems? *Recommendations:* Leveraging and strengthening current monitoring systems to focus on tracking outcomes and results is key to be able to guide policies including decisions on program scale-up or end. This can be achieved by a) introducing indicators on employment outcomes (wage increases, placement rates, and business survival rates) in addition to inputs and outputs; b) conducting periodic evaluations; c) developing rigorous impact evaluations of strategic programs; and d) introducing or upgrading M&E systems where they are weak or don't exist.	*Recommendations:* Reforms to the design of labor regulations could eliminate distortive disincentives for workers and businesses by • Integrating job-search requirements into UI eligibility; • Reducing incentives for unnecessary labor disputes while streamlining dispute resolution by creating automatic mechanisms for some types of labor disputes, and revising and strengthening the mediation and negotiation mechanisms; and • Analyzing mandated nonwage labor costs to understand the effects of each (social security contributions, unemployment funds, labor-related taxes) and considering whether selected fine-tuning could more effectively support the desired social contract of worker protections and growth of formal sector employment and wages.

table continues next page

Table OB.1 Summary Skills and Jobs Agenda for Brazil, by Program Area *(continued)*

<table>
<tr><td colspan="3">IN SEARCH OF CONNECTING THE POOR TO BETTER, MORE PRODUCTIVE JOBS (GOAL 2)</td></tr>
<tr><td colspan="3">CHAPTER 5: Productive Inclusion Policies to Better Connect the Poor with More Productive Jobs</td></tr>
<tr><td>[Adapting] Skills Development/PRONATEC</td><td>[Adapting] Active Labor Market Programs</td><td>Self-Employment Support in Rural Areas</td></tr>
<tr>
<td>*Policy concern:* Which key adjustments to Skills Development/PRONATEC contents, pedagogies, and services would best ensure access of the poor to enhanced employment opportunities?

Analysis: Of all PRONATEC training slots, 40% are targeted to the poor. Dropout rates remain high. For many poor and vulnerable job seekers, difficulties in retaining jobs, ineffective job-search mechanisms (mostly informal networks), and limited access to child care are the main employability constraints, not technical skills. Moreover, increased coordination between PRONATEC and an adapted public employment service (SINE) could improve placement rates among PRONATEC beneficiaries.</td>
<td>*Policy concern:* Which key adjustments to ALMPs would best connect the poor to jobs in urban areas?

Analysis: Most SINE clients coincide with the targeting group of productive inclusion: they are working poor who face diverse employability challenges. Productive inclusion policies will involve not only training but also a comprehensive integration of those programs with (a) "customized" placement services that better serve client needs, (b) added "soft skills" training (including communication and conflict resolution skills), and (c) apprenticeships and other hands-on training components. In short, the goal is to better link social assistance not only to training (such as PRONATEC) but also to Brazil's several ALMPs, including SINE's intermediation services as well as entrepreneurship support and start-up incentives provided by SEBRAE (Brazilian Micro and Small Business Support Service). The availability of a more complete set of interventions beyond PRONATEC could also strengthen social workers' role, thus better leveraging their presence on the ground, and their knowledge and relationship with those in need, in the productive inclusion agenda.</td>
<td>*Policy concern:* How could Brazil strengthen rural productive inclusion policies to better connect the poor to more-productive, higher-earning jobs?

Analysis: Because employment is concentrated in low-productivity (family) agriculture, maximizing the earnings potential of these businesses is critical. But although these programs will promote incomes for many, for others upward mobility will mean moving to the nonagriculture sector. In this context, training and entrepreneurship programs adapted to their skills and experience are helpful.

Recommendations: Brazil could promote the efficiency and sustainability of the integrated model of rural development and social assistance by
• Establishing M&E systems to evaluate the results of programs on employability and income generation, thus enabling evidence-based program expansion and design adjustment;</td>
</tr>
</table>

table continues next page

22

Table OB.1 Summary Skills and Jobs Agenda for Brazil, by Program Area *(continued)*

Recommendations: Brazil could promote employment and earnings among the poor by

- Including in PRONATEC training soft skills targeted to the poor and increased accessibility to child and elder care, transportation subsidies, night courses, and other support for the poor;
- Diversifying support in urban areas beyond PRONATEC through synergies with the adapted intermediation and entrepreneurship programs;
- Improving coordination and services integration between PRONATEC, social assistance, and labor programs (common processes and goals); and
- Improving equity in PRONATEC expansion by (a) better aligning programs with beneficiary profiles; and (b) redistributing PRONATEC training slots across municipalities and subjects to correspond with low-skilled labor market supply and demand.

Recommendations: Toward the goal of diversifying support and making existing programs more efficient and sustainable, key strategic areas include the following:

- Diversify urban productive inclusion beyond PRONATEC through synergies with ALMPs;
- Adapt public employment services (SINE) and other ALMPs to better serve the poor, such as through better alignment of services with beneficiary profiles and local labor markets;
- Expand support to address employment barriers beyond technical skills by adding soft-skills and more hands-on components to PRONATEC while increasing students' or trainees' accessibility to child and elder care, transportation subsidies, night courses, and other support for the poor; and
- Strengthen M&E systems to provide adequate data on the job placement rates of trainees who completed the courses and on earnings or wage increases associated with program participation, as well as business survival and expansion linked with entrepreneurship support, thus enabling evidence-based program expansion and design adjustment.

- Profiling family farmers (including their experience in programs by type of activity) and using the results to decide how to best allocate benefits, and continuing to encourage the use of Cadastro Único/NIS for targeting of rural development programs;
- Expanding support to enhance producers' market orientation and access to markets beyond the quotas for public procurement;
- Promoting private sector partnerships, including with the financial system, to improve access to credit and technology; and
- Adapting and improving access to rural entrepreneurship (microenterprise) programs and expanding access to hands-on, community-based training and skills certification to enhance people's productivity.

In addition, establishing or strengthening M&E systems to trace outcomes and support program expansion is a key priority for rural and urban productive inclusion programs.

Note: TVET = technical vocational education and training; M&E = monitoring and evaluation; PRONATEC = National Program for Access to Technical Education and Employment; SINE = National Employment System; SEBRAE = Brazilian Micro and Small Business Support Service; ALMP = active labor market program; UI = unemployment insurance; FGTS = Severance Indemnity Fund; NIS = social identification number. Cadastro Único (Single Registry) is the Brazilian federal government's database that identifies and characterizes low-income households to support their access to social programs.

Notes

1. Aggregate data are from the Total Economy Database, January 2014 update, The Conference Board, New York, http://www.conference-board.org/data/economydatabase. Firm-level results on labor productivity are from Maciente, Silva, and Gukovas (2015).

2. The minimum wage also affects the poor because social benefits such as the social pension are indexed to the minimum-wage annual increase.

3. Social assistance in addition to education has greatly contributed to addressing these challenges. For example, Brazil's conditional cash transfer program, Bolsa Família, decreases dropout rates and increases the likelihood of grade promotion but has limited effects on learning outcomes (Silva, Proença, and Cireno 2015). Compensating for bad schools and remedying early disadvantages are long-term endeavors that require additional policy agendas.

4. In Brazil, universal child care is available *only* for children of ages four years or older.

5. Active labor market programs (ALMPs) help with job search and matching, improve employability, and connect people to more productive employment. They include job-search assistance and labor intermediation services (National Employment System, SINE), training and apprenticeships, programs to promote entrepreneurship, support to self-employment, and special programs targeted at youth or other vulnerable groups. Labor market regulations and institutions include the minimum-wage policy, labor courts, and support systems for the unemployed (for example, unemployment insurance [Subsidio de Desemprego] and the Severance Indemnity Fund [Fundo de Garantia do Tempo e Serviço, FGTS]).

6. Cadastro Único (Single Registry) is the Brazilian federal government's database that registers and characterizes low-income households (including income, family composition, location, and so on) to provide information that social programs use to select new beneficiaries.

7. PRONATEC is an umbrella program coordinating a variety of existing and new vocational education and training policies, including courses in two modalities: Technical Education (TEC) and Initial and Continuing Training Programs (FIC). Under this program, the Ministry of Education has established partnerships with several other ministries (including Social Development, Tourism, and Communication) to identify and select potential trainees for technical courses.

8. PRONATEC's TEC courses are generally considered preemployment technical education, are longer, and offer upward permeability with the education system. Its FIC courses are generally for the current workforce, consisting of short-duration vocational training and aiming to improve workers' qualification by upgrading their skills.

9. The University for All Program (PROUNI) is a federal program that provides scholarships to poorer students to study in private universities.

10. Financing of Higher Education Students (FIES) is a federal program that provides financing to students who want to pursue a higher-education degree at a private university.

11. "Sistema S" is the training arm of the Confederation of Industry (CNI). It includes nine institutions, including SENAI (the National Service of Industrial Education), SENAR (the National Rural Training Service), SENAC (the National Commercial Training Service), and others. The Brazilian Constitution establishes that these

institutions must use part of the revenues passed on to them for designated educational and training purposes.

12. The constitution also introduced specific labor-related laws (for instance, regarding indexation between social benefits and the minimum wage) that imply that changes in labor regulations have many spillovers to other policies.

13. Although there is no single way to increase job attachment without creating disincentives for productivity, the recent government proposal to increase the minimum employment duration necessary for UI entitlement can reduce UI spending. However, assessing the proposal's effect on UI coverage will be key, particularly among the low-skilled, who tend to have shorter employment spells.

14. Firms' costs for formal employees include the 13th-month salary—an extra monthly salary (8.33 percent of annual salary) payable by the employer each year in December. Employers also pay transportation costs (around 1 percent, up to 6 percent); social security charges (National Institute of Social Security [INSS]/FGTS) on the 13th-month salary (2.98 percent); a vacation bonus (2.78 percent, or one-third of one month's salary when the employee takes vacations); and social security charges (INSS/FGTS) on the vacation bonus (1 percent). In addition, firms have to pay the FGTS penalty of 40 percent (4.5 percent) when dismissing an employee. Finally, depending on the sector, additional payments are required for food staples and health insurance. Hence, nonwage costs can total up to 70 percent of total compensation (James 2011).

15. In Brazil, microenterprises (microempresa) are those with gross annual revenue up to R$240,000 per year, and small businesses (empresa de pequeno porte) are those with gross annual revenue between R$240,000 and R$2,400,000 per year (General Law of Micro and Small Enterprises [Law 123, 2006]).

16. The Brazil Sem Miséria strategy, launched in June 2011, is aimed at eradicating extreme poverty in Brazil. The strategy has three axes: income support, access to services, and productive inclusion. It is an umbrella strategy that coordinates, improves, or expands existing programs. In addition to the "productive inclusion" axis discussed in this report, the "income support" axis expanded the coverage and benefits of the government's flagship conditional cash transfer program, Bolsa Família, which now benefits more than 14 million families and is internationally regarded as a success, costing around 0.6 percent of Brazil's GDP (Brazil, Ministry of Social Development and Fight against Hunger 2013). The "access to services" axis expanded access to child care, housing, and basic health and education services for the poor.

17. Brazil has a long history of supporting micro and small businesses through the Brazilian Micro and Small Business Support Service (Serviço Brasileiro de Apoio às Micro e Pequenas Empresas, SEBRAE). Created in 1972 as a public institution, SEBRAE became a private nonprofit organization in 1990, with the mission of promoting the sustainable and competitive development of small businesses. Types of support provided includes training and technical assistance.

18. The Institute for Applied Economic Research (IPEA) is a federal public foundation (linked to the Secretariat of Strategic Affairs of the Presidency of the Republic) that "provides technical and institutional support to government actions—enabling the formulation and reformulation of public policies and Brazilian development programs." Its mission is to "enhance public policies that are essential to Brazilian development by producing and disseminating knowledge and by advising the state in its strategic decisions" (IPEA website, http://www.ipea.gov.br).

References

Almeida, Rita, Nicole Amaral, and Fabiana de Felicio. 2015. "Mapping Institutions and Policies in Technical Education and Vocational Training (TVET) in Brazil." Policy report—background paper for this report, World Bank, Washington, DC.

Almeida, Rita, Leandro Anazawa, Naercio Menezes-Filho, and Ligia Vasconcellos. 2015. "Technical and Vocational Education and Training in Brazil: Micro Evidence from Brazil." Research paper—background paper for this report, World Bank, Washington, DC.

Brazil, Ministry of Social Development and Fight against Hunger. 2013. *Plano Brasil Sem Miséria [Brazil without Extreme Poverty Plan]: Two Years of Results*. Progress report, Ministry of Social Development and Fight against Hunger, Government of Brazil, Brasilia.

Bruns, Barbara, David Evans, and Javier Luque. 2012. *Achieving World-Class Education in Brazil: The Next Agenda*. Directions in Development Series. Washington, DC: World Bank.

de Hoyos, Rafael, Rogers Halsey, and Anna Popova. 2015. "Out of School and Out of Work: A Diagnostic of NiNis in Latin America." Background paper for "Out of School and Out of Work: Challenges and Solutions around the NiNis in Latin America." Regional study, World Bank, Washington, DC.

de Negri, F., and L. R. Cavalcante, eds. 2014. *Produtividade no Brasil: Desempenho e Determinantes*. Brasilia: IPEA.

di Villarosa, Francesco. 2015. *Favela Pilot Study on Productive Inclusion*. Policy report—background paper for this report, World Bank, Washington, DC.

DIEESE (Inter-Union Department of Statistics and Socioeconomic Studies). 2011. *Rotatividade e flexibilidade no mercado de trabalho*. [Turnover and Flexibility in the Labor Market.] São Paulo: DIEESE.

Dutz, Mark. Forthcoming. "Productivity and Competitiveness for Shared Prosperity in Brazil." Concept note, World Bank, Washington, DC.

Evans, David K., and Katrina Kosec. 2012. *Early Child Education: Making Programs Work for Brazil's Most Important Generation*. World Bank Study. Washington, DC: World Bank.

Gerard, Francois, and Gustavo Gonzaga. 2012. "Social Insurance under Imperfect Monitoring: Labor Market and Welfare Impacts of the Brazilian UI program." Working Paper 039, Network of Applied Economics (REAP).

Gill, Indermit. 2002. *Brazil Jobs Report*. Report 24408-BR, World Bank, Washington, DC; Institute for Applied Economic Research, Brasilia.

IBGE (Brazilian Institute of Geography and Statistics). 2002. *National Sample Survey of Households (PNAD)*. Rio de Janeiro: IBGE.

———. 2010. *National Sample Survey of Households (PNAD)*. Rio de Janeiro: IBGE.

———. 2013. *National Sample Survey of Households (PNAD)*. Rio de Janeiro: IBGE.

———. 2014. *Monthly Employment Survey (PME)*. Rio de Janeiro: IBGE.

ILO (International Labour Organization). 2011. *Key Indicators of the Labour Market*. 7th ed. Geneva: ILO.

ILO (International Labour Organization), OECD (Organisation for Economic Co-operation and Development), and World Bank Group. 2014. *G20 Labour Markets:*

Outlook, Key Challenges and Policy Responses. Report prepared for the G20 Labour and Employment Ministerial Meeting, Melbourne, September 10–11.

James, Gary. 2011. "Business Basics in Brazil: Big Opportunities, Challenges Go Hand in Hand." *Journal of Accountancy* (November): 34. http://journalofaccountancy.com /issues/2011/nov/20114143.html.

Leichsenring, Alexander, Joana Silva, and Rafael Proença. 2015. "Formal Employment Insertion among the Poor and Vulnerable in Brazil between 2008 and 2011." Research paper—background paper for this report, World Bank, Washington, DC.

Maciente, Aguinaldo, Joana Silva, and Renata Gukovas. 2015. "Employment Creation, Labor Productivity, and Firms' Dynamics." Research paper—background paper for this report, World Bank, Washington, DC.

Marra, Karla, Jociany Luz, Joana Silva, and Renata Gukovas. 2015. *Mapping of the Current Network of Active Labor Market Programs (ALMPs)*. Policy report—background paper for this report, World Bank, Washington, DC.

OECD (Organisation for Economic Co-operation and Development). 2012. "Education GPS: The World of Education at Your Fingers." OECD Education GPS. http:// gpseducation.oecd.org.

Oviedo, Ana Maria. 2015. "Labor Market Regulations and Institutions in Brazil." Policy paper—background paper for this report, World Bank, Washington, DC.

Schwartzman, Simon, and Claudio de Moura Castro. 2013. *Estudo e Trabalho da Juventude Brasileira*. [Study and Work of Brazilian Youth.] Research report, Institute for Labor and Society (IETS), Rio de Janeiro.

Silva, Joana, Renata Gukovas, and Luiz Caruso. 2015. "The Wage Returns and Employability of Vocational Training in Brazil: Evidence from Matched Provider-Employer Administrative Data." Research paper—background paper for this report, World Bank, Washington, DC.

Silva, Joana, Rafael Proença, and Flávio Cireno. 2015. "Impacts of the Bolsa Família Program on Education: A Regression Discontinuity Approach." Research paper—background paper for this report, World Bank, Washington, DC; Ministry of Social Development and Fight against Hunger, Brasilia.

World Bank. 2012. *World Development Report 2013: Jobs*. Washington, DC: World Bank.

———. 2013. *World Development Report 2014: Risk and Opportunity*. Washington, DC: World Bank.

Zylberstajn, Eduardo, and Joana Silva. 2015. "Earnings Consequences of Labor Turnover: The Case of Brazil." Research paper—background paper for this report, World Bank, Washington, DC.

CHAPTER 1

Brazilian Labor Markets: Main Achievements and Remaining Challenges

Skills and Jobs Achievements in Brazil since 2000

Remarkable Progress in Average Earnings and Employability

Brazilian labor markets performed remarkably well in the past 15 years in terms of employment, labor market participation, and labor earnings growth. Unemployment in Brazil declined steadily between 2002 and 2014, as shown in figure 1.1. The unemployment rate fell from 12.9 percent in 2002 to 4.9 percent in 2014 (hitting a historic low of 4.3 percent in December 2013—one-third the rate of the early 2000s).[1] Meanwhile, the total number of people employed grew by an annual average of 2.1 percent between 2000 and 2014. Figure 1.1 also illustrates the steady rise of labor income, which grew by an annual average of 2 percent in real terms and reached a historic high of $R2,078 (US$665) per month in February 2014.[2] These trends occurred even as the overall labor force participation rate grew from about 68 percent in 2000 to 70 percent in 2014 and as the female participation rate grew from 56 percent to 59 percent.[3]

In contrast with earlier periods, formal employment expanded greatly, exceeding informal employment since 2007. Since 2002, formal jobs (as a percentage of the workforce) increased by more than 13 percentage points (figure 1.2) as Brazil's private sector created a total of more than 19 million formal jobs (Maciente, Silva, and Gukovas 2015).[4] In 2007, the share of formal employment exceeded that of informal employment for the first time.[5] Along with the increase in formal employment came decreases in informal employment (mainly since 2004); unemployment; and to a smaller extent, the share of the population out of the labor force. The share of self-employed workers and employers remained fairly stable throughout this period (Zylberstajn and Silva 2015). Annual transition rates into formal jobs (table 1.1) indicate that an average of 34 percent of all unemployed and 31 percent of all informal workers moved into

Figure 1.1 Unemployment Rate and Average Labor Earnings, 2002–14

Source: Based on the Monthly Employment Survey (Pesquisa Mensal de Emprego; PME), Brazilian Institute of Geography and Statistics, Rio de Janeiro.
Note: R$ = reais; R$1= US$0.34 (April 2, 2015). Graph displays PME data for every month but has markers for only two months per year to avoid cluttering information on the x-axis. Based on data for selected metropolitan regions in which PME is representative.

Figure 1.2 Workforce Formality and Informality in Brazil, 2001–14

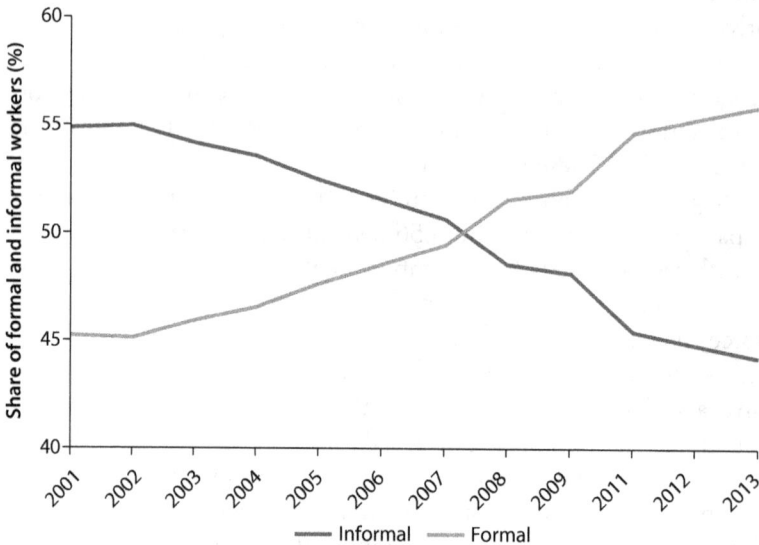

Source: Based on the National Household Survey (Pesquisa Nacional por Amostra de Domicilio, PNAD), Brazilian Institute of Geography and Statistics, Rio de Janeiro.
Note: "Informal" workers include the self-employed as well as those who lack a signed employment card (carteira assinada) and who therefore do not contribute to social security. The figure omits 2010 data because the PNAD did not collect data for 2010, a year when Census data was collected. However, the PNAD and Census survey data were not compatible in this regard.

Table 1.1 Annual Transition Rates and Associated Changes in Median Earnings in Metropolitan Areas of Brazil, 2011–13

percentage

		Final LM status (t + 1)					
	t/t+1	*Formal employee*	*Informal employee*	*Self-employed*	*Unemployed*	*Out of LF*	*Total*
Initial LM status (*t*)	Formal employee	83	4	3	2	8	100
		2.23	**−4.66**	**−7.24**	**n.a.**	**n.a.**	
	Informal employee	31	35	14	4	15	100
		16.15	**3.59**	**0.59**	**n.a.**	**n.a.**	
	Self-employed	8	7	64	1	14	100
		17.03	**2.39**	**−4.41**	**n.a.**	**n.a.**	
	Unemployed	34	10	7	17	32	100
		n.a.	**n.a.**	**n.a.**	**n.a.**	**n.a.**	
	Out of LF	8	4	5	3	80	100
		n.a.	**n.a.**	**n.a.**	**n.a.**	**n.a.**	

Source: Zylberstajn and Silva 2015.

Note: LF = labor force; *t* = start year (2011 or 2012); *t*+1 = final year (2011 or 2012); n.a. = not applicable. Numbers in black designate annual transition rates; numbers in bold designate average changes in median earnings associated with the respective transition. "Informal" employees include those who lack a signed employment card (*carteira assinada*) and who therefore do not contribute to social security.

formal employment each year between 2011 and 2013 (Zylberstajn and Silva 2015). Among those who are out of the labor force, however, only about 8 percent move into formal jobs each year. Transitions into formality increased earnings more than transitions to any other labor market status (Zylberstajn and Silva 2015).

At the aggregate level, total employment expanded with gains concentrated in construction and retail at the expense of agriculture and, to some extent, manufacturing. Shifts in sectoral employment since 2002 have reflected economywide structural transformation. Retail and construction output increased, but agriculture and manufacturing output decreased. Hence, as figure 1.3 shows, the shares of "other services" (such as transport, communications, education and health, public administration, personal services, etc.) and construction employment increased during this period, while agriculture and manufacturing employment decreased. Maciente, Silva, and Gukovas (2015) show that sectoral employment in formal labor markets is remarkably stable (more than 80 percent of workers stay in the same sector year on year), so the new entrants play an important role in big sectoral employment expansions. They also show that the younger workers (below 40 years old) tend to enter manufacturing and retail, while older workers are more likely to enter the agriculture and construction sectors and therefore will be affected differently by long-term sectoral trends as well as business cycle fluctuations.

Importantly, total employment creation recently slowed and has even contracted in some sectors. For instance, manufacturing employment decreased by 3.9 percent between September 2013 and September 2014.[6] As shown in

Figure 1.3 Employment Trends in Brazil, by Sector, 2002–13

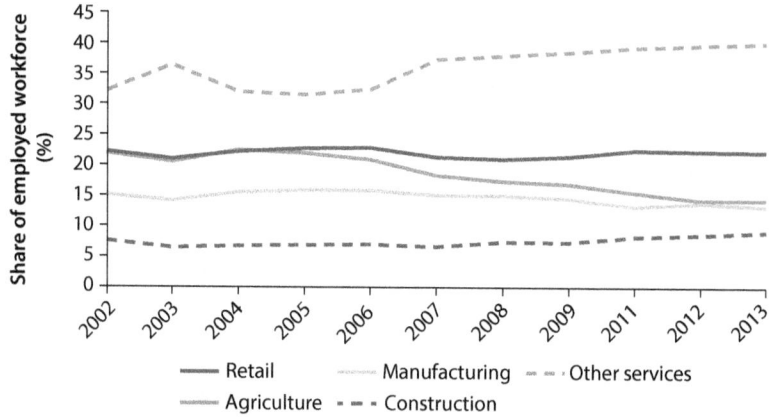

Source: Based on the National Household Survey (Pesquisa Nacional por Amostra de Domicilio, PNAD), Brazilian Institute of Geography and Statistics, Rio de Janeiro.
Note: The figure omits 2010 data because the PNAD did not collect data for 2010, a year when Census data were collected. However, the PNAD and census survey data were not compatible in this regard. "Other services" include transport, communications, education and health, public administration, personal and domestic services.

figure 1.3, the 2002–13 employment trends were as follows, in order of the fastest- to slowest-growing employment sectors:

- *Agricultural* employment contracted over the period, with an average annual decline of –1.4 percent.
- *Manufacturing* employment grew by an average 1.1 percent per year.
- *Construction* was the fastest-growing sector between 2002 and 2013, sustaining above-average annualized employment growth of 3.8 percent.
- *Retail* employment grew at an average annual rate of 1.9 percent.
- *Other services* employment grew at the average annual rate of 4.1 percent, with *public administration* employment growing by an average of 2.7 percent per year, although starting from a very low level (5 percent of total employment in 2002).

At the state level, the evolution of output and employment shares across sectors also show important differences. Commodity price shocks affected states differently (Bastos 2014). For example, in states with a strong agriculture and mining presence, the output share tended to peak around 2008, particularly in Espírito Santo, Maranhão, Pará, Rio de Janeiro, and Sergipe. In the remaining broad sectors considered, trends in output shares were more homogeneous and consistent with those of the economy as a whole. This evidence is consistent with the hypothesis that the behavior of these shares was predominately influenced by macroeconomic factors common to the country as a whole. Bastos (2014) also shows that, looking at employment shares across broad sectors and federal states, once again sectoral trends in the allocation of labor are generally consistent with those displayed for the whole economy, despite some heterogeneity across states in both levels and trends. Annex table 1A.4 shows the labor and poverty status, by state.

The workforce became more skilled, as secondary education coverage expanded significantly. The average educational level of the labor force rose by more than 50 percent between 1995 and 2010, driven by the rapid expansion of secondary education. Brazilians 25 years and older had 7.2 years mean years of schooling in 2010, up from 4.6 years in 1995 (UNDP 2014). Schooling of students from lower-income households increased the most because the extension of coverage during these years favored those households (World Bank 2013). However, overall secondary education coverage increased significantly over the period. According to the School Census (Censo Escolar), the number of students enrolled in secondary education (Ensino Médio) increased from 4 million in 1992 to 8.3 million in 2010 (INEP 2014). Similarly, completion rates in both primary and secondary education have steadily increased over the past decade and a half (OECD 2012; Todos Pela Educação 2012), as shown in figure 1.4, panel a. Educational attainment also improved: for example, between 2003 and 2012, the Program for International Student Assessment (PISA) math scores in

Figure 1.4 Basic Education Completion and Student Math Performance in Brazil and Selected Countries

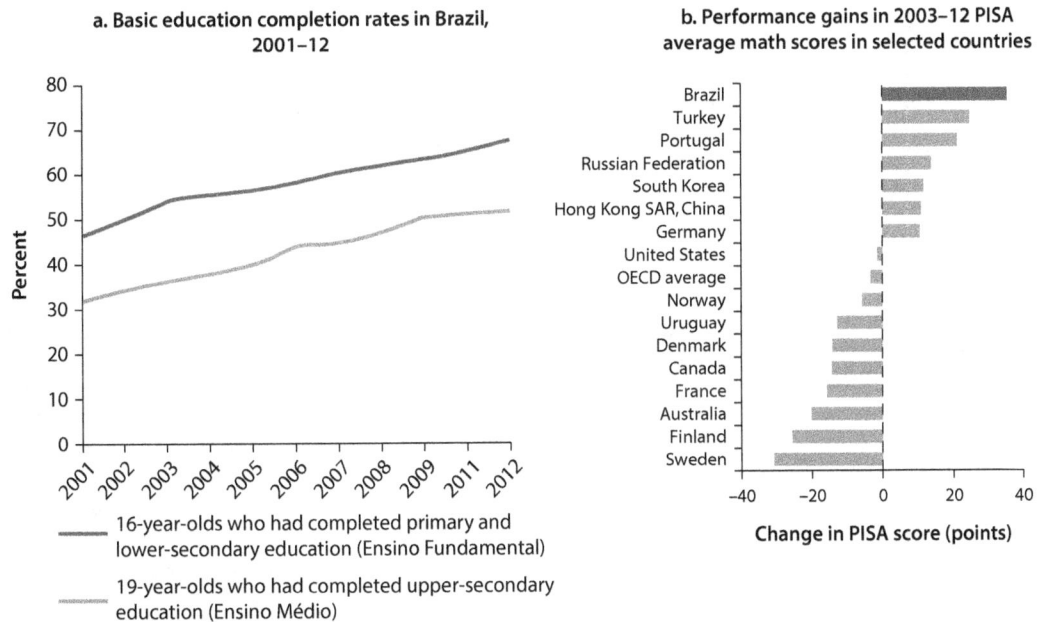

a. Basic education completion rates in Brazil, 2001–12

16-year-olds who had completed primary and lower-secondary education (Ensino Fundamental)

19-year-olds who had completed upper-secondary education (Ensino Médio)

b. Performance gains in 2003–12 PISA average math scores in selected countries

Change in PISA score (points)

Sources: OECD 2012; Todos Pela Educação 2012.
Note: The figure omits 2010 data because the National Sample Survey of Households (Pesquisa Nacional por Amostra de Domicilio, PNAD) did not collect data for 2010, a year when Census data were collected. However, the PNAD and Census survey data were not compatible in this regard.

Sources: OECD 2005, 2014.
Note: PISA = Program for International Student Assessment; OECD = Organisation for Economic Co-operation and Development; SAR = special administrative region.

Brazil increased by 35 points (figure 1.4, panel b)—the largest increase among all participating countries (OECD 2014). Significant improvements were also found in reading and science.

Although the schooling level of the workforce increased, it came up from a very low level, and average educational levels remain low in Brazil relative to comparable countries. The 2012 PISA found that two-thirds of Brazilian 15-year-olds were "low achievers" in math (although this share is markedly lower than the 75 percent share in 2003). And the 2012 average PISA scores in math, reading, and science, while all improved since 2000, lag behind the 2012 OECD averages. In each case, the improvements in Brazilian students' performance can be explained by "improvements in the economic, social, and cultural status of the student population" (OECD 2014).

Improved Labor Market Outcomes, Particularly among the Poor

There were significant strides in labor market outcomes of the poor since 2000. In Brazil during this period, labor earnings at the bottom of the per capita income distribution increased at much higher rates than for those at the top, as shown in figure 1.5, panel a. Over the same period, the relative supply of skilled labor increased more among the poor than the nonpoor, contributing to an increase in average earnings (figure 1.5, panel b). Similarly, the wage premium decreased between the Southwest and Northeast regions, where most of the poor live (Ferreira, Firpo, and Messina 2014).

Figure 1.5 Changes in Skilled Labor and Wages in Brazil, by Income Distribution, 2002–13

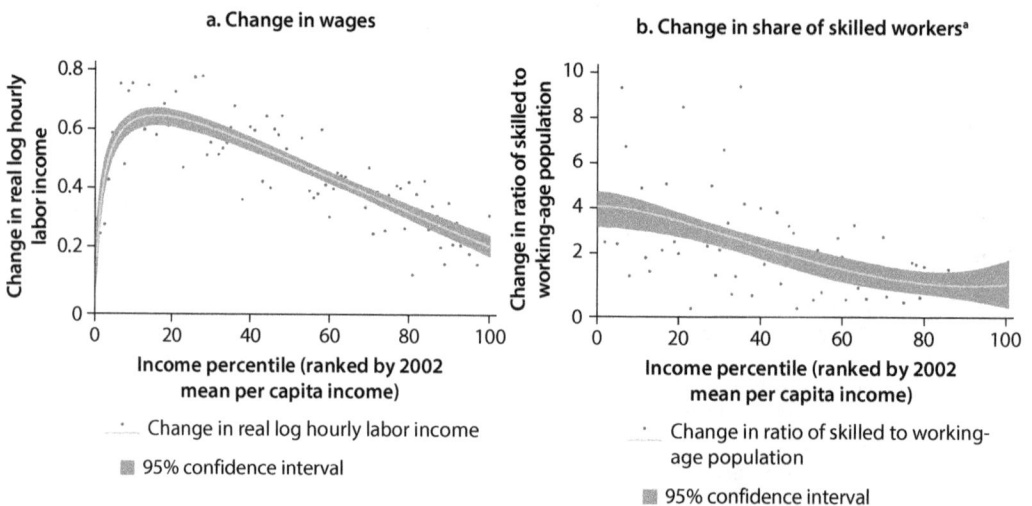

a. Change in wages

b. Change in share of skilled workers[a]

Change in real log hourly labor income — *y-axis panel a*
Income percentile (ranked by 2002 mean per capita income) — *x-axis panel a*

Change in real log hourly labor income
95% confidence interval

Change in ratio of skilled to working-age population — *y-axis panel b*
Income percentile (ranked by 2002 mean per capita income) — *x-axis panel b*

Change in ratio of skilled to working-age population
95% confidence interval

Source: Based on the National Household Survey (Pesquisa Nacional por Amostra de Domicilio, PNAD), Brazilian Institute of Geography and Statistics, Rio de Janeiro.
a. "Skilled workers" are those with 11 or more years of education. "Working-age" individuals are at least 18 years old.

Formal labor market insertion also increased more among the poor than the nonpoor. The disadvantaged segments of the population participated more in employment and increased their share of higher-paying, formal jobs. Merging administrative records of the Ministry of Social Development and Fight against Hunger with social security records, Leichsenring, Silva, and Proença (2015) find that the share of the poor who gained formal employment expanded from 10.5 percent in 2008 to 16 percent in 2011 (considering only the beneficiaries of Brazil's Bolsa Família conditional cash transfer program, that is, those registered in Cadastro Único with monthly per capita income below R$140, or US$47.60).[7] Among the vulnerable (defined as those registered in Cadastro Único with monthly per capita incomes between R$140 and R$270, or US$47.60–US$91.80), formal employment insertion increased at a similar rate (from 14.1 percent to 20 percent). These trends are in sharp contrast with formal labor participation among the nonpoor, which increased at a much smaller rate (from 48.9 percent in 2008 to 50.6 percent in 2011), as shown in figure 1.6.

Young workers who completed high school drove the increase in formal labor market insertion among the poor. As of 2008, the poor who had entered the formal labor market were primarily less-educated working adults, in particular,

Figure 1.6 Insertion in Formal Employment of Poor vs. Nonpoor in Brazil, 2008–11

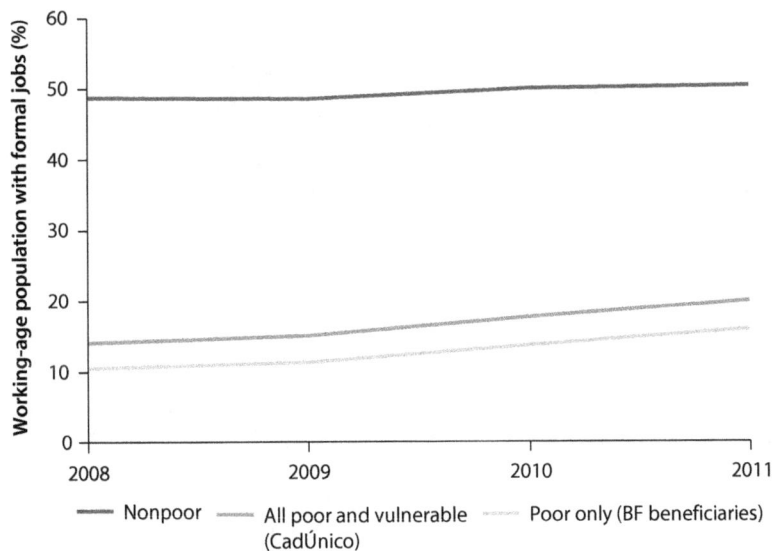

Source: Leichsenring, Silva, and Proença 2015.
Note: BF = Bolsa Família (conditional cash transfer program); "CadÚnico" = Cadastro Único ("Single Registry"), the Brazilian federal government's database that registers and characterizes low-income households (including income, family composition, location, and so on) to provide information that social programs use to select new beneficiaries; "Poor" = Bolsa Família beneficiaries (no more than R$140 [US$47.60] monthly per capita income); "Nonpoor" = everyone else.

workers between 29 and 39 years of age who had completed only elementary school (Leichsenring, Silva, and Proença 2015). Between 2008 and 2011, the growth (by age and education) in insertion in formal employment among the poor came from younger, more-educated workers entering the labor market: 18- to 24-year-olds who had completed high school made up the group whose share increased the most (figure 1.7). This influx of young and educated workers shifted the profile of the poor with formal jobs quickly. By 2011 the poor who held formal jobs were mostly young, relatively educated workers (Leichsenring, Silva, and Proença 2015).

Figure 1.7 Variation in Formal Employment Insertion Rates of Poor and Nonpoor in Brazil, by Age Group and Educational Attainment, 2008–11

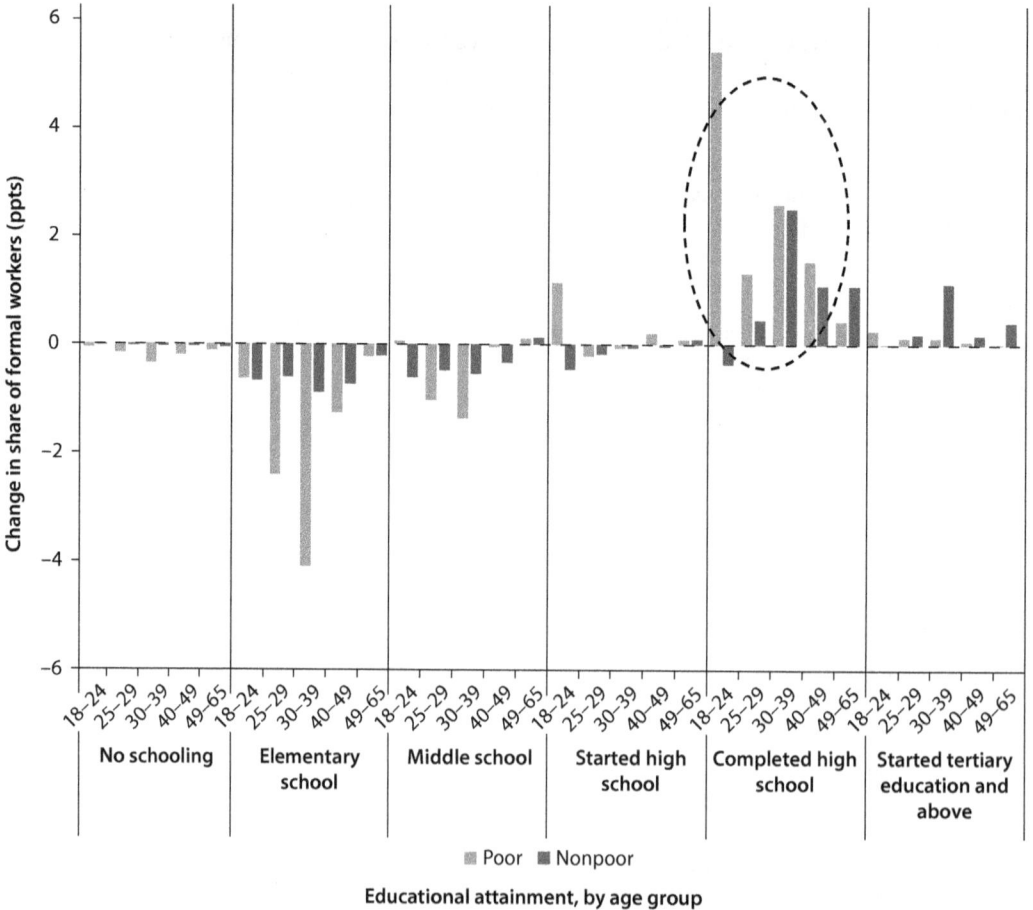

Source: Leichsenring, Silva, and Proença 2015.
Note: ppts = percentage points; "Poor" = Bolsa Família beneficiaries; "Nonpoor" = everyone else. For both the poor and the nonpoor, we computed the share of each age-group and education combination in 2008 and 2011. Bars represent the change in share of formal workers made up by the poor or nonpoor for each age-group and education combination between 2008 and 2011.

Poverty and Inequality Reduction from Pro-Poor Labor Markets

Poverty and inequality decreased in the past 15 years in Brazil. Moderate poverty has fallen from 24.7 percent in 2001 to 8.9 percent in 2014 (using a poverty line of R$140 [US$47.60] monthly per capita income, the threshold of the Bolsa Família conditional cash transfer program). Similarly, extreme poverty declined sharply during the same period, from 9.9 percent to 4 percent (using a poverty line of R$70) (World Bank 2013).[8] Although income inequality remains high, the progress made since the early 2000s is remarkable. Between 2001 and 2013, the Gini coefficient dropped by six points, from 0.59 to 0.53, as shown in figure 1.8, panel a.[9] Per capita income among individuals in the bottom two quintiles of the distribution grew annually by 6.5 percent during the 2002–12 period, nearly twice as fast as the mean growth rate of the whole population (3.6 percent) (World Bank, forthcoming). Along with higher average earnings, inequality in labor earnings declined significantly in Brazil (Ferreira, Firpo, and Messina 2014).

Improvements in labor market outcomes were the main driver of reductions in poverty and inequality in the 2000s. The reduction in labor income inequality could have happened either because (a) both top and bottom quintiles' earnings were rising, but the bottom was rising faster; or (b) the bottom quintiles' earnings were rising, and the top quintiles' earnings were falling. Each explanation would have different implications for poverty. As discussed earlier, Brazil experienced trends consistent with option (b), which has larger effects on poverty. Most (two-thirds) of the poverty reduction and about half of the inequality reduction can

Figure 1.8 Economic Inequality Trends and Determinants in Brazil and Other Selected Latin American Countries

a. Economic inequality trends, 2002–13

b. Determinants of inequality reduction in Brazil, 2001–11

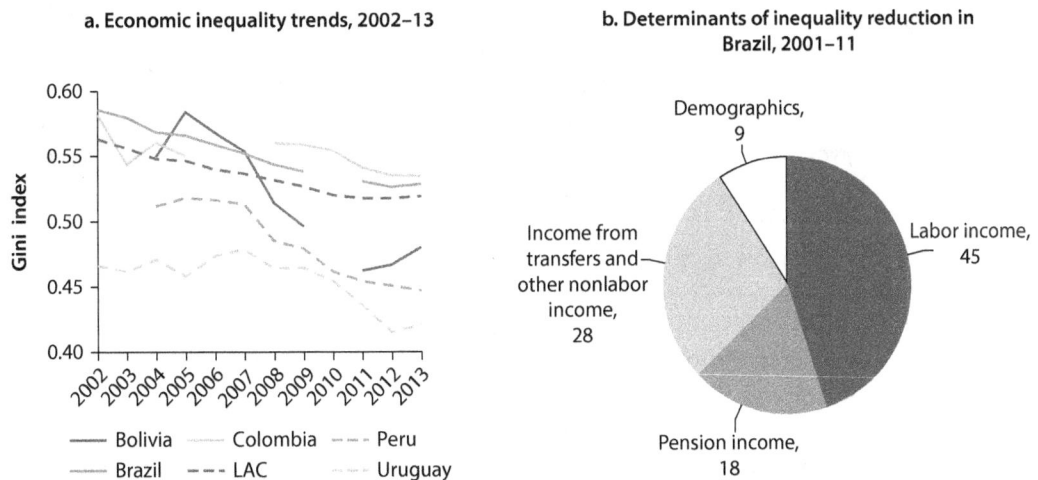

Source: LAC Equity Lab tabulations of SEDLAC (CEDLAS and the World Bank) and World Development Indicators (WDI).
Note: LAC = Latin America and the Caribbean. The Gini index represents a nation's income distribution, from zero (expressing perfect equality) to one (expressing maximal inequality).

Source: Based on Azevedo, Inchauste, and Sanfelice 2013.
Note: The factors contributing to inequality reduction are derived from Shapley-Barros decomposition methods. Demographics factors include working-age population and employment rate.

Table 1.2 Labor Market Status among the Poor and Nonpoor in Brazil, 2011
percentage

	Poor	Nonpoor
Employer	1.2	98.8
Salaried worker	5.2	94.8
Formal	2.2	97.8
Informal	16.0	84.0
Self-employed	13.7	86.3
Unpaid	58.3	41.7
Unemployed	46.0	54.0

Source: Bianchi-Santarrosa and Lopez-Calva 2014.
Note: "Poor" = Per capita household monthly income below R$140, or US$47.60. "Nonpoor" = Per capita household monthly income above R$140. "Unpaid" refers to workers who receive no payment, either from volunteer work or from family work.

be attributed to lower inequality in labor incomes, which resulted from increased employment rates and real earnings of the poor and decreased real earnings of the rich (Azevedo et al. 2013; Barros et al. 2010; Ferreira, Firpo, and Messina 2014; World Bank, forthcoming), as shown in figure 1.8, panel b.

Exiting from poverty between 2003 and 2011 was significantly associated with insertion in formal employment along with structural unemployment reduction, increased salaried job opportunities, and increased informal-job wages. Given the value of the minimum wage and the poverty line determined by the Brazilian government, a household is unlikely to be in poverty if at least one member has a formal job. Unsurprisingly, poverty, when broken down by labor market status, is associated with unemployment and working without pay (Bianchi-Santarrosa and Lopez-Calva 2014), as shown in table 1.2.[10] The poverty rate is lower, albeit significant, among the self-employed, but it is far below average for employers and salaried employees. Unemployed and unpaid workers are more likely to stay in poverty. Although informality is more strongly associated with people who remain in poverty than those who escape it, a nontrivial share of people who exited poverty between 2003 and 2011 is still made up of informal workers, indicating that other factors beyond formalization also play a role in helping lift people out of poverty. These factors include structural unemployment reduction, increased salaried job opportunities, and increased informal-job wages.

Two Critical Goals to Sustain Earnings and Employability Increases: Raise Labor Productivity, and Connect the Poor to More Productive Jobs

Continued progress in employment and labor earnings will depend on achieving a first critical goal: *raising labor productivity*. Although wages have been growing, labor productivity (using aggregate and firm-level data) has been low and stagnant over the past decade. Faster growth in wages than in labor productivity generated an increasing gap between these two aggregates. This trend implies rising unit labor costs, which erode the competitiveness of the tradable sector. Hence, raising labor productivity is needed to sustain future wage increases.

Continued improvements in livelihoods of the poor will depend on achieving a second critical goal: *connecting the poor to better, more productive jobs.* Over the past 15 years, economic growth has been pro-poor, associated with (a) increased earnings primarily from low-skilled, low-productivity occupations; and (b) increased skills development and labor market participation of the poor (including in the formal employment). Sustaining this pro-poor earnings growth is essential (as box 1.1 discusses) but also a challenge for four main reasons:

- Earnings increases at the bottom of the wage distribution were highly influenced by a minimum-wage policy that links its annual change to gross domestic product (GDP) growth.[11] In the current context of lower growth, high earnings increases through this channel might be more difficult.
- Brazil remains a highly unequal country, and the poor's endowments in terms of skills and education, as well as access to and ownership of capital and land, lag behind those of the nonpoor, making mobility of these workers across jobs and access to and retention of high-productivity jobs harder, particularly in weaker labor markers.

Box 1.1 Why Focusing on Jobs for the Poor Matters

To sustain both labor earnings growth and reductions in poverty and inequality, it is critical to focus on the need for "inclusive" labor productivity growth. This goal goes beyond, but intersects with, the goal of increasing labor productivity for all. For labor earnings growth to be *sustained*, it must be accompanied by increased labor productivity. For labor earnings growth to be *pro-poor*, it must most benefit those with lower earnings and be accompanied by opportunities for the poor and disadvantaged to upgrade their own productivity and convert skill gains into sustainable incomes.

In the current context of lower growth and tighter fiscal constraints, investment in the skills and labor programs for the poor is even more important for two key reasons.

First, there is an argument for skill upgrading to improve competitiveness overall. The poor are a large portion of the labor force, and improving their skills will benefit the economy as a whole. Making skills and labor policies more inclusive is valuable toward this goal and requires specific actions to adapt these policies to better reach and serve the poor.

Second, it is important not to reverse the wage and employment gains that were the key drivers of inequality and poverty reduction. Sustaining pro-poor earnings growth in tighter labor markets is not guaranteed. In Brazil, the poor's endowments in terms of skills and education are lower, their access to supporting services is more restricted, and they work in sectors with bleaker prospects—making them more vulnerable to job loss, less protected when this occurs (given their lower average tenures in formal labor markets, which limit access to social security), and less mobile across jobs.

- Converting higher skills into "sustainable" incomes is harder for the poor as they face a number of mutually reinforcing barriers to employability beyond technical skills.
- The poor are most likely to work in sectors with bleaker prospects, such as agriculture and construction.

Goal 1: Raise Labor Productivity to Sustain Future Wage Increases

Labor productivity remains low in Brazil compared with other middle-income countries, despite a significant increase in workforce education. In the past three decades, as shown in figure 1.9, Brazil's labor productivity started from a low level, and its growth has been much slower than that of either developed countries (such as Germany and the United States) or of developing-country comparators (such as Argentina and China).[12] In 2014, labor productivity in Brazil was equivalent to one-fourth the productivity in Germany, less than one-third the productivity in the Republic of Korea, and less than one-fifth the productivity in the United States. It also remains below the Latin American and OECD averages. Moreover, labor productivity grew by an average of only 1 percent per year between 1995 and 2009—far slower than the growth in several Asian economies (for example, China, Japan, and Korea) and the United States (Macedo and Esteves 2012). Almost all sectors experienced this low growth in labor productivity, the exceptions being the automobile, financial services, insurance, extractive

Figure 1.9 Labor Productivity in Selected Countries, 1950–2014

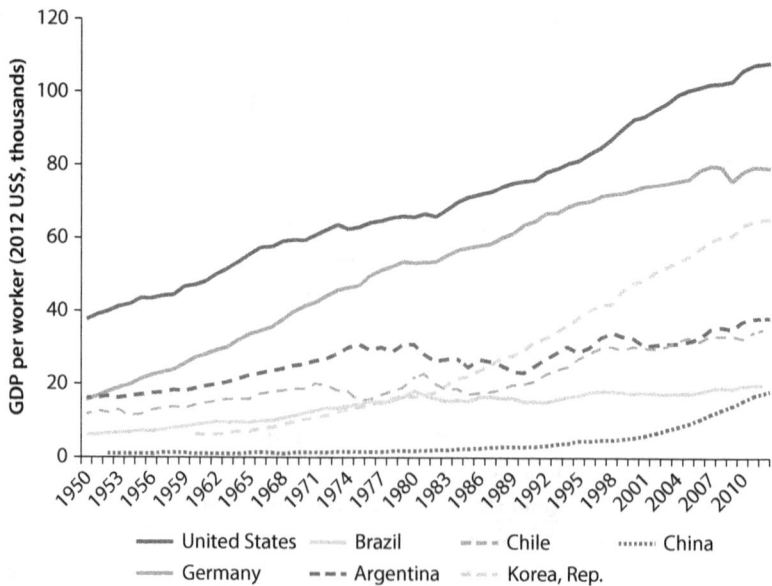

Source: Total Economy Database, January 2014 update, The Conference Board, New York, http://www.conference-board.org/data/economydatabase.

Figure 1.10 Labor Productivity and Wage Indexes in Brazil and Advanced G20 Economies, 1999–2012

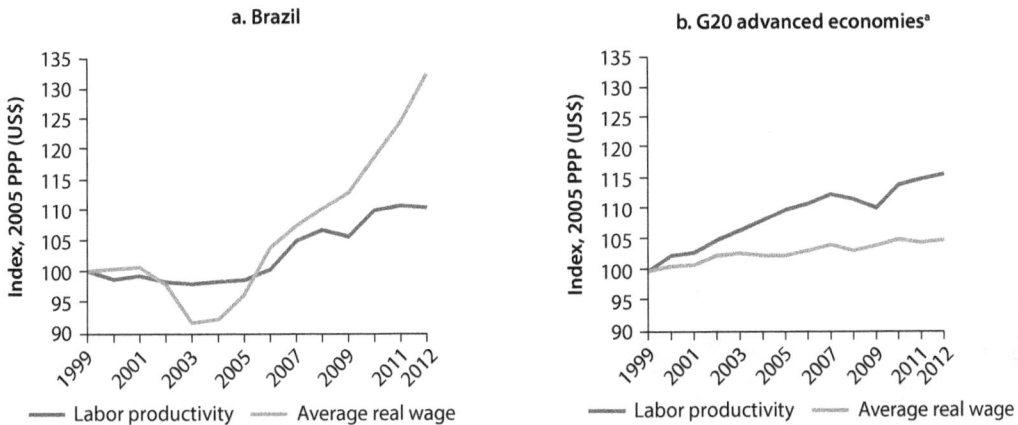

a. Brazil

b. G20 advanced economies[a]

Labor productivity — — Average real wage

Sources: Total Economy Database, January 2014 update, The Conference Board, New York, http://www.conference-board.org/data /economydatabase; ILO, OECD, and World Bank Group 2014.
Note: G20 = Group of Twenty; PPP = purchasing power parity. Labor productivity is defined as GDP per employed person (in constant 2005 PPP US$ for all countries). 1999 = 100.
a. Both indexes are based on a weighted average of all the countries in the group that takes into account labor productivity and the size of paid employment. The G20 advanced economies are Australia, Canada, France, Germany, Italy, Japan, the Republic of Korea, the United Kingdom, and the United States.

industries, and agriculture sectors. Importantly, labor productivity in technology-intensive manufacturing sectors even decreased between 2000 and 2009 (Bonelli 2005; Fonseca 2012; Macedo and Esteves 2012). This trend of stagnant labor productivity is also confirmed using firm-level data. Data on the value added per worker in manufacturing firms show that the distribution of firm-level productivity remained remarkably stable in the 2000s (Maciente, Silva, and Gukovas 2015).

In the 2000s, labor earnings grew faster than labor productivity in Brazil, making increased labor productivity imperative to keep labor costs from rising so fast that they hurt competitiveness and job creation. Since 2004, gains in real wages have significantly outpaced labor productivity growth (figure 1.10, panel a)—in stark contrast to trends in the Group of Twenty (G20) advanced countries (figure 1.10, panel b). This implies rising unit labor costs, which erode the competitiveness of the tradable sector. Brazil's recent slowdown in growth and investment is causing labor demand to contract, in turn exerting pressures on employment and wages in the absence of productivity growth. At the firm level, the disconnect between productivity and wage growth is also apparent: among more than one-third of manufacturing firms, value added per worker in 2012–13 increased slower than minimum wage, putting at risk further employment and wage gains, particularly among firms with high concentration of workforce in wage levels around the minimum wage.[13] Although changes in rent sharing between wages and investment can help avoid imediate employment adjustments, these changes are easier to sustain in the context of a positive demand shock. However, economic prospects appear significantly more moderate than in

Figure 1.11 Formal Job Creation, Unemployment, and Nonemployment Rates in Brazil

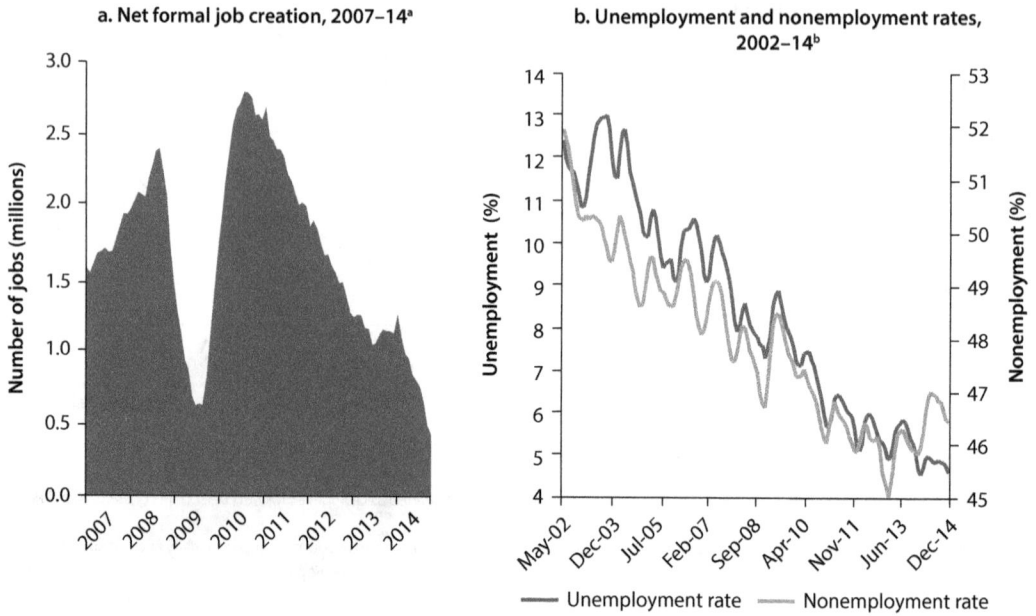

a. Net formal job creation, 2007–14[a]

b. Unemployment and nonemployment rates, 2002–14[b]

—— Unemployment rate   —— Nonemployment rate

Source: Zylberstajn and Silva 2015.
Note: Both graphs track the moving three-month average.
a. Net formal job creation shows net formal employment gains or losses (jobs created minus jobs lost).
b. "Nonemployment" refers to the working-age population (age 18 years and older) that is out of work and not searching for a job. A person is unemployed if jobless but searching for a job (that is, in the labor force).

the 2000s, with the deceleration of China and a slowdown of domestic demand playing pivotal roles. In addition, after the mid-2020s, Brazil is likely to face a contracting labor force, which will force the country to rely increasingly on labor productivity growth instead of new entrants into the labor market to sustain high economic growth (Gragnolati et al. 2011).

Job creation is already slowing in Brazil. Figure 1.11 (panel a) shows a striking deceleration in net formal job creation starting in the second half of 2010 (Zylberstajn and Silva 2015). While the economy was creating more than 2.5 million jobs in mid-2010, this figure declined to fewer than 0.5 million jobs in mid-2014. Notably, while job creation has slowed down significantly, the unemployment rate has remained more resilient. This can be explained by the decreasing labor force participation rate (that is, more working-age people are now out of the labor force and as they are not actively searching for jobs they are not counted as unemployed), as shown in figure 1.11, panel b (Zylberstajn and Silva 2015). If the labor force participation had remained at the same level, the unemployment rate would be higher. Importantly, annual transition rates into nonemployment[14] in recent years (2011–14) indicate that an increasingly high share of the unemployed are leaving the labor force (from 30 percent in 2010–12 to 34 percent in 2013–14), as are many of the self-employed (21 percent in 2013–14), informal workers (16 percent in 2013–14), and formal workers (9 percent in 2013–14). Among those out of the labor force, most (80 percent in 2013–14) remain inactive, and this percentage remains remarkably stable (Zylberstajn and Silva 2015).

On the demand side, job creation is skewed toward "new small firms" or "new small establishments of old, large (multiestablishment) firms" that generally grow slowly as they age, hindering the prospects for labor productivity growth. In most developing countries, net job creation is typically concentrated in young (and not necessarily small) firms (World Bank 2014). In contrast, most of the job creation in Brazil comes from either "new and small" firms (less than one year old and up to 10 workers) or "old and large" firms (more than 30 years old and with more than 1,000 employees) (figure 1.12, panel a)—and a similar pattern was

Figure 1.12 Net Job Creation in Brazil, by Business Age and Size, 2013

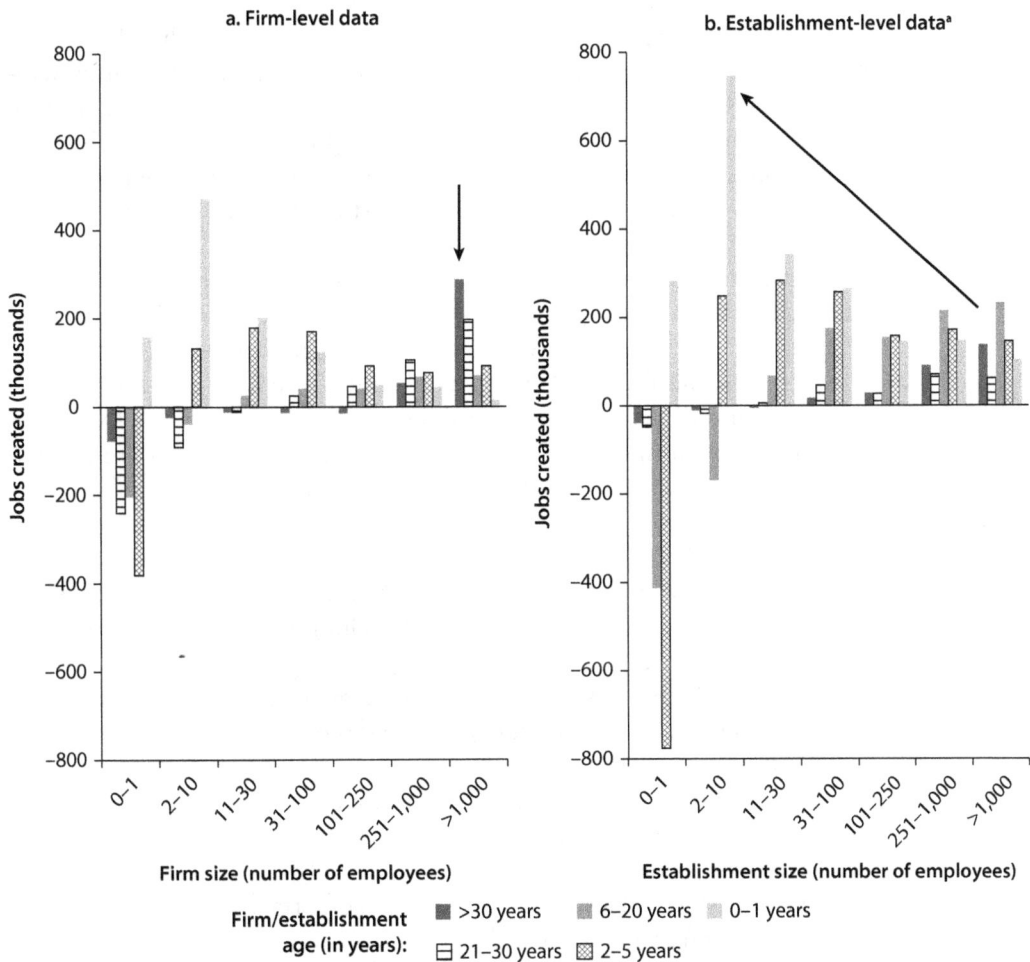

Source: Maciente, Silva, and Gukovas 2015.
Note: Negative net job creation resulted when total employment in 2013 was lower than that in 2012.
a. Each firm can have multiple establishments.

observed throughout the 2000s (Maciente, Silva, and Gukovas 2015). Few firms enter the market at large scale, and microfirms have low or negative net job creation because firm closure is high. The concentration of a large share of job creation in "old and large" firms registered in Brazil is atypical, representing potentially good news for productivity because these firms are generally the most productive and skill-intensive. However, using establishment-level information, this concentration is no longer present (figure 1.12, panel b). In contrast, a higher concentration of job creation in found among new entrants with 2–10 employees. Maciente, Silva, and Gukovas (2015) show that the concentration of high job creation in "old, large firms" (reported using firm-level information) for the most part consists of job creation in "new small establishments of old, large (multiestablishment) firms." This distinction matters for policies aimed at supporting firms' productivity, because such policies are usually targeted based on "firm," not "establishment," size.

The firms expected to be the most productive and skilled-labor-intensive are hiring relatively fewer workers in Brazil's private sector. Brazilian firms with workforces of above-average education are less dynamic in terms of job creation. Furthermore, within firms, the higher the increase in workers' average educational level, the lower the net job creation (Maciente, Silva, and Gukovas 2015). In addition, the high-productivity firms are not growing more than the low-productivity firms. This dynamic can constrain labor productivity growth prospects.

For firms, the skill package of the "right workers" is increasingly complex, requiring that skills development policies focus on developing "demand-based competencies" and "noncognitive" skills. In today's private sector, further raising workers' technical skills without linking them to demand may not translate into greater use of those skills in production (Maciente, Silva, and Gukovas 2015), as shown in figure 1.13, panel a. Furthermore, employers are increasingly demanding socioemotional skills, such as attitude in the workplace commitment, accountability, good customer relations, and the ability to work in a team (Busso et al. 2012), as shown in figure 1.13, panel b. These collective pressures on both workers and firms make it urgent to rethink skills development (technical education and vocational training) policies in Brazil, which is the focus of chapter 2.

High nonwage labor costs also can erode competitiveness and thus impede firms' investment in innovation and training and prospects for job creation—key priorities for renewed labor market regulations. Brazil is an outlier when it comes to high nonwage costs such as social insurance expenditures and labor-related taxes, with nonwage labor costs contributing more than 33 percent of total labor costs, as discussed in detail in chapter 3 (ILO 2014). High formal employment costs could lead to the substitution of formal jobs for informal jobs in response to contraction on the demand for final goods and services. To the extent that employers make this substitution, formal employment will fall more than the change in total employment levels. Another possible response is that employers could make adjustments that would decrease productivity—for

Figure 1.13 Workforce Skill Use and Firms' Skill Demand in Brazil and Other Latin American Countries

a. Skills used by formal workforce in Brazil, 2003–13

b. Formal firms' demand for skills, by type, in selected Latin American countries, 2010

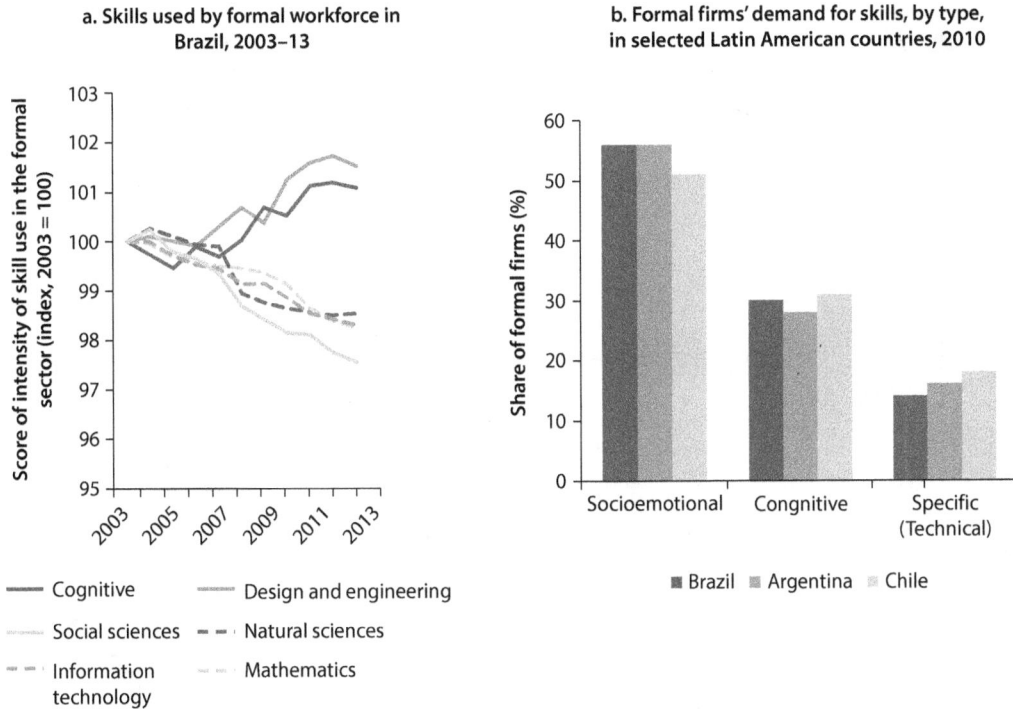

Legend for panel a:
— Cognitive
— Design and engineering
— Social sciences
– – Natural sciences
– – Information technology
– – Mathematics

Legend for panel b:
■ Brazil ■ Argentina ▫ Chile

Source: Maciente, Silva, and Gukovas 2015.
Note: Data were generated from Brazil's Annual Social Information Report (RAIS) for formal employees only. For each occupation, skill scores were computed based on matching job classifications in the United States Occupational Information Network (ONET) with those in the Brazilian Classification of Occupations (CBO) and aggregating them into 21 skill factors (such as cognitive skills, design and engineering skills, and so on). For the economy as a whole, an average score on each skill factor was determined by weighting the scores for each occupation on each factor by the average number of employees in that occupation during each year. The average score was then normalized to 100 for 2003 to show changes across years. For more details on the skill factors computation methodology and definitions, see Maciente 2013.

Source: Busso et al. 2012.
Note: The data were generated from the Demand for Skills Survey conducted among firms in Argentina, Brazil, and Chile. "Socioemotional" skills include attitude in the workplace, commitment, accountability, good customer relations, and ability to work in a team. "Cognitive" skills include knowledge-based skills (language and communication, reading, writing, problem solving, and critical thinking).

example, decreased investments in training, new technologies, or better management techniques. The discussion of how incremental reforms of labor regulation linked with nonwage labor costs, along with more efficient mechanisms of income support in case of dismissal and forms of resolution of labor disputes, could support firms' productivity while also protecting workers is the focus of chapter 3.

Brazil's more productive, innnovative firms take longer than similar firms in other Latin American countries to fill job vacancies, as shown in figure 1.14, panel a. This disparity is particularly high among skilled, high-productivity workers (Almeida and Jesus Filho 2011). In addition, once the matching takes

Figure 1.14 Average Job Vacancy Duration and Worker Tenures, Selected Countries

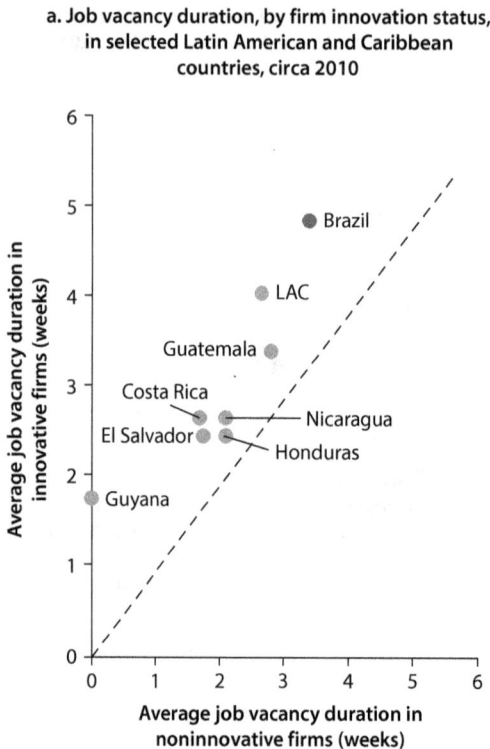

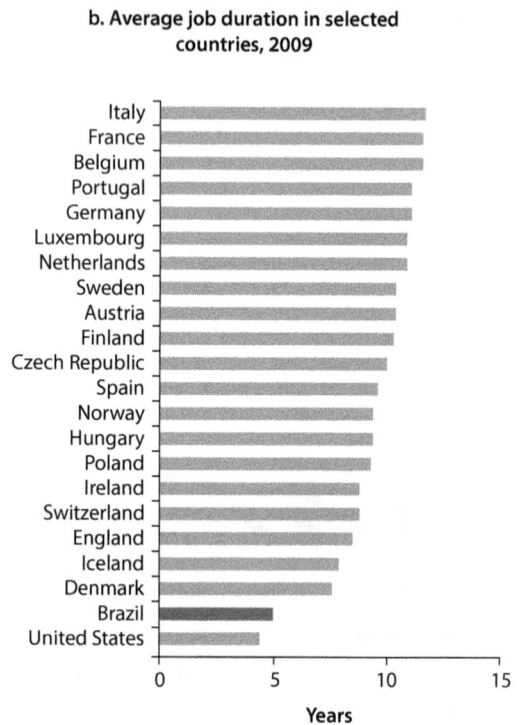

a. Job vacancy duration, by firm innovation status,
in selected Latin American and Caribbean
countries, circa 2010

b. Average job duration in selected
countries, 2009

Source: Almeida and Jesus Filho 2011.
Note: LAC = Latin America and the Caribbean. For definitions of
"innovative" and "noninnovative" firms and methodology, see Almeida
and Jesus Filho 2011.

Source: DIEESE 2011.

place, it lasts less in Brazil than in other countries (DIEESE 2011), as shown in figure 1.14, panel b. This impedes labor productivity and leaves a gap that efficient job-matching support through renewed labor programs could fill. Low job attachment decreases firms' incentives to invest in training, having a negative impact on labor productivity. More efficient job intermediation services could help fill this gap, as discussed in detail in chapter 4.

Goal 2: Connect the Poor to Better, More Productive Jobs

As discussed earlier, labor income increases were largely responsible for Brazil's reductions in poverty and inequality over the past 15 years. However, striking gaps remain between the incomes of the poor and the middle class, largely reflecting differences in their labor incomes. In 2013, the average hourly wage of those in the bottom income quintile was only 15 percent of that of the top quintile, and their average earnings were 4 percent of those of the top quintile, as shown in figure 1.15.[15] Average per capita income of those in the third quintile

Figure 1.15 Decomposition of Average Monthly Income of the Poor and Middle Class in Brazil, 2013

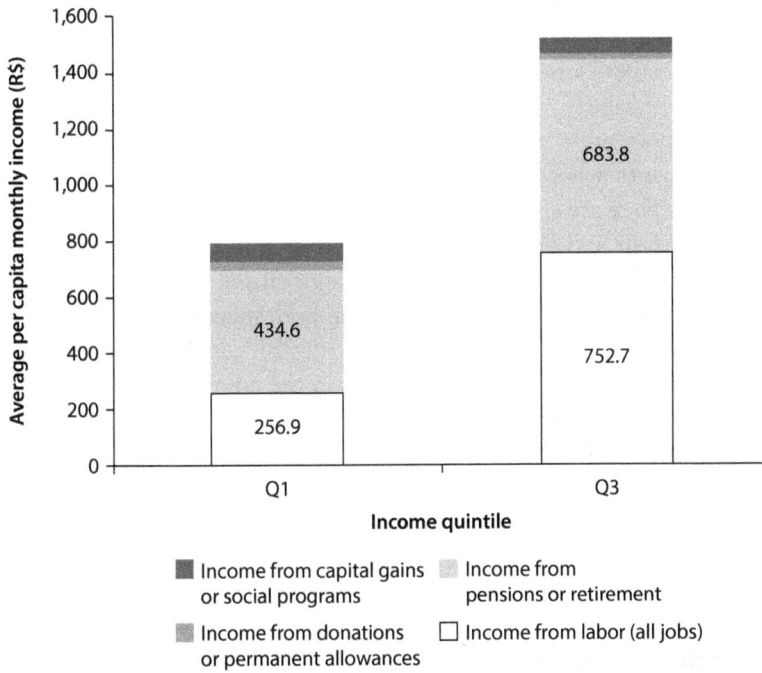

Source: Based on the National Household Survey (Pesquisa Nacional por Amostra de Domicilio, PNAD), Brazilian Institute of Geography and Statistics, Rio de Janeiro.
Note: R$ = reais; Q1 = bottom income quintile (0–20 percent of households based on per capita income); Q3 = middle income quintile (41–60 percent of households based on per capita income).

of income distribution (roughly the "middle class") is almost double the incomes of those in the poorest two quintiles. Decomposition of sources of average incomes shows that although middle-class pension income is higher, it is labor income that accounts for most of the difference. In fact, average labor income in the third (middle) quintile is almost triple that of the bottom quintile. As will be shown later, this is not surprising given the high prevalence of unpaid or low-paying jobs among the poor, especially in rural areas.

In rural areas, employment is largely concentrated in low-earning (or unpaid) agriculture activities in the informal sector. Annex table 1A.1 describes the labor market profile of rural residents. Two-thirds of all agricultural workers in rural areas have low-paying, low-productivity jobs, with 62.5 percent producing goods for their own consumption, 22.5 percent being unpaid, and 9.7 percent being self-employed, for whom working is not enough to escape poverty.[16] Most non-agricultural workers (67 percent) are informal and have, on average, better-paying jobs than do agricultural workers.[17] In almost every respect of labor outcomes, those in the bottom quintiles fare worse in rural areas. The poor have a lower labor force participation rate overall (about 12 percentage points lower for the poorest quintile than the richest quintile), and the gap is especially high for females and youth. Among employees in poor families, informality is more than double that of the better-off (approximately 90 percent in the poorest quintile compared with 42 percent in the top quintile). Most of the rural poor work as either agricultural or livestock laborers (59.3 percent) or agricultural or livestock producers (18 percent).

The urban poor are a more heterogeneous group, some of whom are unemployed and most of whom are working poor, whether they are wage earners or self-employed. They are also more heterogeneous than the rural poor in terms of employment sector and occupation, as shown in annex table 1A.3. They work mostly as domestic workers (13.7 percent), agricultural workers (11.7 percent), helpers in civil construction (7.2 percent), and salespeople (6.4 percent).[18] The unemployment rate in these areas is 7.2 percent, which is above the national average (6.6 percent). Among all urban residents in the labor force, 31.2 percent are self-employed and 56.3 are wage earners. One-fifth all urban workers work in low-earning, low-productivity self-employment.

Despite the progress, in Brazil there are large differences between the poor and nonpoor in terms of unemployment rates, types of employment, and occupations. Most of the poor work, as shown in annex table 1A.2.[19] However, the poor (in the bottom income quintile) are much more likely to be engaged in unpaid activities, to work part-time, or to be low-paid self-employed than the middle class (the third and fourth income quintiles).[20] The working poor are engaged mainly in agriculture, trade and retail, and domestic services, whereas the middle class works mostly in trade and retail or in manufacturing. The top two most common occupations among the poor are "laborer" and "producer in agriculture and livestock" and, to a smaller extent, "domestic worker." Among the middle class, the most common occupations are "salesperson (stores and markets)" and "laborer in agriculture and livestock."

Formal labor market insertion and job retention of the poor remain limited, particularly among older, poorly educated individuals who might not be able to return to formal education. As shown earlier in figure 1.6, despite a significant increase, insertion in formal labor markets remains limited among the poor (only 20 percent of the poor hold formal jobs versus 50.6 percent among the nonpoor in 2011). Among the poor, those who are formally employed are less educated, with 23.8 percent having completed only elementary school and only 3.4 percent having completed university, against 20.7 percent of the nonpoor having a university degree (Leichsenring, Silva, and Proença 2015). When they do obtain formal jobs, they are lower-quality formal jobs: the poor tend to participate more in sectors that demand less qualification, in smaller firms, and in jobs of shorter duration that pay less. Formal job retention and reentry also present challenges for the poor: fewer than half of the poor stay in a formal job for more than 20 months. And after losing a formal job, the poor take much longer to find another one: only 25 percent reenter a formal job within the next two years (Leichsenring, Silva, and Proença 2015), as shown in figure 1.16. Moving to formal employment is the labor market transition associated with

Figure 1.16 Duration of Formal Employment among the Poor and Nonpoor in Brazil, 2008–12

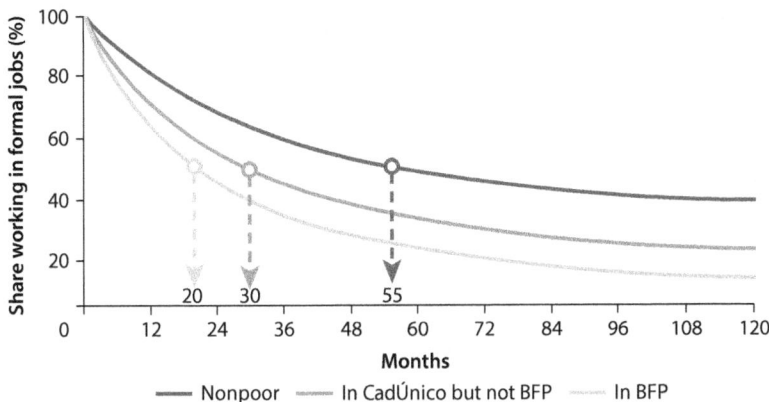

Source: Leichsenring, Silva, and Proença 2015.
Note: "Poor" refers to both Bolsa Família program (BFP) beneficiaries and people registered in Cadastro Único (CadÚnico), the federal database of low-income households. "Nonpoor" refers to those not registered in CadÚnico. Circled data points represent median formal job duration.

the highest wage increase (a median earnings increase of 17 percentage points for the self-employed and 16 percentage points for informal workers in 2013). But the poor are still much more likely to leave the labor force and much less likely to transition from informal to formal jobs or remain in the formal sector, as shown in table 1.3.[21]

Sustaining pro-poor earnings growth is not guaranteed for several main reasons. First among them, minimum-wage policy highly influenced the earnings increases at the bottom of the wage distribution; in the current context of lower growth, high earnings increases through this channel might be more difficult. Earnings increased between 2004 and 2013 primarily in low-skilled, low-productivity occupations at low wage levels (Maciente, Silva, and Gukovas 2015), as shown in figure 1.17, panel a.[22] This trend was highly influenced by a minimum-wage policy (cross-hatched portion of figure 1.17, panel b) as well as the decrease in gaps between urban and rural residents, formal and informal workers, and men and women (Ferreira, Firpo, and Messina 2014).[23] Moving forward, as the minimum wage annual changes are linked to GDP growth whose prospects are bleaker than in the previous decade, high earnings increases through this channel might be more difficult to achieve. Similarly, at the lower current levels of the wage gaps across gender and location, further gains might take longer, particularly in tighter labor markets that might hit the poorest the hardest.

Second, Brazil remains a highly unequal country: the poor's skills and education lag behind, and these gaps are hard to reverse, making job mobility and insertion in high-productivity jobs harder, particularly in tighter labor markers. There are striking differences between the educational attainment of the poor (bottom income quintile) and that of the nonpoor. The overwhelming majority of adults (18 and older) in the bottom quintile have below-primary education

Table 1.3 Transition Rates of Formal and Informal Salaried Workers in Brazil, by Labor Status and Income Quintile, 2011–13

percentage

		Final LM status (t+1)						
	t/t+1	*Out of LF*	*Unemployed*	*Self-employed*	*Employer*	*Informal*	*Formal*	*Total*
	1st income quintile (poorest)							
Initial LM	Out of LF	83	2	5	0	3	6	100
status (*t*)	Unemployed	31	13	9	1	11	35	100
	Self-employed	30	2	56	1	6	6	100
	Employer	100	0	0	0	0	0	100
	Informal	22	9	19	0	31	19	100
	Formal	9	0	1	2	6	82	100
	Total	75	3	7	0	4	10	100
	5th income quintile (richest)							
	Out of LF	81	3	4	0	4	7	100
	Unemployed	34	13	6	0	10	36	100
	Self-employed	11	1	64	8	6	10	100
	Employer	7	0	22	58	4	9	100
	Informal	14	3	13	3	33	34	100
	Formal	8	2	3	1	4	83	100
	Total	25	2	13	5	7	48	100

Source: Based on the Monthly Employment Survey (Pesquisa Mensal de Emprego, PME) conducted by the Brazilian Institute of Geography and Statistics, Rio de Janeiro, from August 2011 to August 2012 and from January 2013 to December 2013.
Note: LM = labor market; LF = labor force. The transition rates have 2013 as their final periods, and the start point is always 16 months before the final month, that is, start period *t* designates a given month from August 2011 to August 2012; and *t*+1 designates an end period 16 months after *t*, that is, a given month from January 2013 to December 2013. "Informal" employees are those who lack signed a employment card (carteira assinada) and who therefore do not contribute to social security.

(62.5 percent) compared with 40.4 percent nationally, as shown in figure 1.18.[24] Only 14.2 percent in the bottom quintile have completed secondary education, compared with 26.1 percent nationally. Finally, only 1.0 percent of those in the bottom quintile have completed tertiary education, compared with 10.1 percent nationally. Conditional cash transfer programs have made important strides in this area. For example, Silva, Proença, and Cireno (2015) show that Brazil's flagship conditional cash transfer program, Bolsa Família, decreases dropout rates and increases the likelihood of grade promotion among the poor. Even so, more schooling does not easily translate into better learning outcomes (measured as higher scores in the Prova Brasil [Brazil Test], a nationwide standardized proficiency test taken in the fifth and ninth grade). Compensating for bad schools and remedying early disadvantages require additional policy agendas, such as improving basic schooling quality and early childhood development in poor areas.

The rural poor, in particular, have lower upward labor mobility than the urban poor. The share of the rural poor working either without pay or for self-consumption increased significantly between 2002 and 2013 (PNAD). The share

Figure 1.17   Changes in Real Wages and Inequality in Brazil

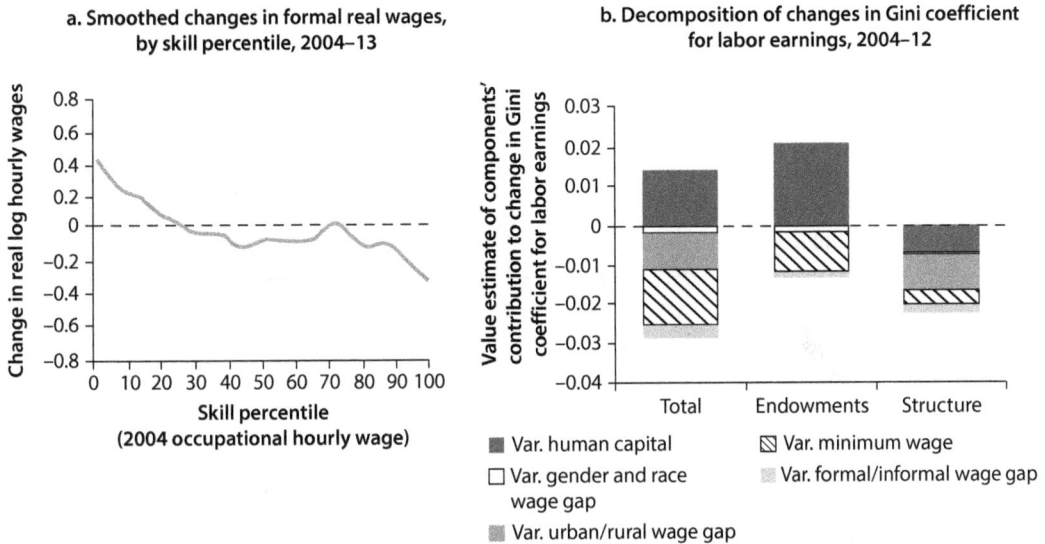

a. Smoothed changes in formal real wages, by skill percentile, 2004–13

b. Decomposition of changes in Gini coefficient for labor earnings, 2004–12

Legend:
- ■ Var. human capital
- ▨ Var. minimum wage
- □ Var. gender and race wage gap
- ▦ Var. formal/informal wage gap
- ▦ Var. urban/rural wage gap

Source: Maciente, Silva, and Gukovas 2015.
Note: Calculations use social security administrative data from the Annual Social Information Report (RAIS) and follow the methodology of Autor and Dorn (2013). Figure shows the 2004–13 changes in wages among 192 detailed occupations (three-digit Brazilian Classification of Occupations [CBO] classifications) encompassing all nonfarm, private sector formal employment in Brazil. Occupations are ranked by skill level, approximated by the mean log wage of workers in each occupation in 2004.

Source: Ferreira, Firpo, and Messina 2014.
Note: A Gini coefficient of zero expresses perfect equality (every resident has the same income), whereas a coefficient of one (or 100 percent) expresses maximal inequality (one person has all income). The paper uses a generalized Oaxaca-Blinder decomposition (recentered influence function [RIF] regression-based decomposition) to assess the contribution of each of the following potential changes in the Gini coefficient for labor earnings: human capital; demographic characteristics of the labor force (race, gender, and location); and labor market institutions (minimum wages). Bars show the contribution of endowments (that is, changes in the composition) and structure (that is, changes in the returns) in each of the variable groups.

below the poverty line decreased over the same period, but only by 4 percentage points. Similar trends took place among the urban poor, but only a small share of urban workers are unpaid, and the share of those below the poverty line decreased dramatically. Given that almost 45 percent of the urban population was above the poverty line in 2013, their labor mobility appears to be significantly higher. As noted before, education appears to be a strong predictor of labor market outcomes. Among the overall rural population, despite a general improvement in education, the types of employment based on educational attainment were even more polarized in 2013 than in 2002: those with primary education or less were much more likely to work either for own consumption or in unpaid jobs in 2013 than before, as shown in figure 1.19.[25] Importantly, looking at self-employment, the poor represent more than half of loan defaulters, making their business prospects bleaker.

Third, converting higher skills into sustainable incomes is more difficult for the poor because they face a number of mutually reinforcing barriers to employability beyond technical skills. Among their employability constraints

Figure 1.18 Educational Attainment and Labor Market Status of the Poor in Brazil, 2013

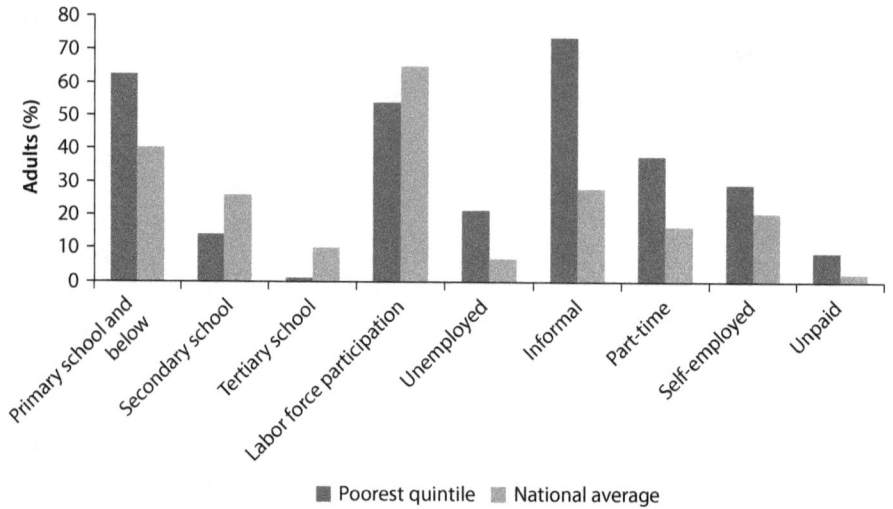

■ Poorest quintile   ▨ National average

Sources: Based on the National Household Survey (Pesquisa Nacional por Amostra de Domicilio, PNAD), Brazilian Institute of Geography and Statistics, Rio de Janeiro.
Note: "Poor" = those in the bottom income quintile (comprising the lowest-earning 0–20 percent of households). "Informal" = workers without a signed employment card (sem carteira). "Part-time" = those working fewer than 30 hours per week in the primary job. "Self-employed" = own-account or unpaid workers. Only adults (individuals 18 years or older) are included in the analysis. "Unpaid" refers to workers who receive no payment, either from volunteer work or from family work.

Figure 1.19 Job Status of the Rural Population in Brazil, by Educational Level, 2002 and 2013

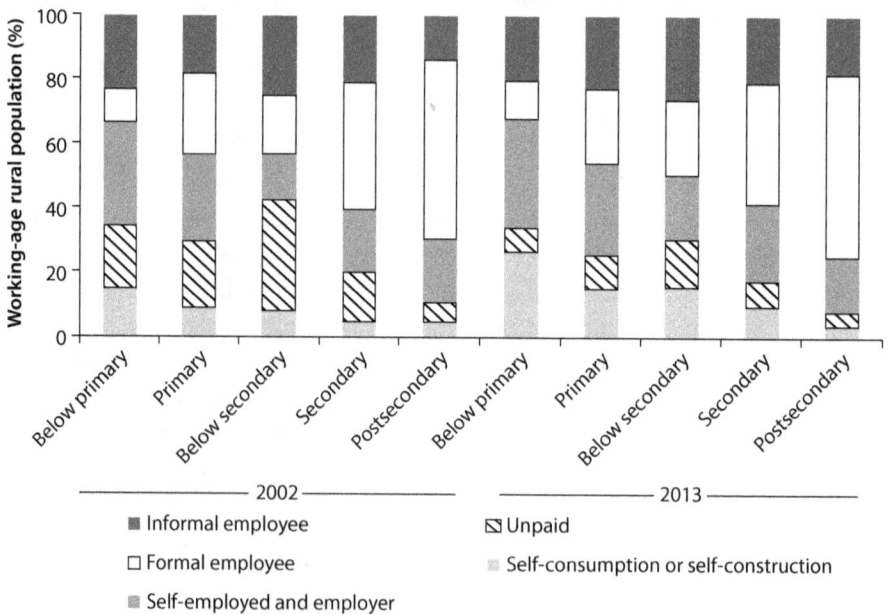

■ Informal employee   ▨ Unpaid
□ Formal employee   ▨ Self-consumption or self-construction
▨ Self-employed and employer

Sources: Based on the National Household Survey (Pesquisa Nacional por Amostra de Domicilio, PNAD), Brazilian Institute of Geography and Statistics, Rio de Janeiro.
Note: "Working-age" refers to the population ages 15 years and older. "Informal employees" are workers without a signed employment card (sem carteira). "Unpaid" refers to workers who receive no payment, either from volunteer work or from family work.

are ineffective job-search mechanisms (mostly informal networks) and limited access to child care.[26] Most Brazilians rely on informal networks to find a job, and the poor are less likely than the rich to have well-connected, high-earning people in their networks. Importantly, access to child care is significantly lower among the worse-off, potentially limiting labor force participation, as shown in figure 1.20.

Fourth, the poor are most likely to work in sectors with bleaker prospects, such as agriculture and construction. Overall, 14 million Brazilians 15 years of age or older are working in rural areas, as shown in annex table 1A.1. Out of all rural jobs, 65 percent are in agriculture, and this share is even higher among the poor (82.4 percent).[27] Other constraints on future job creation prospects in agriculture include the process of structural transformation (such as labor shifts to nonfarm employment in rural and urban areas) and bleaker prospects for the businesses that had benefited from the commodity boom (in soybeans, sugar cane, and so on). Moreover, between 2008 and 2011, the poor increased their insertion in formal employment mostly in manufacturing and construction, which are also declining.

Figure 1.20 Employability Constraints of the Brazilian Poor beyond Skills and Education

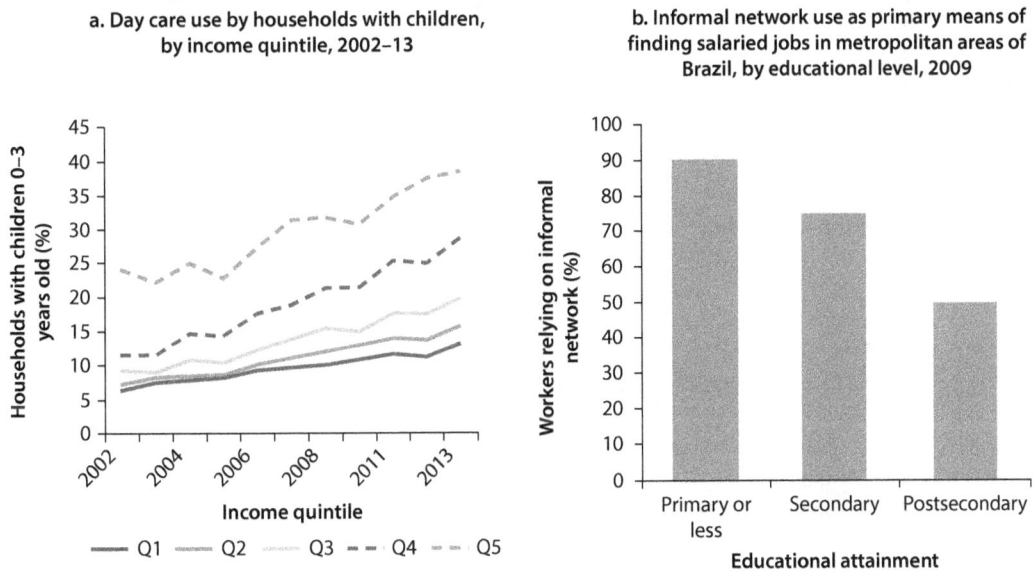

a. Day care use by households with children, by income quintile, 2002–13

b. Informal network use as primary means of finding salaried jobs in metropolitan areas of Brazil, by educational level, 2009

Source: Based on the National Household Survey (Pesquisa Nacional por Amostra de Domicilio, PNAD), Brazilian Institute of Geography and Statistics, Rio de Janeiro.
Note: Figure omits 2010 data because PNAD did not collect data for 2010, a year when census data were collected. However, the PNAD and census data were not compatible in this regard. Q1 = bottom income quintile (0–20 percent of households based on per capita income); Q2 = 21–40 percent; Q3 = 41–60 percent; Q4 = 61–80 percent; Q5 = 81–100 percent.

Source: Mazza 2011.

In this context, to sustain progress in inequality and poverty, renewed productive inclusion policies are needed to connect the poor to better, more productive jobs. Inclusive productivity growth is needed to ensure that disadvantaged segments of the population participate in the growth process by upgrading their own productivity and converting it into sustainable incomes. Given the challenges of the poor described in this chapter, the strategic approaches to connect the poor to more productive jobs will include (a) promoting their skills; (b) helping them transition to better-paid formal and informal jobs; and (c) retaining high-paying, high-productivity jobs. These approaches will require different priorities in urban and rural areas, as chapter 5 discusses in detail.

Annex 1A: Complementary Tables

Table 1A.1 Labor Market Profiles of Rural and Urban Residents in Brazil, 2013
percentage

	Rural	Urban	Total
Labor force participation	66.95	65.01	65.30
Female	51.62	54.87	54.43
Youth	55.44	57.14	56.87
Unemployed	3.15	7.20	6.58
Working in agriculture	64.61	5.08	14.56
Low earnings	65.92	56.99	63.81
Self-consumption	62.49	75.37	65.21
Unpaid	22.45	11.30	20.10
Self-employed, earnings below poverty line	9.67	6.67	9.04
Employer, earnings below poverty line	0.08	—	0.06
Employee, earnings below poverty line	5.31	6.66	5.60
Non-low earnings	34.08	43.01	36.19
Self-employed, earnings above poverty line	53.23	32.78	45.77
Employer, earnings above poverty line	2.50	5.17	3.47
Employee, earnings above poverty line	44.27	62.05	50.75
Total			
Self-consumption or self-construction	32.41	25.22	30.31
Unpaid	11.65	3.78	9.34
Self-employed or employer	31.87	27.48	30.59
Formal employee	7.93	21.93	12.04
Informal employee	16.13	21.58	17.73
Working in nonagricultural occupations	35.39	94.92	85.44
Low earnings	8.88	2.37	2.80
Self-construction	2.93	5.01	4.57
Unpaid	36.94	37.18	37.13
Self-employed, earnings below poverty line	29.24	22.04	23.55
Employer, earnings below poverty line	—	0.40	0.32
Employee, earnings below poverty line	30.89	35.38	34.44

table continues next page

Table 1A.1 Labor Market Profiles of Rural and Urban Residents in Brazil, 2013 *(continued)*

	Rural	*Urban*	*Total*
Non-low earnings	91.12	97.63	97.20
Self-employed, earnings above poverty line	22.61	18.90	19.13
Employer, earnings above poverty line	2.20	4.17	4.05
Employee, earnings above poverty line	75.19	76.93	76.82
Total			
Self-consumption or self-construction	0.26	0.12	0.13
Unpaid	3.28	0.88	1.04
Self-employed or employer	25.20	23.05	23.20
Formal employee	41.94	57.06	56.06
Informal employee	29.32	18.89	19.57

Source: Based on the National Household Survey (Pesquisa Nacional por Amostra de Domicilios, PNAD) conducted by the Brazilian Institute of Geography and Statistics, Rio de Janeiro.
Note: — = not available. Data are based on the working-age population (ages 15 years and older) and pertain to individuals' main jobs only.

Table 1A.2 Labor Market Profiles in Brazil, by Income Quintile, 2013

	Q1		*Q3 and Q4*	
Unemployment rate (%)	17.23		6.11	
Average hourly wage (R$)	3.2		7.26	
Median hourly wage (R$)	2.2		4.4	
Average income from labor (monthly, R$)	241.0		911.7	
Median income from labor (monthly, R$)	180.0		804.0	
Hours worked (weekly)	32.3		39.7	
Employed, unpaid (%)	8.7		1.7	
Employed, for self-consumption (%)	23.7		3.6	
Self-employed and employers (%)	29.6		21.6	
Employees, total (%)	38.1		73.2	
Employees, informal sector (%)	73.6		28.0	
Three most common sectors (%)	Agriculture	55.0	Trade and reparation	19.0
	Trade and reparation	10.0	Manufacturing	14.0
	Domestic services	9.0	Agriculture	13.0
Three most common occupations (%)	Laborer in agriculture and livestock	39.0	Salesperson (stores and markets)	8.0
	Producer in agriculture and livestock	11.0	Laborer in agriculture and livestock	8.0
	Domestic worker	8.0	Domestic worker	6.0

Source: Based on the National Household Survey (Pesquisa Nacional por Amostra de Domicilios, PNAD) conducted by the Brazilian Institute of Geography and Statistics, Rio de Janeiro.
Note: R$ = reais; Q1 = bottom income quintile (0–20 percent of households based on per capita income); Q3 = 41–60 percent; Q4 = 61–80 percent.

Table 1A.3 Labor Market Profiles of the Poor in Brazil, Urban and Rural, 2013

	Urban		Rural		Total	
	Q1	All	Q1	All	Q1	All
Average monthly per capita income (R$)	94.9	1,061.3	100.6	529.2	97.1	981.5
Average hourly wage (R$)	3.8	12.4	2.3	6.0	3.2	11.6
Median hourly wage (R$)	2.8	5.6	1.8	3.7	2.2	5.5
Average monthly income from labor (R$)	349.2	1,604.6	150.6	633.3	241.0	1,449.9
Median monthly income from labor (R$)	283.9	946.2	9.5	378.5	179.8	898.9
Years of education	6.3	8.4	4.7	5.2	5.7	7.9
Maximum level of education (%)						
Below primary	56.0	35.7	73.0	67.2	62.5	40.4
Primary school	13.1	11.4	9.9	9.4	11.9	11.1
Below secondary	10.0	8.0	8.0	6.7	9.2	7.8
Secondary	17.7	28.4	8.5	13.2	14.2	26.1
Post-secondary	3.2	16.6	0.7	3.5	2.3	14.6
Labor force participation (%)	47.7	65.0	65.0	67.0	54.3	65.3
Female labor force participation	36.9	54.9	47.9	51.6	40.7	54.4
Youth labor force participation	35.1	57.1	46.9	55.4	39.6	56.9
Unemployed (%)	34.4	7.2	5.9	3.2	21.4	6.6
Employer (%)	0.4	3.7	0.2	1.5	0.3	3.7
Employed, unpaid (%)	3.4	2.3	13.1	8.7	8.7	2.3
Employed, for self-consumption (%)	9.1	4.5	35.8	21.0	23.7	4.5
Self-employed (%)	30.9	20.6	27.9	28.0	29.3	28.0
Employee, total (%)	56.2	69.0	22.9	40.8	38.1	40.8
Employee, informal sector	68.6	25.6	83.7	51.0	73.6	28.0

	Urban, Q1		Rural, Q1		Total, Q1	
Five most common occupations (%)	Laborer in agriculture and livestock	59.0	Laborer in agriculture and livestock	15.0	Laborer in agriculture and livestock	39.0
	Producer in agriculture and livestock	10.0	Domestic worker	14.0	Producer in agriculture and livestock	11.0
	Fisherman and hunter	3.0	Helper in civil construction	7.0	Domestic worker	8.0
	Domestic worker	3.0	Salesperson (stores and markets)	6.0	Helper in civil construction	4.0
	Miller	2.0	Bricklayer	5.0	Salesperson (stores and markets)	3.0

Source: Based on the National Household Survey (Pesquisa Nacional por Amostra de Domicilios, PNAD) conducted by the Brazilian Institute of Geography and Statistics, Rio de Janeiro.
Note: R$ = reais; Q1 = bottom income quintile (0–20 percent of households based on per capita income). All = all income quintiles.

Table 1A.4 Labor Market and Poverty Status in Brazil, by State, 2013

percentage

	State		State		State	
	Urban	Rural	Urban	Rural	Urban	Rural
	RO		RN		PR	
Unpaid and self-consumption	2.29	8.35	2.16	5.31	1.86	2.60
Self-employed or employer below poverty line	0.41	1.26	1.38	0.93	0.17	0.14
Employee below poverty line	0.66	0.63	1.23	1.38	0.38	0.16
Self-employed or employer above poverty line	14.41	10.46	18.09	4.47	15.42	3.87
Employee above poverty line	53.38	8.16	56.15	8.90	68.73	6.67
	AC		PB		SC	
Unpaid and self-consumption	1.62	9.46	3.94	8.24	2.30	3.53
Self-employed or employer below poverty line	0.72	1.74	1.29	0.96	0.18	0.15
Employee below poverty line	1.80	0.90	2.57	1.21	0.20	0.07
Self-employed or employer above poverty line	14.67	7.43	17.36	3.74	13.89	5.37
Employee above poverty line	52.34	9.34	53.62	7.07	66.94	7.38
	AM		PE		RS	
Unpaid and self-consumption	3.46	6.03	2.51	4.74	2.65	7.39
Self-employed or employer below poverty line	1.68	1.82	1.24	1.64	0.26	0.27
Employee below poverty line	1.74	0.30	1.91	0.85	0.33	0.07
Self-employed or employer above poverty line	19.87	4.88	16.25	4.73	14.00	6.78
Employee above poverty line	56.76	3.46	58.76	7.39	62.52	5.74
	RR		AL		MS	
Unpaid and self-consumption	1.08	4.78	2.65	9.72	1.36	2.39
Self-employed or employer below poverty line	0.72	0.72	1.37	1.27	0.37	0.03
Employee below poverty line	1.26	0.27	2.60	2.24	0.58	0.17
Self-employed or employer above poverty line	17.93	7.12	12.06	4.53	15.51	1.64
Employee above poverty line	60.99	5.13	52.32	11.25	70.51	7.43
	PA		SE		MT	
Unpaid and self-consumption	2.43	9.67	2.61	6.13	1.45	2.51
Self-employed or employer below poverty line	1.41	3.23	1.23	1.54	0.20	0.33
Employee below poverty line	1.73	1.01	2.06	1.07	0.56	0.16
Self-employed or employer above poverty line	16.51	9.58	16.38	7.04	14.00	5.02
Employee above poverty line	44.27	10.16	49.33	12.62	66.48	9.28
	AP		BA		GO	
Unpaid and self-consumption	1.07	1.46	8.72	31.76	1.63	1.92
Self-employed or employer below poverty line	1.45	0.68	5.10	7.87	0.33	0.05
Employee below poverty line	1.65	0.48	8.14	6.01	0.56	0.05
Self-employed or employer above poverty line	22.02	3.30	66.74	22.05	17.82	2.36
Employee above poverty line	64.69	3.20	186.45	32.32	69.48	5.80
	TO		MG		DF	
Unpaid and self-consumption	3.29	11.82	2.79	5.23	0.47	0.22
Self-employed or employer below poverty line	0.72	1.03	0.25	0.36	0.27	0.00
Employee below poverty line	1.03	0.69	0.63	0.35	0.22	0.07
Self-employed or employer above poverty line	17.44	5.35	15.18	3.65	13.57	1.06
Employee above poverty line	49.84	8.80	64.23	7.35	81.46	2.65

table continues next page

Table 1A.4 Labor Market and Poverty Status in Brazil, by State, 2013 *(continued)*

	State		*State*		*State*	
	Urban	*Rural*	*Urban*	*Rural*	*Urban*	*Rural*
	MA		*ES*		*CE*	
Unpaid and self-consumption	6.60	20.36	1.35	4.18	3.57	12.16
Self-employed or employer below poverty line	1.64	2.57	0.56	0.23	1.47	2.19
Employee below poverty line	1.78	1.67	0.86	0.33	2.49	1.79
Self-employed or employer above poverty line	11.74	8.35	16.61	5.07	15.73	4.42
Employee above poverty line	33.46	11.82	63.56	7.25	47.62	8.57
	PI		*RJ*		*SP*	
Unpaid and self-consumption	5.83	12.87	0.46	0.17	0.81	0.33
Self-employed or employer below poverty line	1.29	3.30	0.49	0.05	0.20	0.01
Employee below poverty line	1.41	1.73	0.36	0.08	0.40	0.03
Self-employed or employer above poverty line	15.52	9.05	19.78	0.66	16.47	0.66
Employee above poverty line	40.17	8.85	75.95	1.99	78.29	2.80

Source: Based on the National Household Survey (Pesquisa Nacional por Amostra de Domicilios, PNAD) conducted by the Brazilian Institute of Geography and Statistics, Rio de Janeiro.
Note: States are abbreviated as follows: Acre (AC), Alagoas (AL), Amapá (AP), Amazonas (AM), Bahia (BA), Ceará (CE), Distrito Federal (DF), Espírito Santo (ES), Goiás (GO), Maranhão (MA), Minas Gerais (MG), Mato Grosso (MT), Mato Grosso do Sul (MS), Pará (PA), Paraíba (PB), Pernambuco (PE), Piauí (PI), Paraná (PR), Rio de Janeiro (RJ), Rio Grande do Norte (RN), Rondônia (RO), Roraima (RR), Rio Grande do Sul (RS), Santa Catarina (SC), Sergipe (SE), São Paulo (SP), Tocantins (TO).

Notes

1. The employment and unemployment rate data are based on the Monthly Employment Survey (Pesquisa Mensal de Emprego, PME), Brazilian Institute of Geography and Statistics, Rio de Janeiro.

2. $R1= US$0.32 (April 2, 2015).

3. The labor participation rate data are based on the National Sample Survey of Households (Pesquisa Nacional por Amostra de Domicílio, PNAD), Brazilian Institute of Geography and Statistics, Rio de Janeiro. In demographic and regional terms, Ferreira, Firpo, and Messina (2014) find that since 2002 there is a rising share of non-white workers in the labor force (18–64 years old)—from 45.5 percent in 2002 to 53.3 percent in 2013—and that although the labor force has continued to urbanize (from 85.6 percent in 2002 to 86 percent in 2013), most of the urbanization trend preceded 2002.

4. The total of 19 million new formal jobs excludes public administration jobs, which accounted for 16 percent of all job creation in Brazil since 2003 and today constitutes 21 percent of all employment. Despite the increase in formality, about 40 percent of employees in Brazil have informal jobs and are therefore not covered by social security—a coverage level below the Latin American and Caribbean average but higher than that of neighboring Southern Cone countries such as Argentina and Uruguay. (The preceding data are derived from the Socio-Economic Database for Latin America and the Caribbean, Universidad Nacional de La Plata [SEDLAC/CEDLAS], accessed January 4, 2015, http://sedlac.econo.unlp.edu.ar/eng/.). In addition, based on the National Sample Survey of Households (PNAD), most agricultural

workers in 2013 (about 59 percent) were either self-employed or worked for self-consumption. In this sector, salaried workers represent 30 percent of the workforce, out of which almost 60 percent are informal. In contrast, 76 percent of nonagriculture workers are salaried, among whom 26 percent are informal.

5. "Informality" in this report refers to those workers who lack a signed employment card (carteira assinada).

6. The September 2013–September 2014 data are based on the Monthly Employment Survey (Pesquisa Mensal de Emprego, PME) conducted by the Brazilian Institute of Geography and Statistics, Rio de Janeiro.

7. Cadastro Único (Single Registry) is the Brazilian federal government's database that registers and characterizes low-income households (including income, family composition, location, and so on) to provide information that social programs use to select new beneficiaries.

8. The poverty line is defined as per capita income of US$4 per day—the international standard across countries in the Latin American and Caribbean region.

9. The Gini index (or Gini coefficient), the most commonly used measure of inequality, is a measure of statistical dispersion representing the income distribution of a nation's residents. A Gini coefficient of zero expresses perfect equality (every resident has the same income), whereas a coefficient of one (or 100 percent) expresses maximal inequality (one person has all the income, and all others have none).

10. Because of the absence of representative panel income data in Brazil, the authors (Bianchi-Santarrosa and Lopez-Calva 2014) have used the synthetic panel approach recently developed by Dang et al. (2011). Income mobility from 2003 to 2011 was predicted based on the associated characteristics possessed in 2011 by individuals of different mobility groups. (Labor market status and formalization indicators are available only for the head of a household.) In addition, observations are restricted for households whose head is between 25 and 55 years of age to control for attrition between the two datasets. Finally, the poverty line used is R$140 (the Bolsa Família Program threshold).

11. The minimum wage also affects the poor because social benefits such as the social pension are indexed to the minimum-wage annual increase.

12. Comparative labor productivity data come from the Total Economy Database, January 2014 update, The Conference Board, New York, http://www.conference-board.org/data/economydatabase.

13. The minimum-wage effect has two dimensions: First, because the annual change in the minimum wage is indexed to the GDP growth rate of two years prior, it can grow faster than labor productivity growth for a large share of firms, affecting their ability to accumulate capital. Second, because many social benefits are indexed to the minimum wage, its growth has fiscal effects. Although these effects can be important, they are not the focus of this report.

14. A person is unemployed if searching for a job (that is, in the labor force) but jobless; a person is nonemployed if jobless, regardless of being in the labor force.

15. The data presented throughout the paragraph are based on the National Household Survey (Pesquisa Nacional por Amostra de Domicilios, PNAD) conducted by the Brazilian Institute of Geography and Statistics, Rio de Janeiro.

16. The data throughout the paragraph are based on the National Household Survey (Pesquisa Nacional por Amostra de Domicilios, PNAD) conducted by the Brazilian Institute of Geography and Statistics, Rio de Janeiro.

17. Of all agricultural employees (constituting 24 percent of all agricultural workers), 67 percent work in the informal sector, and only 33 percent in the formal sector.

18. The data presented throughout this paragraph are based on the National Household Survey (Pesquisa Nacional por Amostra de Domicilios, PNAD) conducted by the Brazilian Institute of Geography and Statistics, Rio de Janeiro.

19. This evidence is confirmed by a recent study on favelas that finds that 17 percent of *favela* residents who receive Bolsa Família work (Data Favela 2015).

20. The findings presented in this paragraph are based on the National Household Survey (Pesquisa Nacional por Amostra de Domicilios, PNAD) conducted by the Brazilian Institute of Geography and Statistics, Rio de Janeiro.

21. This finding, as shown in table 1.3, is based on on the Monthly Employment Survey (Pesquisa Mensal de Emprego, PME) conducted by the Brazilian Institute of Geography and Statistics, Rio de Janeiro.

22. In contrast to Autor and Dorn (2013), Maciente, Silva, and Gukovas do not find evidence of wage polarization in Brazil. Applying the same methodology as described in figure 1.17, panel a, to the National Household Survey (Pesquisa Nacional por Amostra de Domicilios, PNAD), similar evidence is found as when using RAIS, which shows that this is not a particular feature of formal labor markets. Similarly, employment shares of occupations ranked by skill level remained fairly stable with no evidence of polarization. Ranking occupations by skill using wage levels of 2004 as above, Maciente, Silva, and Gukovas (2015) also analyze the change in the employment share and find that it remained fairly stable across the period. Hence, while the number of jobs in each occupation increased significantly, there was no significant change in the composition of employment.

23. The minimum wage also affects the poor through the other social benefits, such as social pensions (Benefício de Prestação Continuada [BPC]), that are indexed to it.

24. Data throughout this paragraph are based on the National Household Survey (Pesquisa Nacional por Amostra de Domicilio, PNAD), Brazilian Institute of Geography and Statistics, Rio de Janeiro.

25. Data throughout this paragraph are based on the National Household Survey (Pesquisa Nacional por Amostra de Domicilio, PNAD), Brazilian Institute of Geography and Statistics, Rio de Janeiro.

26. In Brazil, universal child care is available *only* for children of ages four years or older.

27. Data throughout the paragraph in the main text and in this note are based on the 2013 National Household Survey (Pesquisa Nacional por Amostra de Domicilios, PNAD) conducted by the Brazilian Institute of Geography and Statistics, Rio de Janeiro. Of all those employed in rural areas, 8.7 percent and 21 percent are engaged in unpaid work or self-consumption, respectively. In addition, 29.5 percent are either self-employed or an employer, 20 percent are formal employees, and 21 percent are informal employees. By comparison, among all workers nationally, 5.4 percent work for self-consumption, 2.3 percent are unpaid, 24.3 percent are either self-employed or an employer, 50 percent are formal employees, and 19.3 percent are informal employees.

References

Almeida, Rita, and Jaime Jesus Filho. 2011. "Demand for Skills and the Degree of Mismatches: Evidence from Job Vacancies in the Developing World." Unpublished manuscript, World Bank, Washington, DC.

Autor, David, and David Dorn. 2013. "The Growth of Low-Skill Service Jobs and the Polarization of the U.S. Labor Market." *American Economic Review* 103 (5): 1553–97.

Azevedo, João Pedro, María E. Dávalos, Carolina Diaz-Bonilla, Bernardo Atuesta, and Raul A. Castañeda. 2013. "Fifteen Years of Inequality in Latin America: How Have Labor Markets Helped?" Policy Research Working Paper 6384, World Bank, Washington, DC.

Azevedo, João Pedro, Gabriela Inchauste, and Viviane Sanfelice. 2013. "Decomposing the Recent Inequality Decline in Latin America." Policy Research Working Paper 6715, World Bank, Washington, DC.

Barros, Ricardo, Mirela Carvalho, Samuel Franco, and Rosane Mendonça. 2010. "Markets, the State, and the Dynamics of Inequality in Brazil." In *Declining Inequality in Latin America: A Decade of Progress?* edited by Luis F. Lopez-Calva and Nora Lustig, 134–74. Washington, DC: Brookings Institution and United Nations Development Programme.

Bastos, P. 2014. "Labor Reallocations Following Exchange Rate Shocks: Evidence from Brazil." Background paper, World Bank, Washington, DC.

Bianchi-Santarrosa, S., and L. Lopez-Calva. 2014. "Poverty Dynamics and the Labor Market in Brazil." Policy note—background paper for this report, World Bank, Washington, DC.

Bonelli, Regis. 2005. *Productivity Performance in Developing Countries, Country Case Studies: Brazil*. Report, United Nations Industrial Development Organization (UNIDO), Vienna.

Busso, Marina, Matías Bassi, Sergio Urzúa, and Jaime Vargas. 2012. *Desconectados: Habilidades, educación y empleo en América Latina*. [Disconnected: Skills, Education, and Employment in Latin America.] Washington, DC: Inter-American Development Bank.

Dang, Hai-Anh, Peter Lanjouw, Jill Luoto, and David McKenzie. 2014. "Using Repeated Cross-Sections to Explore Movements in and out of Poverty. *Journal of Development Economics* 107: 112–28.

Data Favela. 2015. "Pesquisa sobre emprego entre os beneficiaries do Programa Bolsa Familia residents em Favelas." Unpublished manuscript, Data Favela, Brasilia.

DIEESE (Inter-Union Department of Statistics and Socio-Economic Studies). 2011. *Rotatividade e flexibilidade no mercado de trabalho.* [Turnover and Flexibility in the Labor Market.] São Paulo, Brazil: DIEESE.

Ferreira, Francisco H. G., Sergio P. Firpo, and Julian Messina. 2014. "A More Level Playing Field? Explaining the Decline in Earnings Inequality in Brazil, 1995–2012." IRIBA (International Research Initiative on Brazil and Africa) Working Paper 12, University of Manchester, United Kingdom.

Fonseca, R. 2012. "Produtividade e crescimento da indústria brasileira." [Productivity and Growth of Brazilian Industry.] *Revista Brasileira de Comércio Exterior* 112: 42–51.

Gragnolati, Michele, Ole Hagen Jorgensen, Romera Rocha, and Anna Fruttero. 2011. *Growing Old in an Older Brazil: Implications of Population Aging on Growth, Poverty, Public Finance, and Service Delivery.* Directions in Development Series. Washington, DC: World Bank.

ILO (International Labour Organization). 2011. *Key Indicators of the Labour Market.* 7th ed. Geneva: ILO.

ILO (International Labour Organization), OECD (Organisation for Economic Co-operation and Development), and World Bank Group. 2014. *G20 Labour Markets: Outlook, Key Challenges, and Policy Responses.* Report prepared for the G20 Labour and Employment Ministerial Meeting, Melbourne, Australia, September 10–11.

INEP (National Institute of Educational Studies and Research Anísio Teixeira). 2014. *Censo Escolar da Educação Básica 2013: Resumo Técnico.* Brasilia: INEP.

Leichsenring, Alexandre, Joana Silva, and Rafael Proença. 2015. "The Insertion in Formal Employment among the Poor and Vulnerable." Research paper—background paper for this report, World Bank, Washington, DC.

Macedo, Mariano, and Luiz Alberto Esteves. 2012. "Produtividade: algumas observações. Um breve retrato da produtividade do trabalho agregada da Economia Brasileira." PowerPoint presentation for Seminário ABDI-IPEA, Rede de Pesquisa "Formação e Mercado de Trabalho," October 26.

Maciente, Aguinaldo. 2013. "The Determinants of Agglomeration in Brazil: Input-Output, Labor and Knowledge Externalities." PhD dissertation, University of Illinois at Urbana-Champaign.

Maciente, Aguinaldo, Joana Silva, and Renata Gukovas. 2015. "Employment Creation, Labor Productivity, and Firms' Dynamics." Research paper—background paper for this report, World Bank, Washington, DC.

Mazza, Jacqueline. 2011. "Fast Tracking Jobs: Advances and Next Steps for Labor Intermediation Services in Latin America and the Caribbean." Technical note, Inter-American Development Bank, Washington, DC.

OECD (Organisation for Economic Co-operation and Development). 2005. *PISA 2003 Technical Report.* OECD, Paris.

———. 2012. "Education GPS: The World of Education at Your Fingers." OECD Education GPS website, http://gpseducation.oecd.org.

———. 2014. *PISA 2012 Results in Focus: What 15-Year-Olds Know and What They Can Do with What They Know.* Brochure on 2012 PISA (Program for International Student Assessment) results, OECD, Paris.

Silva, Joana, Rafael Proença, and Flávio Cireno. 2015. "Impacts of the Bolsa Família Program on Education: A Regression Discontinuity Approach." Research paper—background paper for this report, World Bank, Washington, DC; Ministry of Social Development and Fight Against Hunger, Brasilia.

Todos Pela Educação (All for Education). 2012. *Anuário Brasileiro da Educação Básica 2012.* [Brazilian Yearbook of Basic Education 2012.] São Paulo: Editora Moderna.

UNDP (United Nations Development Programme). 2014. *Human Development Report 2014. Sustaining Human Progress: Reducing Vulnerabilities and Building Resilience.* New York: UNDP.

World Bank. 2013. *World Development Report 2014: Risk and Opportunity*. Washington, DC: World Bank.

———. 2014. *Doing Business 2015: Going Beyond Efficiency*. Washington, DC: World Bank.

———. Forthcoming. "Achieving Sustainable Shared Prosperity for Brazil's Third Century of Independence. A Systematic Country Diagnostic." World Bank, Washington, DC.

Zylberstajn, Eduardo, and Joana Silva. 2015. "Earnings Consequences of Labor Turnover: The Case of Brazil." Research paper—background paper for this report, Institute of Economic Research Foundation, University of São Paulo (FIPE-USP); World Bank, Washington, DC.

Skills Development Programs to Help Workers Become More Employable and Productive

Introduction

Brazil can continue to build upon the progress achieved in educational coverage and quality, not only to prepare a high-quality workforce but also to extend opportunities to the most vulnerable, who may lack relevant qualifications for an increasingly competitive labor market. Brazil's progress in expanding education coverage and quality has been extensively discussed and documented (Bruns, Evans, and Luque 2012). However, many challenges remain. For example, average schooling is only 8.4 years (completion of only lower-secondary education) and the educational quality is low, and 18.7 percent of 18- to 24-year-olds are neither in school nor at work (de Hoyos, Halsey, and Popova 2015). Within this context, technical vocational education and training (TVET), and in particular technical education (TEC), provides options for learning an applied vocation and for keeping at-risk and unmotivated youth in school through the upper-secondary level, while vocational training provides opportunities to adapt a low-qualified or unqualified labor force, update obsolete skills, and prepare workers for new opportunities in new or fast-growing sectors. Interestingly, the share of students enrolled in TEC at the upper-secondary level is low by international standards (13.5 percent of total upper-secondary enrollment, which is substantially below the 46 percent Organisation for Economic Co-operation and Development [OECD] average in 2011) (OECD 2012).

Since 2011, Brazil has invested significantly in vocational training and TEC through the flagship program PRONATEC, aiming to foster economic opportunities for all—especially the poorest and most vulnerable, who often drop out of formal school. The National Program for Access to Technical Education and Employment (PRONATEC) is an umbrella program coordinating a variety of existing and new vocational education and training policies, including courses in two modalities: Technical Education (TEC) and Initial and Continuing Training Programs (FIC). Under this program, the Ministry of Education (MEC) has established partnerships with several other ministries (including Social Development; Labor and Employment; Tourism; and Communication) to identify and select potential trainees for technical courses. The program offered 8.8 million training slots between 2011 and 2014, and it includes an important focus on reaching the poor and disadvantaged populations (for a detailed description, see Feres 2012). PRONATEC is thus tweaking the traditional panorama of TVET in Brazil, whereby TEC had primarily reached students of high socioeconomic backgrounds and vocational training was geared toward the needs of larger firms (Canali 2009; Almeida, Amaral, and Felicio 2015). Nevertheless, various design and implementation issues may be hindering the efficiency and effectiveness of this flagship program. This chapter discusses some of these issues, also offering a broader perspective of the challenges and opportunities faced by the country's overall TVET system.

Even though persistent weaknesses in the general education system may be hampering the TVET system's effectiveness, TVET in Brazil has several strong and well-designed features. Positive features of the TVET system include (a) a strong articulation of general and technical skills across tracks at the secondary level (Schwartzman and Moura Castro 2013; Almeida et al. 2015; Almeida, Amaral, and Felicio 2015); and (b) a well-coordinated set of diverse, short-duration courses that often yield good employability and productivity results (Silva, Gukovas, and Caruso 2015). However, as the general education system still faces multiple quality challenges (Bruns, Evans, and Luque 2012), the effectiveness of TVET programs may be limited by weak foundations of the general education system and limited opportunities for second-chance education programs.

Brazil could fine-tune the design and implementation of its TVET system, including PRONATEC, to enhance its efficiency and sustainability in producing a more productive workforce. The TVET system faces important challenges, including (for several providers) little coordination with the private sector in TEC (Almeida, Amaral, and Felicio 2015). Moreover, while Brazil has good administrative datasets and strong monitoring of TEC and vocational training programs through the National System of Vocational Education and Information Technology (SISTEC), these are not regularly used to track employability and inform policy. Anticipating a period of fiscal consolidation, PRONATEC's efficiency and labor market results are even more critical. Moreover, most PRONATEC expansion happened through the Sistema S (S System) network of course providers, whose trainings have high quality and returns (Silva, Gukovas, and Caruso 2015).[1] This expansion was anchored on the gratuity agreement between Sistema S and the government, establishing that 60 percent of total revenues from taxes directed at Sistema S are used to provide subsidized training. However, this allocation is now being met. Looking forward, the expansion will likely rely on a more diverse set of training providers, which will inevitably bring new challenges, including quality certification and accreditation issues (Almeida, Amaral, and Felicio 2015).

This chapter identifies challenges and discusses concrete opportunities for incremental modifications to strengthen TVET delivery and ultimately PRONATEC's focus on the skills needed for the labor market. Even though there is no "one-size-fits-all" solution to Brazil's complex TVET delivery challenges, the key strategic priorities for PRONATEC and the delivery of TVET include the following:

- *Strengthening monitoring and evaluation (M&E) systems* (building on the country's strong administrative data) to measure results by tracking learning and labor market outcomes (employability and earnings increases) of trainees, systematically using that information to inform program expansion, and making it also available to students and trainees so they can make more informed decisions
- *Improving partnerships with the private sector and access to apprenticeships,* thus better aligning training offerings and content with employers' needs
- *Guaranteeing the quality and relevance of program content,* including through more innovative curricula and pedagogies, a strong attention, and articulation to, core foundational skills (cognitive and socioemotional); and stronger technical preparation for teachers and trainers, including greater linkage with sector experience
- *Making career guidance available* to support students' school-to-work transition and older trainees' sector or job redeployment

Although all of these reforms are important, promoting evidence-based policy making through better M&E systems is an essential first step to begin adjusting program resources and content depending on labor and business needs. Without strong M&E systems, PRONATEC's TEC and FIC will not have a solid mechanism of ensuring internal efficiency or aligning course content with the needs of the labor market. Also critical is the fact that skills needed for productivity and economic growth require a sequenced and well-articulated combination of education, training, and labor market programs and institutions (Banerji et al. 2010). Any skills development and upgrading policy for Brazil should keep in mind these critical elements for success.

While this chapter focuses on reforms of skills development programs to raise labor productivity (Goal 1), it reserves for chapter 5 a more detailed discussion on how to adapt skills programs, including PRONATEC, to better serve the needs of the poor by connecting them with more productive jobs (Goal 2). Chapter 5 discusses in greater depth the need for the inclusion of "soft skills" modules and hands-on components and apprenticeships that better address the employability barriers of the poor and strengthen links with entrepreneurship support. In urban areas—and when job demand is strong—it emphasizes the importance of promoting links with public employment services to ensure that trainees are not discouraged.

Existing Skills Development Policies

Despite impressive progress in education coverage over recent decades, Brazil faces obstacles concerning both low educational quality and individuals' completion of upper-secondary education, renewing the focus on TVET. Over the past 20 years, school enrollments for students aged 7–14 years have steadily increased (from 80.9 percent in 1980 to 96.7 percent in 2010). However, and despite being one of the world's largest economies, Brazil has a population whose average schooling is 8.4 years, corresponding to the completion of only a lower-secondary education (Bruns, Evans, and Luque 2012). In fact, no segment of the Brazilian education system crystallizes the quality gap with OECD and East Asian countries as clearly as secondary school. Furthermore, there is evidence that the returns to education have been falling (figure 2.1), reducing students' incentives to invest in it (Aedo and Walker 2012). Within this context, TVET arises as an option for learning an applied vocation and keeping at-risk and unmotivated youth in school through the upper-secondary level. It is also a way to adapt a low-skilled or unqualified labor force and prepare workers for new opportunities in new or fast-growing sectors.

Figure 2.1 Education Earnings Premiums in Selected Latin American and Caribbean Countries, 1990–2008

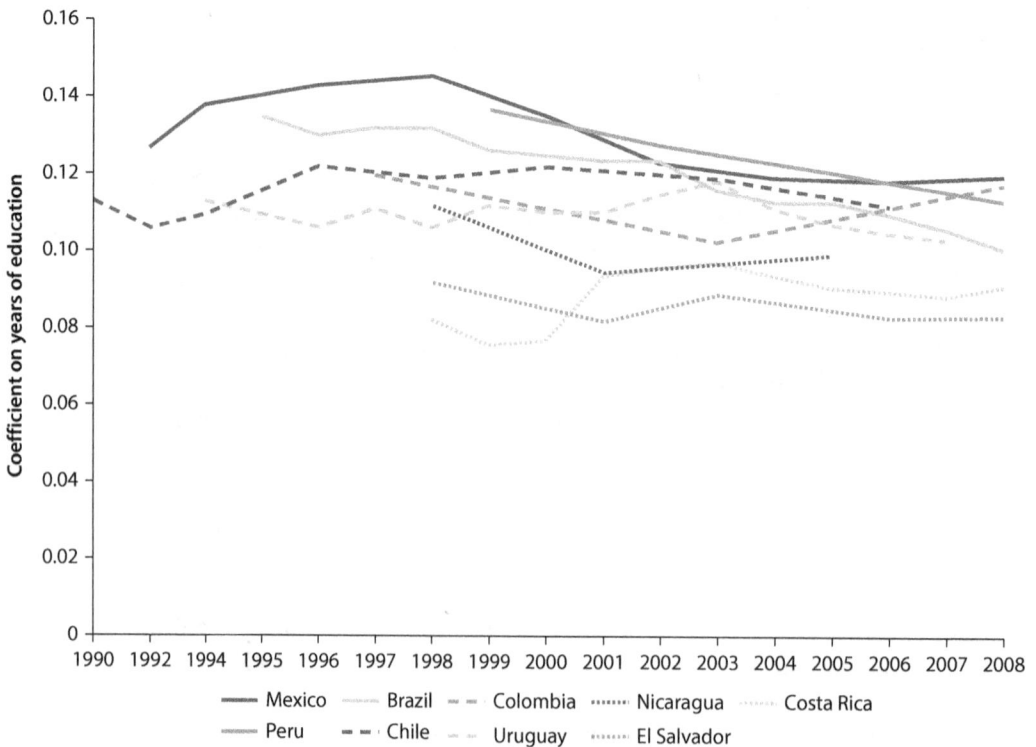

Source: Aedo and Walker 2012, based on Gasparini et al. 2011.
Note: Figure reports the coefficients on years of education variable from Mincer-style monthly earnings regressions.

In the years ahead, education policies that deliver high-quality educational foundations to all students are essential to strengthen the impacts of TVET policies. Even though this chapter will focus on technical skills, it is crucial to ensure that new cohorts of Brazilian workers develop strong foundations in basic education, from early childhood through secondary education (including both regular and special tracks) and second-chance education programs. As discussed in Bruns, Evans, and Luque (2012), a high percentage of secondary students in Brazil are enrolled in night shifts, which deliver only four hours of instruction a day, compared with seven hours or more in most OECD countries and even longer school days in leading East Asian countries. Infrastructure is also lacking: Brazilian schools lack the libraries, science labs, and computer and language facilities that most OECD students enjoy. In addition, the curriculum is often oriented toward memorization, and almost every state secondary school system faces a severe shortage of qualified math and science teachers. As a result, policies to improve basic education should continue to be a priority for Brazil, including second-chance or adult education for youth and adults with low educational attainment for their age (an approach called Educação de Jovens e Adultos [EJA], also referred to as "Supplementary Education").

Even though enrollments in secondary and postsecondary TEC have recently grown significantly, the share of Brazilian students enrolled in TEC at the upper-secondary level is still low by international standards. From 2007 to 2011 alone, enrollment in TEC (at the secondary level) in Brazil grew by 60 percent, from 780,000 to 1.25 million students (INEP 2013). Nevertheless, TEC in 2011 still represented only 13.6 percent of total upper-secondary enrollment (approximately 8 million students), as shown in figure 2.2 (OECD 2011). This number is still considerably lower than the TEC enrollment levels in countries such as France, Germany, Portugal, and Spain, where enrollments in TEC reach about 40 percent of the total number of students enrolled in the upper-secondary level. The OECD average is 46 percent. There is also some anecdotal evidence that skills shortages may be hurting the more innovative firms (for example, Aedo and Walker 2012), although this may be explained by the shortages in selected occupations such as architects or engineers (Menezes-Filho 2012).

TVET delivery in Brazil is divided primarily between short-duration FIC courses (vocational training) and long-duration TEC courses and involves multiple providers. FIC courses are short-term vocational training programs usually directed at improving existing workers' qualifications and not tied to the formal education system. The Sistema S (S System) network of providers has a key role in the delivery of these courses: each year it trains approximately 3.5 million students (making it the fifth-largest training provider in the world), and it is responsible for more than 80 percent of total PRONATEC FIC provision. Other providers include federal institutes, state and municipal school networks, and private providers (INEP 2013; Almeida, Amaral, and Felicio 2015; Brazil, Court of Accounts 2015). TEC courses are longer-term programs that do form part of the formal education system and have upward permeability. They are mostly offered at the secondary and postsecondary levels.[2] Almeida, Amaral,

Figure 2.2 Upper-Secondary Technical Education Enrollments, Selected Countries, 2011

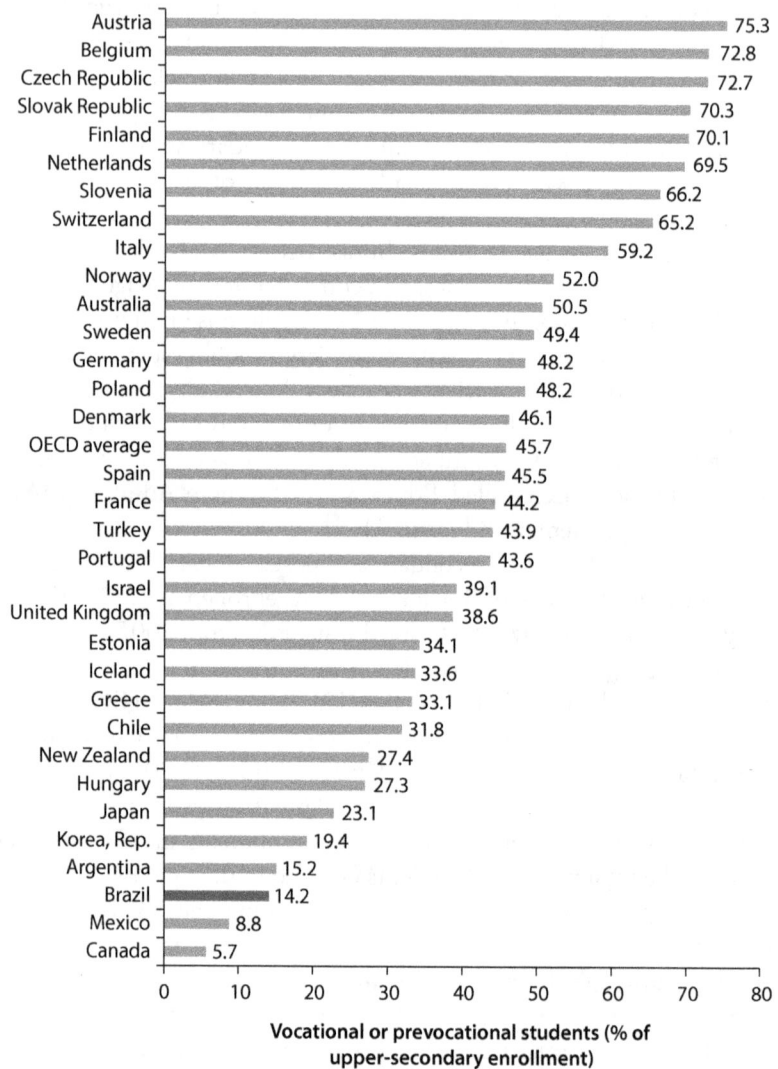

Austria	75.3
Belgium	72.8
Czech Republic	72.7
Slovak Republic	70.3
Finland	70.1
Netherlands	69.5
Slovenia	66.2
Switzerland	65.2
Italy	59.2
Norway	52.0
Australia	50.5
Sweden	49.4
Germany	48.2
Poland	48.2
Denmark	46.1
OECD average	45.7
Spain	45.5
France	44.2
Turkey	43.9
Portugal	43.6
Israel	39.1
United Kingdom	38.6
Estonia	34.1
Iceland	33.6
Greece	33.1
Chile	31.8
New Zealand	27.4
Hungary	27.3
Japan	23.1
Korea, Rep.	19.4
Argentina	15.2
Brazil	14.2
Mexico	8.8
Canada	5.7

Vocational or prevocational students (% of upper-secondary enrollment)

Source: OECD 2011.
Note: OECD = Organisation for Economic Co-operation and Development. Table reports the percentage of upper-secondary students enrolled in vocational or prevocational programs.

and Felicio (2015) explore data from INEP administrative records and break down the distribution of enrollments for TEC at secondary or postsecondary level across the different providers as of 2011. They show that enrollments in private account for 47 percent of total enrollments, while Sistema S accounts for 41 percent, state TVET systems account for 9 percent, and federal TVET systems for 3 percent. In addition, TEC includes tertiary-level technical education (Tecnológico) that is mainly delivered by federal technical education institutes (institutos federais).

Beyond PRONATEC, a comprehensive mapping of the TVET system reveals four facts worth highlighting. First, the broader TVET system displays permeability between tracks at the upper-secondary and tertiary levels (Almeida, Amaral, and Felicio 2015), as shown in figure 2.3. TEC is not a dead-end track.[3] Second, and related to this (as this report will further discuss), TEC students have greater wage returns than their peers in an academic upper-secondary track and are also more likely to proceed to tertiary education, an unusual phenomenon for TEC in Latin America. This permeability is an important feature to strengthen and maintain in the system.[4] Third, technical and academic subjects are generally well integrated in the Brazilian system of education, ensuring that technical students also have at least ongoing education in critical foundational subjects such as math, science, and Portuguese, even when they choose a technical track. The three main alternative tracks at the upper-secondary level (Integrado, Concomitante, and Subsequente) all combine technical courses with general courses at the secondary level. Fourth, it includes a well-coordinated set of diverse, short-duration vocational training courses whose quality and returns are very diverse (Almeida et al. 2015), but for some providers (such as the S System) often yield good employability and productivity results (Silva, Gukovas, and Caruso 2015).

In addition to FIC courses for which MEC is responsible, the Ministry of Labor and Employment and state secretariats of labor offer "qualification" programs: short-term vocational training for a predefined occupation designed to meet a specific industry or local demand.[5]

Figure 2.3 Brazil's TVET System: Vertical and Horizontal Permeability across Technical and Academic Tracks, and TEC and FIC modalities

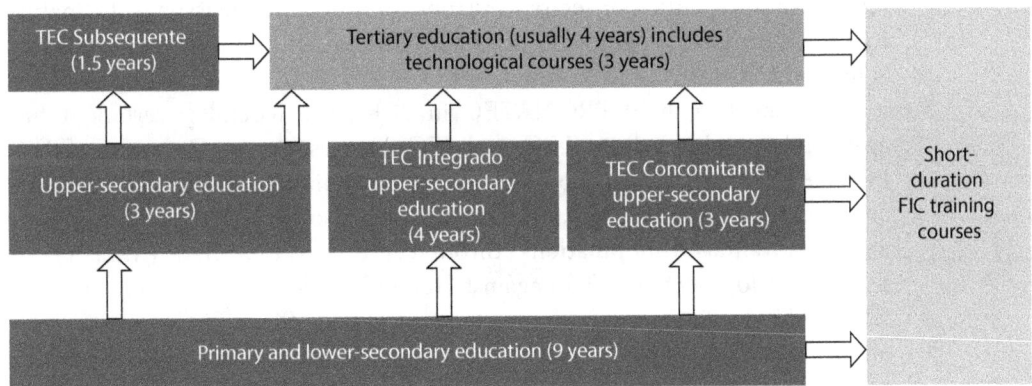

Source: Almeida, Amaral, and Felicio 2015. © World Bank. Further permission required for reuse.
Note: TEC = Technical Education modality of PRONATEC (National Program for Access to Technical Education and Employment); FIC = Initial and Continuing Training modality of PRONATEC. "Technological" courses are tertiary-level technical courses delivered mainly by federal technical education institutes. "TEC Subsequente" includes technical courses for students who have already concluded an academic upper-secondary program. "TEC Integrado" includes academic and vocational courses offered as one program in the same school. "TEC Concomitante" is a complementary, but separate, technical program for students who are completing an academic upper-secondary program, which is frequently carried out in two separate schools.

Student payment for TVET also varies by provider, state, or municipality as well as by student profile (whether a federal or state social program beneficiary). TVET programs are free of charge to students enrolled in any public institution within the federal or state networks. In Sistema S, however, payment can vary: some students study for free through subsidies from public social programs such as Bolsa Trabalhador or under the new Free-of-Charge Vacancies Agreement (Acordo de Gratuidade) signed between Sistema S and the government. If an employer pays for TVET courses (typically FIC courses through Sistema S), the students will also not be directly charged. In this case, payment is the responsibility of the employer soliciting the courses for its employees. Students who do not fall under one of these beneficiary categories and wish to take courses through Sistema S will be charged, although the fee varies according to the program or state.

Many technical programs in Brazil, whether of short or long duration, still do not require apprenticeships or other types of workplace learning as part of the curriculum, partly because employer involvement is difficult to obtain (Almeida, Amaral, and Felicio 2015). Although some states, such as Ceará, have implemented joint programs with local industry to provide paid internships for graduates, this practice is neither uniform nor fully integrated into the TVET curriculum. TVET providers still have no de facto legal obligation to offer apprenticeships or other forms of workplace learning for TEC. However, the National Catalogue of Technical Courses indicates that apprenticeships and workplace learning can be carried out *in addition to* the required minimum classroom hours for TEC, not *in place of* this classroom time. From employers' perspective, as the chapter 4 discusses in detail, the Apprentice Law of 2000 mandates that all medium-size and large firms fill 5–15 percent of their professional workforce with youth apprentices. However, these opportunities are neither exclusive to TEC students nor available in all regions, municipalities, or sectors. Further complicating the issue is the inability of certain TEC programs to offer apprenticeships in areas where industry is limited.

Since the launch of PRONATEC in 2011, the federal government has aggressively expanded its TEC and FIC courses. As of December 2014, PRONATEC had offered more than 8 million training slots to TEC students and vocational trainees. Notably, the program also focuses on reaching poor and disadvantaged populations through PRONATEC-MDS (Ministry of Social Development and Fight against Hunger), under which 40 percent of all PRONATEC training slots are targeted to the poor. Since PRONATEC's creation, enrollments financed by the program grew by approximately 60 percent for TEC at the upper-secondary level and more than quadrupled for vocational training (Brazil, Ministry of Education 2014), as shown in figure 2.4. Overall, PRONATEC vacancies tend to concentrate disproportionately in shorter-term FIC courses.

A critical question, however, is whether PRONATEC—and TVET program delivery more generally—is cost-effective and financially sustainable. Are the

Figure 2.4 PRONATEC Enrollments, by Type, 2011–14

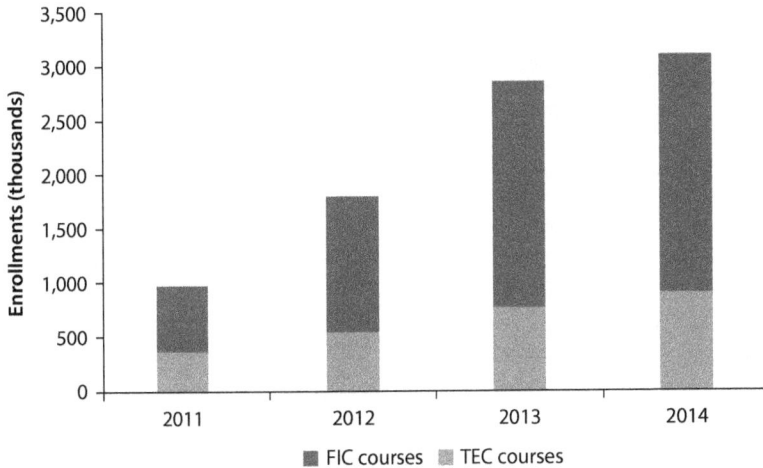

Source: Brazil, Ministry of Education 2014; Brazil, Court of Accounts 2015.
Note: PRONATEC is the National Program for Access to Technical Education and Employment. "FIC" refers to short-term courses (Initial and Continuing Training Programs). "TEC" refers to technical education courses at the upper-secondary level. The 2014 data include enrollments as of May 2014.

skills being taught and the programs being offered well aligned with the needs of the labor market? Is TVET reaching the populations and fields where it can make the greatest impact? In reviewing the evidence, one fact was striking: *there is virtually no evidence, either nationally or subnationally, on PRONATEC's cost-effectiveness*. It thus becomes critical to assess PRONATEC's fiscal efficiency, given that significant total spending (estimated at approximately 0.06 percent of gross domestic product) has produced still largely unknown results (for lack of any systematic evaluation) on the trainees' short- and medium-term employability and productivity. The information gaps concerning the effectiveness of TVET programs in general are also striking, especially given Brazil's strong administrative data and high technical capacity.

In Brazil, the TEC track (for some modalities and providers) has more impact than general education on employability and labor earnings. Recent empirical evidence shows that upper-secondary TVET has large and varied impacts on earnings compared with the returns of completing general secondary education. Almeida et al. (2015) use pre-PRONATEC data (from IBGE 2007) to show that, overall, TEC students see wage premiums of 9.7 percent over their peers who complete only academic upper-secondary education (figure 2.5, panel a). These higher returns, however, vary somewhat by provider and are more concentrated in certain sectors such manufacturing and information technology (figure 2.5, panel b). The authors also show that many graduates in certain technical fields hold jobs not directly related to their main fields of study (figure 2.7)—suggesting that possible skills gaps or mismatches require deeper examination if students in these fields often end up working in other

Figure 2.5 Wage Premiums for Technical Education Graduates Relative to Academic Upper-Secondary Graduates, 2007

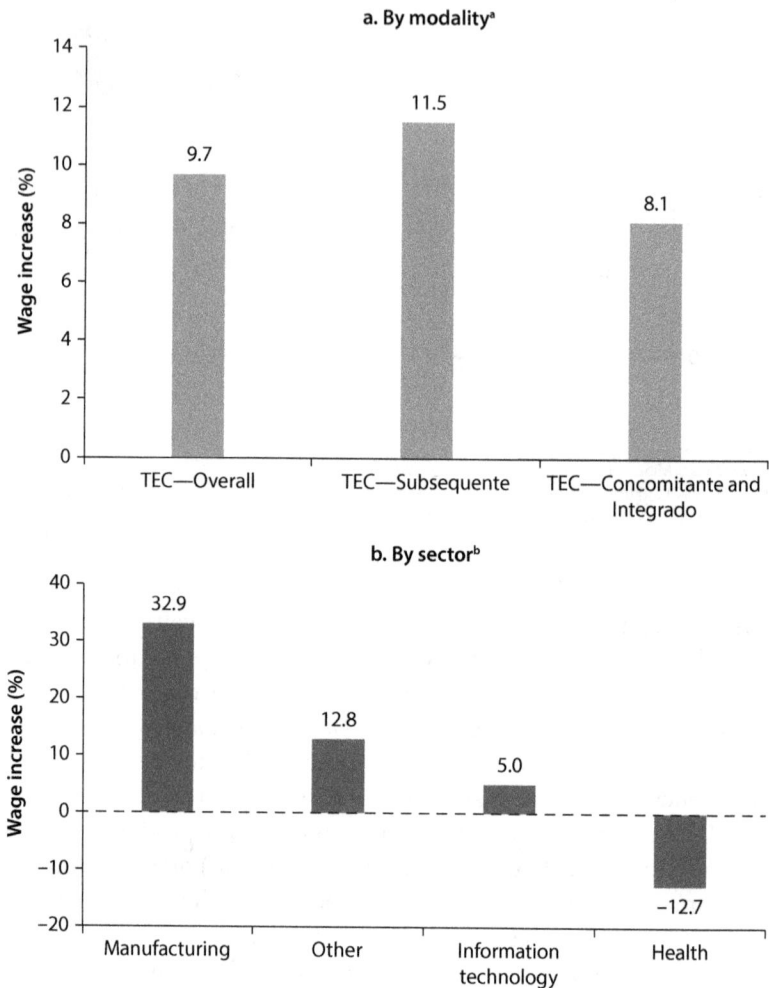

a. By modality[a]

b. By sector[b]

Source: Almeida et al. 2015.

Note: Figure reports the propensity score matching estimates of the wage premiums for graduates in the technical track at the upper-secondary level using data from IBGE (2007).

a. Graph reports the returns by type of training modality: Overall (including all modalities), Subsequente, Comcomitante, or Integrado. "TEC—Subsequente" is a technical program for students who have already concluded an academic upper-secondary program. "TEC—Integrado" includes academic and vocational courses offered as one program in the same school. "TEC—Concomitante" is a complementary, but separate, technical program for students who are completing an academic upper-secondary program, frequently carried out in two separate schools. "TEC—Overall" graduates (including Concomitante, Subsequente, and Integrado) averaged a 9.7 percent higher hourly wage than graduates of the general upper-secondary academic track. Similarly, TEC—Subsequente graduates averaged an 11.5 percent higher hourly wage. TEC—Concomitante and TEC—Integrado graduates averaged an 8.1 percent higher hourly wage.

b. Graph reports overall wage returns for technical education graduates relative to general academic upper-secondary graduates by the sector of current activity. "Other" includes other courses that are not classified as manufacturing, information technology, management, agriculture, or health.

areas despite the potentially higher returns in their own fields of study. In addition, graduates of the technical track tend to be more employable or more likely to be actively searching for a job (Almeida et al. 2015).[6]

Furthermore, upper-secondary TEC tends to attract students of higher socioeconomic background relative to general-track students; this is a challenge as PRONATEC aims to expand coverage of the most vulnerable, mainly through the expansion of FIC courses. Yet the large wage returns from TEC are present even after accounting for the fact that TEC graduates tend to be from better-off households. The socioeconomic disparity between TEC and general-track students is a somewhat historical feature of the Brazilian system. Figure 2.6 breaks down these groups of students as of 2007, illustrating that among TEC students, 17 percent or less came from the two poorest income quintiles while most students came from the two wealthiest quintiles (Almeida, Menezes-Filho, and Anazawa 2014). In contrast, approximately 40 percent of the general academic track students came from the bottom two income quintiles. Furthermore, students in the technical track (especially in the Integrado modality) were likelier than general upper-secondary students to proceed to university. Students who continued on to tertiary education also tended to come from the Integrado modality, which are some of the more-selective TEC schools and offer preparation for tertiary-level entrance exams like the national exam at the end of high school (Exame Nacional do Ensino Médio, Enem).[7] This pre-PRONATEC profile

Figure 2.6 Profile of Upper-Secondary Students, by Educational Track and Income Quintile, 2007

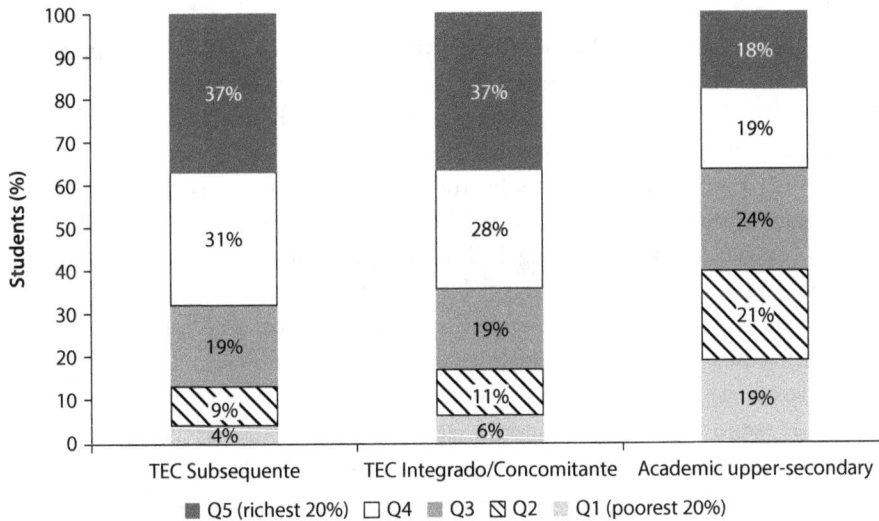

Source: Almeida, Menezes-Filho, and Anazawa 2014.
Note: TEC refers to students enrolled in technical education at the upper-secondary level. TEC Subsequente is a technical program for students who have already concluded an academic upper-secondary program. TEC Integrado includes academic and vocational courses offered as one program in the same school. TEC Concomitante is a complementary, but separate, technical program for students who are completing an academic upper-secondary program, frequently carried out in two separate schools.

of technical students is an important consideration for the continued expansion of the federal program, as it seeks to expand access to TEC generally but also emphasizes reaching the beneficiaries of several of Brazil's social programs for low-income and underserved populations.

This "bias" in the profile could partly result from the heavier course load associated with the Brazilian secondary technical track relative to the general academic track. Students in the secondary technical track must complete an average of 800–1,200 more classroom hours than required in the general academic track. This workload naturally exacerbates existing socioeconomic inequalities by presenting an additional barrier for students who cannot afford not to work during these longer periods. This is especially the case for students in the Subsequente or Concomitante modalities of TEC, where the technical courses tend to take up more time in the school curricula. For programs in some regions or sectors, students must complete additional hours in workplace learning such as apprenticeships.

Interestingly, however, evidence shows that many technical-track students end up taking jobs in fields that were not in their fields of study. A snapshot of recent technical graduates as of 2007 showed that a high share of TEC graduates actually end up working outside their main fields of study (Almeida et al. 2015). In the health sector, for example, more than 40 percent of graduates of health-related technical programs worked in non-health-related occupations (figure 2.7, panel a), and 52 percent of those who studied industrial TEC courses ended up in nonindustrial manufacturing fields (figure 2.7, panel b). It will be critical to understand this phenomenon and its implications for the returns to this type of education, as PRONATEC continues to expand its supply of technical and professional courses and slots.

Among the short-duration vocational training courses (FIC), those provided by Sistema S have high returns that vary in magnitude by type of course. As figure 2.8 shows, among all students of Sistema S FIC courses between 2007 and 2012, apprenticeship courses had the greatest impact on wages, increasing them by 24 percent, although these students have a lower baseline in terms of both wages and qualifications (Silva, Gukovas, and Caruso 2015). Habilitation courses (longer courses, averaging 1,200 hours, for current high school students or recent graduates) increased wages by 4 percent. These courses have returns comparable to those associated with European technical tracks of significantly longer duration. The other modalities (initiation, qualification, and technical skills upgrading) appear to increase wages by 1–3 percent, even after controlling for a wide range of observables and for workers' and firms' fixed effects, as shown in figure 2.8 (Silva, Gukovas, and Caruso 2015). Interestingly, as discussed in detail in chapter 5, in spite of lower socioeconomic backgrounds, subsidized PRONATEC trainees have better wage returns than unsubsidized trainees to vocational training provided by the Sistema S providers. However, they have a significantly lower probability of formal labor market insertion than other trainees after completing training, even after controlling for observables (such as age, educational level, and training modality).

Figure 2.7 Occupational Distribution of Health and Industrial TEC Graduates in Brazil, by Economic Sector, 2007

percent

a. Distribution of health TEC graduates

Transport, storage, and communication, 2
Public administration, 10
Manufacturing industry, 8
Construction, 1
Accomodation and food, 3
Agriculture, 1
Domestic services, 5
Education, health, and social services, 57
Trade and repairs, 13

b. Distribution of industrial TEC graduates

Accommodation and food, 3
Agriculture, 1
Construction, 6
Transport, storage, and communication, 8
Public administration, 7
Trade and repairs, 23
Education, health, and social services, 4
Manufacturing industry, 48

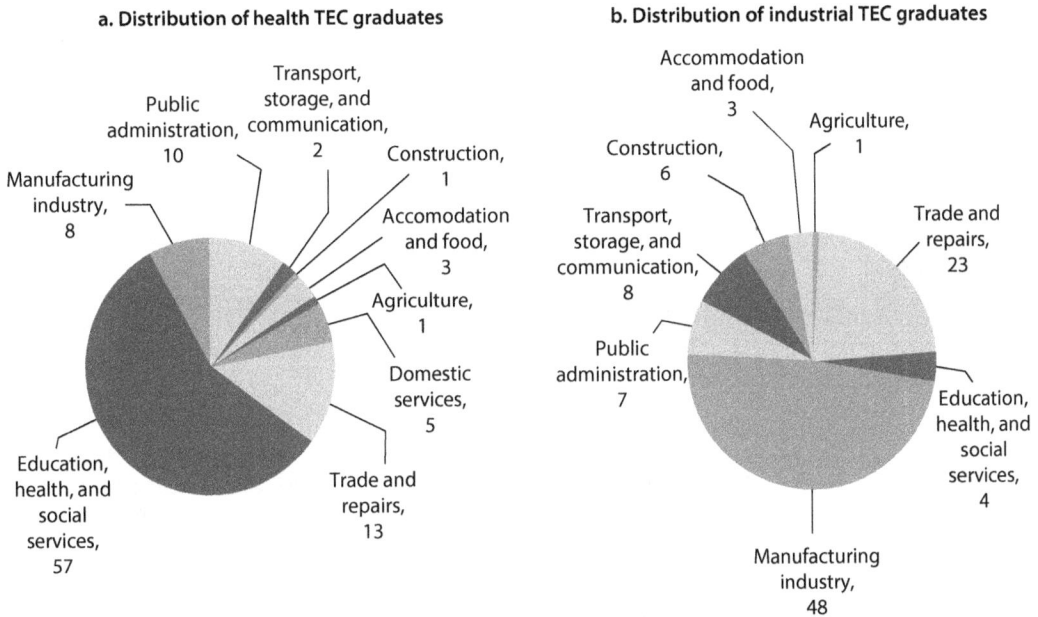

Source: Almeida et al. 2015.
Note: Charts display the percentages of graduates working in designated sectors who had completed, as of 2007, an upper-secondary technical (TEC) course in the health field (panel a) and in the industry (manufacturing) field (panel b).

PRONATEC FIC expansion occurred mainly through the Sistema S provider network, but the gratuity quota is now being fulfilled, and expansion through higher reliance on a more diverse set of providers might bring new challenges. As figure 2.9 shows, approximately 80 percent of PRONATEC's FIC course enrollments from its 2011 inception through May 2014 have occurred through Sistema S (Brazil, Ministry of Education 2014). This expansion was anchored on the gratuity agreement quota between Sistema S and the government (establishing that 60 percent of total revenue from taxes directed at Sistema S will be used to provide subsidized training) that is now being fulfilled. As the providers are diversified beyond Sistema S, the new challenges could include quality certification and accreditation issues (Almeida, Amaral, and Felicio 2015). Furthermore, in the months ahead, private provision is likely to become more relevant across all segments, including for TEC courses, because PRONATEC recently began financing students taking both FIC and TEC courses from private postsecondary education providers (through Financing of Higher Education Students [FIES] and the University for All Program [PROUNI]). In this context, it is critical to:

- Improve the regulatory framework to strengthen quality certification and accreditation of private providers (including through the National Professional Certification and Initial and Continuing Training [CERTIFIC] Network);[8]

Figure 2.8 Formal Wage Returns to Vocational Training from Sistema S Providers, by Course Type, 2007–12

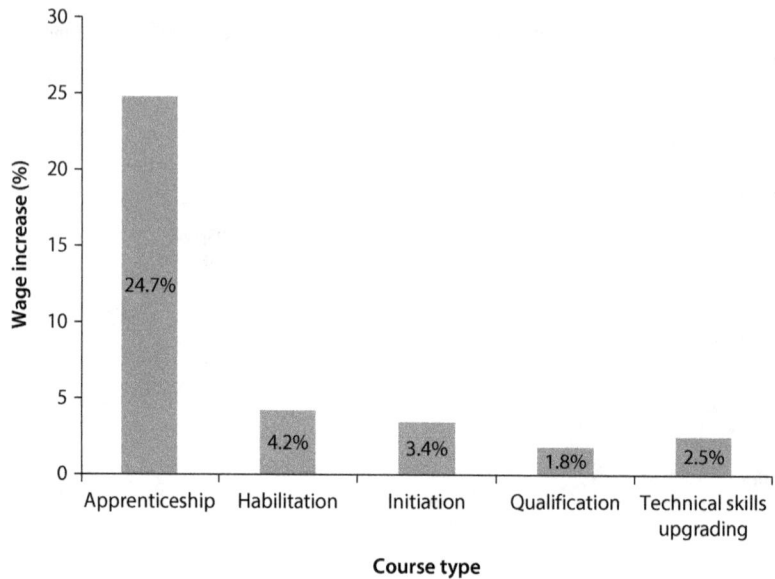

Source: Silva, Gukovas, and Caruso 2015.

Note: PRONATEC = National Program for Access to Technical Education and Employment. Wage returns are estimated by comparing trainees of Sistema S (National Service for Industrial Training, SENAI) who found formal jobs with comparable formal workers who hadn't received training, in a difference-in-differences estimation. Data came from the Annual Social Information Report (RAIS), merged with SENAI trainee-level records. It covered five training modalities: apprenticeships (for those enrolled or with completed high school); habilitation (long courses, averaging 1,200 hours, for current high school students or recent graduates); qualification (short courses, averaging 200 hours, to build workers' skills for particular jobs); technical upgrading (to upgrade workers' skills for particular jobs); and initiation (to prepare workers for low-complexity functions).

- Adjust course contents to the demands of the most vulnerable groups; and
- Link or complement the vocational training with other interventions including job-search support at the end of the training programs or building in soft-skills modules into the training curricula.

The Way Forward: A Policy Agenda

Higher-quality, more cost-effective, and sustainable delivery of TEC and vocational training—particularly of PRONATEC programs—is a necessary avenue to foster labor productivity. Five key areas that can contribute to improving PRONATEC's efficiency and sustainability as it continues to expand and, consequently, to improving the quality and effectiveness of TVET in Brazil more generally include strengthening M&E systems; improving private partnerships and access to apprenticeships; developing a career guidance framework; improving TVET program quality and relevance; and focusing on TVET innovation, particularly through hands-on learning.

Figure 2.9 Distribution of PRONATEC Course Providers Serving Bolsa Formação Beneficiaries, 2011–14

percent

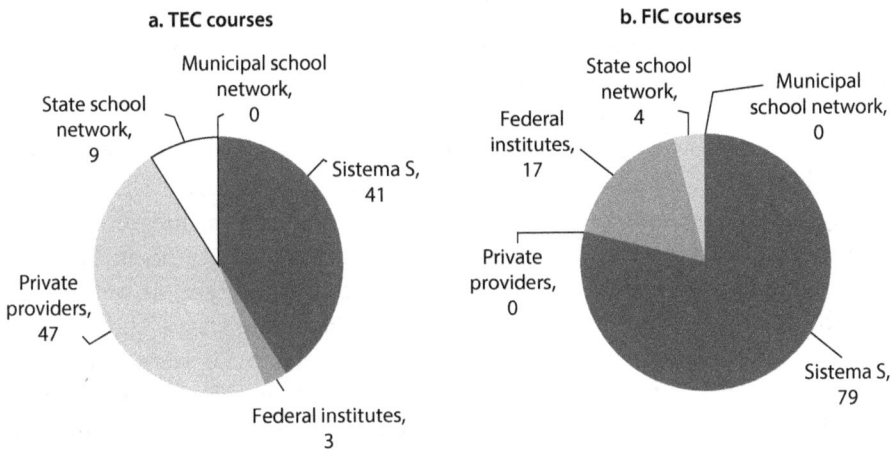

a. TEC courses

- Municipal school network, 0
- State school network, 9
- Sistema S, 41
- Private providers, 47
- Federal institutes, 3

b. FIC courses

- State school network, 4
- Municipal school network, 0
- Federal institutes, 17
- Private providers, 0
- Sistema S, 79

Source: Brazil, Ministry of Education 2014.
Note: PRONATEC = National Program for Access to Technical Education and Employment. "FIC" (Initial and Continuing Training Programs) refers to short-term courses and "TEC" to technical courses at the upper-secondary level. Figure reports data only for beneficiaries of Bolsa Formação, which offers free TEC courses for low-income students enrolled in public secondary education and FIC courses for vulnerable social groups. "Sistema S" refers to the National Service for Apprenticeship, which includes several institutions that provide technical vocational education and training courses. Although public technical education is already free, those enrolled through Bolsa Formação also receive financial support for course materials, transportation, and meals. The 2014 data include course offerings as of May 2014.

Strengthening M&E Systems

First and foremost, Brazil needs to improve M&E systems to trace outcomes and inform program expansion. Strong M&E systems are especially important for tracking and improving the quality and relevance of TVET for the labor market. To date, and in spite of the high quality of the data available, Brazil continues to lack a solid M&E system that (a) tracks provider quality or course performance; (b) includes objective measures of student knowledge (captured by nationwide standardized tests); and (c) provides information on job placement rates or the impacts on wages of vocational training programs, or on students' transition rates to tertiary education for TEC programs.[9] Through the National System of Vocational Education and Information Technology (SISTEC), MEC tracks a range of socioeconomic characteristics for all students who have completed or are completing technical courses at the upper-secondary and tertiary level (ensino tecnológico). However, SISTEC does not systematically cover all the supply of all these courses and does not track students into higher education or into the labor market. If data were available, evaluations could assess the cost-effectiveness of many PRONATEC interventions specifically (such as Bolsa Formação, e-Tec Brasil, or Brasil Profissionalizado)[10] as well as their most effective delivery mechanisms. In addition, while general secondary education has a modern system of student assessment, national exams like Enem are not compulsory for all students completing upper-secondary education, regardless of their track. Consequently, there is no way to evaluate learning and the quality of technical schools. In addition, few federal or state technical schools measure their performance based on the insertion of students into the labor market—information that could systematically guide and inform policy implementation.

Other countries faced similar operational challenges, and their experience could help Brazil in this reform. An international comparison showed that policy makers are using several indicators systematically to measure system quality and labor market outcomes of graduates. These indicators include the proportion of trainees with jobs in the short and medium term as well as sustainability and quality measures of these jobs (including wages, contract formality, and nonwage benefits). In Brazil, the Pernambuco state has set an innovative M&E system of vocational system collecting this type of information. It is therefore critical to capitalize on opportunities for further research and evaluation (Almeida, Amaral, and Felicio 2015). These core indicators can be complemented by others—for example, employers' perceptions of the trainees' quality. Beyond collecting information on these indicators, the use of this information in supporting the career guidance of students and trainees and helping to disseminate information provided by "labor observatories" is key, and Australia, Chile, Turkey, and the United States are pioneers in these domains (box 2.1).

Box 2.1 M&E Systems, Work-Related Websites, and Counseling in Australia, Chile, Turkey, and the United States

Even though Brazil has outstanding administrative data and information on technical vocational education and training (TVET) programs, the information tends to focus on program take-up rather than on posttraining employability and earnings increases. There is thus an urgent need to improve these monitoring and evaluation (M&E) systems, not only by promoting the more systematic measurement of results but also by ensuring a "feedback loop" to implementation. A strong M&E system can also be the backbone for a system of career guidance and information dissemination for a host of stakeholders, including students and trainees, training providers, and policy makers. Several countries have moved in this direction, building strong M&E systems that help provide up-to-date, reliable information for decision making at all levels.

In Australia, the National Centre for Vocational Education Research (NCVER) conducts systematized M&E that underpins TVET policy. NCVER is a not-for-profit company owned by state, territory, and federal ministries, and is dependent on the Australian Department of Industry, which is responsible for skills development, research, and innovation policies. NCVER has been recognized nationally, and internationally, as a leader in TVET research. Much of the work it

box continues next page

Box 2.1 M&E Systems, Work-Related Websites, and Counseling in Australia, Chile, Turkey, and the United States *(continued)*

conducts is used by policy makers, training providers, and the private sector to align and improve TVET provision throughout the country.

In Chile, the MiFuturo online platform (http://www.mifuturo.cl) provides information on the students' and trainees' average wage and percentage employed three and six months after previous-year course completion, by course subject and region. The information is accessible through an easy-to-use website that helps students and trainees make more-informed decisions. MiFuturo also features information on educational requirements and exams for various careers and jobs, options for financial aid, current and expected returns to different levels of education, and projected growth of different occupations. In the United States, the *Occupational Outlook Handbook* (*OOH*) serves a similar purpose. Underpinned by solid data from the U.S. Bureau of Labor Statistics, the *OOH* provides students as early as middle school an opportunity to explore the educational requirements and expected career trajectories and salaries for different fields and occupations.

In Turkey, the M&E system tracks final policy results, and the government surveys samples of trainees who have completed the course each year, collecting information on three key indicators: (a) the trainees' insertion rate in labor markets and retention rates in the jobs 3, 6, and 12 months after training completion; (b) the insertion costs (total program budget divided by the number of trainees employed upon course completion); and (c) the posttraining average wage increase of the trainees. The results are disaggregated by student gender, student age, type of program, type of job (formal or informal), type of provider, and region.

In the United States, the state of Virginia is also using such information to help inform the development of career clusters, in which trained career counselors work with students as early as the seventh grade to develop academic and career plans of study (ACPs). These ACPs are mandatory but malleable plans intended to guide students in thinking about their career interests while also ensuring that students are building a strong, adequate foundation in academic and technical subjects that will allow for transitions in and out of different career pathways and occupations later in life as their interests and circumstances evolve over their lifetimes.

Sources: Aedo 2013; Almeida, Amaral, and Felicio 2015.

Improving Private Partnerships and Access to Apprenticeships

Second, Brazil should improve partnerships with the private sector and access to apprenticeships to more closely align the supply of TVET courses with the quantity and quality of the skills demanded by the labor market and preferred by students.[11] This is a challenge at both the national and subnational levels, given the diversity of local labor market needs and the large diversity within states. To address this challenge, innovative governance arrangements could be considered within a sector approach—for example, through the use of *skills councils* or similar skills ecosystems. At the state level, TVET providers could invite local representatives from different sectors of the economy (such as industry, commerce, tourism, and services) to present their stances on the types of occupations or professionals in greatest demand (as Sistema S already does in a large extent; see, for example, Schwartzman and Moura Castro 2013). These inputs from local representatives could be complemented by both quantitative and qualitative information on the job placement rates of students from different types of TVET programs. Programs that more easily place students in jobs, especially high-quality jobs, should be further supported and see their number of slots expanded. In addition, TVET programs should increasingly build partnerships with employers to create work-place learning—such as through apprenticeships—as part of the curriculum. Workplace learning stands out as one of the best ways to promote TVET learning that is both aligned with labor market needs and builds and strengthens socioemotional skills. For the student, workplace learning provides a strong learning environment because it offers real, on-the-job training experience that makes it easier to acquire both hard and soft skills. It also facilitates a two-way flow of information between employers and potential employees, making recruitment more effective or less costly to the employer. Only in this way can the Brazilian model become more cost-effective. The Republic of Korea, for example, has an interesting science, technology, engineering, and math (STEM) education model that incorporates explicit formalized partnerships with the private sector. In addition, early evidence suggests that Brazilian employers increasingly demand both socioemotional skills (including persistence and self-control) and nonroutine cognitive and interpersonal skills, which workplace learning often helps to strengthen (Aedo and Walker 2012).[12] To our knowledge, almost no TVET program in Brazil strongly emphasizes these types of skills. Box 2.2 describes some international examples of partnering with firms for vocational training.

Developing a Career Guidance Framework

Third, Brazil should develop a strategic career guidance framework based on a solid information system to help guide students and their families when making educational and career decisions. Brazil currently lacks such a system (see, for example, Neri 2010). These interventions are critical to help reverse the negative stigma that persists around TEC. International experience shows that these services are important and help focus student attention on the differences between career paths as well as their associated rates of return. However, developing a career guidance framework—including qualified guidance professionals and up-to-date information systems as portals for students and their families—rests on the establishment of a strong, systematic M&E system to provide reliable, timely data for these needs.

Focusing on Better-Prepared Technical Teachers and Trainers

Fourth, Brazil should improve TVET quality and relevance through better-prepared technical teachers and trainers. Improving teacher and trainer preparedness is only one component of improving quality and relevance of education and training, but it is a critical one.[13] For example, Almeida, Amaral, and Felicio (2015) show that the quality challenge is deeply linked with the difficulties in hiring and retaining highly qualified teachers who have an up-to-date command of the

---

Box 2.2 Vocational Training Results from Greater Partnering with Firms: Lessons from China, India, and Korea

As private corporations and public sector institutions join forces to improve vocational training, agreements between private sector employers and community colleges are pulling the educational curriculum toward market needs, as in the following examples:

- China Vocational Training Holdings specializes in matching students with jobs in the Chinese car industry by keeping masses of data on both students and companies.
- In India and other countries, some firms direct high school students to focused, fully funded training that uses digital technology advances. For example, call centers and more-sophisticated outsourcing companies (in the legal and accounting fields) run three-month training programs that build the capabilities of new hires to follow computer-prompted responses to meet client needs. Many such new hires then learn on the job and even move to next-level management positions and beyond.
- Korea has created a network of vocational high schools, labeling students as "young meisters" (from the German, "master craftsmen") to counteract the country's obsession with academic laurels. The Meister High Schools provide free education and give graduates the opportunities to either begin stable employment after graduation, to serve the army as a noncombatant in one's own area of expertise, or to enter college with three-year work experience.
- Korea also regulated that all polytechnics must undertake regular visits to companies to keep their curricula updated, and companies themselves are regularly invited to visit campuses to provide input. In addition, partnership agreements are regularly signed between technical and vocational schools at the secondary and tertiary levels and companies to allow practitioners to teach in those schools and to allow those schools to offer in-service training to the companies' employees.

Sources: Mok 2010; KRIVET 2015.

---

latest technical knowledge in their fields. Although the quality of TVET teachers in federal institutes and Sistema S is generally considered good, public sector hiring policies still leave few opportunities for teachers to easily move between teaching and other occupations in their fields. This permeability across academia and the labor market is of critical importance for keeping TVET curricula up to date and relevant to the labor market. Especially in the most remote areas, it is difficult to keep a teacher's knowledge up to date because it is difficult to find and recruit teachers with relevant experience. The importance of up-to-date knowledge also poses a constraint for adding, dropping, or modifying existing TVET programs because the specialized skills evolve, yet teachers spend little time in industry, and hiring new teachers and reallocating existing teachers where needed can be difficult. At the same time, the lack of job security and benefits packages for private sector TVET teachers—an occupation that does not attract the strongest candidates—leaves the quality of TVET provision in private institutions uneven, if not lacking. This report argues that it is critical, especially in the public network, to promote more flexible contracts that allow teachers to be well trained for teaching while also obtaining sectoral experience.

Focusing on TVET Innovation

Finally, Brazil should focus on TVET innovation through pedagogies and curricula that combine attention to core foundational skills while promoting hands-on learning. Rarely do TVET pedagogies use real-life case studies or focus on solving firms' real-world challenges. In addition, TEC rarely incorporates the latest technologies. Nor does it offer a set of physical tools that enable students to apply their learning in new and innovative ways. Curricula and pedagogies should incorporate the latest technologies. Access to relatively low-cost but high-tech infrastructure is increasingly available through "maker-space" and "fab-lab" laboratories that many technical schools and universities around the world are either building in-house or linking their classrooms to within their cities and communities (see box 2.3).

Box 2.3 TVET Innovation: Fab Labs

Fab Labs—short for fabrication laboratories—are low-cost, high-tech laboratories that can increasingly be linked to technical and vocational education providers at both the secondary and tertiary levels, ultimately making TVET delivery in the country more innovative and cost-effective.

They began as an outreach project of the Center for Bits and Atoms (CBA) at the Massachusetts Institute of Technology (MIT) to give the public access to design and manufacturing tools previously available only to engineers at big companies or large research universities. By contrast, these smaller workshops typically need little more than a large room and are relatively cheap to set up, costing between $50,000 and $100,000. They consist of high-tech but versatile, easy-to-learn technologies and tools that enable the user to build and prototype "almost anything." These types of laboratories are also often complemented by classes that use innovative methodologies and project-based learning that teach users to turn their ideas into products and apply them to solving local problems. These types of lab models have cropped up in different parts of the globe and have been used to create solutions ranging from simple household needs such as Wi-Fi antennas or warning sensors (in case a cow strays into the family garden) to more-complex solar and wind-powered turbines or analytical instruments for agriculture, health care, and other industries.

Fab Labs and similar models of low-cost, high-tech, easy-to-use laboratories are increasingly being linked to institutions that provide technical and vocational education at both the secondary and tertiary levels, particularly in the United States. These labs often are integrated into the technical education curriculums, and teachers build lab time into their lesson plans. The labs give students an opportunity for hands-on experience, allowing them to develop both strong technical skills and an innovative and entrepreneurial mindset that is applicable to industries ranging from hairdressing to renewable energies and that facilitates lifelong learning.

Source: Almeida, Amaral, and Felicio 2015 (based on MIT's Center for Bits and Atoms website, http://cba.mit.edu/); Fuller and Unwin 2012.

Adapting Skills Development Programs to the Needs of the Poor and Vulnerable

Of particular additional concern are the challenges of expanding PRONATEC effectively to the poorest and most vulnerable—challenges that chapter 5 discusses in detail. PRONATEC faces imminent challenges in addressing the skill needs of the poor, many of whom have dropped out of the formal schooling system and need a qualification for the labor market. The discussion in Silva, Gukovas, and Caruso (2015) and the international evidence in many developing countries (Almeida, Behrman, and Robalino 2012; Almeida et al. 2012) also show that, in addition to the recommendations above, and specifically for this group, it is important to complement the trainings with soft skills (such as perseverance and team work). In urban areas—and when job demand is strong—links with public employment services are especially important to ensure that trainees are not discouraged. And in rural areas, it is essential to rethink flexible delivery models that can extend high-quality programs to the most-remote areas. These rural strategies often attract more females and should involve short technical courses combined with literacy skills, soft-skills, and (for some segments) entrepreneurial skills training. Furthermore, for many of the most vulnerable, course content needs to be simplified or adapted to their skills. Finally, as discussed above, developing quality certification for the wide set of private providers is critical to ensure that these programs pay off. These certification systems must recognize prior training and working experience to ensure that the private sector can better assess the life-long learning and ultimately create incentives for older workers to invest in vocational training. Chapter 5 details further how Brazil can improve skills development of the poor and vulnerable through its productive inclusion strategies.

Notes

1. "Sistema S" is the training arm of the Confederation of Industry (CNI). It includes nine institutions, including SENAI (the National Service of Industrial Education), SENAR (the National Rural Training Service), SENAC (the National Commercial Training Service), and others. The Brazilian Constitution establishes that these institutions must use part of the revenues passed on to them for designated educational and training purposes.

2. Within state schools, TEC programs are also offered in three modalities with varied course loads and time frames: (a) "Integrado," covering academic and vocational courses offered as one program in the same school; (b) "Concomitante," covering complementary, but separate, technical courses for students in an academic upper-secondary program, either as an integrated program or taken in parallel (two separate schools); and (c) "Subsequente," an option for students who have completed an academic upper-secondary education and want to complement their education with a technical program.

3. Two important background papers to this report map policies and institutions in TVET and shorter-term courses delivered by multiple providers (Almeida, Amaral, and Felicio 2015; Marra et al. 2015). The latter is partly based on an extensive

initiative, led by the World Bank Education Global Practice, called System Assessment Benchmarking for Education Results (SABER) (World Bank 2013).

4. Vertical and horizontal permeability in an education system is a key element in promoting socioeconomic mobility. A system that offers multiple pathways to exit and enter the education system, and that recognizes accumulated learning, allows students to pursue different educational levels throughout their lifetimes. Maintaining a flexible set of options to retrain or increase their skill levels as their personal set of interests or the needs of the labor market change keeps young people and adults from hitting dead ends in their educational and career tracks. This is especially critical for technical education (TEC) students and those from lower socioeconomic classes, who often enter the labor market at a younger age.

5. Contracted educational institutions usually provide these short-duration "qualification" programs, often in partnership with the ministry or state secretariat sponsoring the program and the main FIC program providers.

6. These positive impacts on earnings had been found by others for Brazil (Neri 2010; Severini and Orellano 2010; Vasconcellos et al. 2010; Reis 2015). Almeida et al. (2015) also show that, after completing the courses, graduates of the technical track at the upper-secondary level are more likely to be working or at least looking for a job than graduates of the academic track. For example, those who completed a general TEC course had a 6.7 percent higher probability of being economically active than the control group.

7. In contrast, students from the Subsequente modality (a TEC program taken after the completion of an academic upper-secondary program) are primarily older, night-course students who work during the day, which may make it less feasible to pursue a tertiary-level program.

8. In 2007, the CERTIFIC Network was created by a ministerial decree originating from MEC and the Ministry of Labor and Employment. The main goal was to improve the existing certification system while also certifying the knowledge that workers have acquired on the job in a wide variety of fields. The CERTIFIC certification is available in fields such as fisheries and aquaculture, music, construction, tourism and hospitality, and electronics, among others. Individuals who are approved through a knowledge assessment receive a diploma, certifying the knowledge and skills they have acquired in that particular field or industry. Those who are not approved may attend a CERTIFIC qualification course to improve their skills and eventually obtain a certification.

9. Almeida, Behrman, and Robalino (2012) discuss the importance of establishing solid M&E frameworks. Brazil, however, is a good example of a country with the capability to leverage existing, comprehensive federal administrative datasets to quantify TVET system impacts in the labor market. For examples of possible approaches, see the methodologies pursued by Silva, Gukovas, and Caruso (2015) and Almeida et al. (2015).

10. e-Tec Brasil is the modality of TVET based on E-Learning network. PRONATEC offers free distance-learning FIC courses and TEC programs, as well as professional qualification programs (Brazil, Ministry of Education 2010). Brasil Profissionalizado is an intervention aimed at strengthening the delivery of TEC and training through secondary-level state networks. This expansion channels federal funding to the states for infrastructure, teacher training, and developing management capacity and peda- gogical practices.

11. This challenge has also been highlighted and discussed in the Brazilian context by Rodríguez, Dahlman, and Salmi (2008) and Schwartzman (2014).

12. "Nonroutine cognitive/analytical skills" consist of thought processes requiring the absorption, processing, and decision making of abstract information. Computer programmers, teachers, lawyers, doctors, nurses, and many other professionals need such abilities intensively. "Nonroutine cognitive/interpersonal skills" characterize personality traits that underlie behaviors such as teamwork, reliability, discipline, and work effort. These are important for both professional occupations and team-based work environments as well as services that establish direct client contact (Aedo and Walker 2012).

13. For a discussion of this challange in other settings, see King and Palmer (2010).

References

Aedo, Cristian. 2013. "Labor Market Observations for Education." PowerPoint presentation for an international TVET seminar at the World Bank, Washington, DC, March 19.

Aedo, Cristian, and Ian Walker. 2012. *Skills for the 21st Century in Latin America and the Caribbean*. Directions in Development Series. Washington, DC: World Bank.

Almeida, Rita, Nicole Amaral, and Fabiana de Felicio. 2015. *Assessing Advances and Challenges in Technical Education in Brazil*. Policy report, World Bank, Washington, DC.

Almeida, Rita, Leandro Anazawa, Naércio Menezes-Filho, and Ligia Vasconcellos. 2015. "Technical and Vocational Education and Training in Brazil: Micro Evidence on the Wage Returns." Research paper—background paper for this report, World Bank, Washington, DC.

Almeida, Rita, Juliana Arbelaez, Maddalena Honorati, Arvo Kuddo, Tanja Lohmann, Mirey Ovadiya, Lucian Pop, Maria Laura Sanchez-Puerta, and Michael Weber. 2012. "Improving Access to Jobs and Earnings Opportunities: The Role of Activation and Graduation Policies." Background paper for the 2012–22 Social Protection and Labor Strategy, World Bank, Washington, DC.

Almeida, Rita, Jere Behrman, and David Robalino, eds. 2012. *The Right Skills for the Job? Rethinking Training Policies for Workers*. Human Development Perspectives Series. Washington, DC: World Bank.

Almeida, Rita, Naércio Menezes-Filho, and Leandro Anazawa. 2014. "A educação profissional e técnica no Brasil: evolução recente e impacto no mercado de trabalho brasileiro." [Professional and Technical Education in Brazil: Recent Evolution and Impact on the Brazilian Labor Market.] Policy note, World Bank, Washington, DC.

Banerji, Arup, Wendy Cunningham, Ariel Fiszbein, Elizabeth King, Harry Patrinos, David Robalino, and Jee-Peng Tan. 2010. "Stepping Up Skills for More Jobs and Higher Productivity." Working paper 55566, World Bank, Washington, DC.

Brazil, Court of Accounts. 2015. *Relatório de Auditoria Anual de Contas*. [Audit Annual Accounts Report.] Tribunal de Contas da União [Federal Court of Accounts], Brasilia.

Brazil, Ministry of Education. 2010. "Educação Profissional e Tecnológica—Projetos e Ações 2010." [Vocational and Technological Education: Projects and Actions 2010.] Ministry of Education, Secretariat of Vocational and Technological Education, Brasília.

———. 2014. "Auditoria de Contas." Ministry of Education, Brasilia.

Bruns, Barbara, David Evans, and Javier Luque. 2012. *Achieving World-Class Education in Brazil: The Next Agenda*. Directions in Development Series. Washington, DC: World Bank.

Canali, Heloisa Helena Barbosa. 2009. "A trajetória da educação profissional no Brasil e os desafios da construção de um ensino médio integrado à educação profissional." [The Path of Vocational Education in Brazil and Challenges of a Middle School Integrated into Professional Education.] Unpublished manuscript. FAE—UFMG University Belo Horizonte, Brazil.

de Hoyos, Rafael, Rogers Halsey, and Anna Popova. 2015. "Out of School and Out of Work: A Diagnostic of NiNis in Latin America." Background paper for "Out of School and Out of Work: Challenges and Solutions around the NiNis in Latin America." Regional study, World Bank, Washington, DC.

Feres, Marcelo. 2012. "PRONATEC—Programa Nacional de Acesso ao Ensino Técnico e Emprego." PowerPoint presentation to World Bank video conference, Brasilia and Washington, DC, November 12.

Fuller, A., and L. Unwin. 2012. "What's the Point of Adult Apprenticeships?" *Adults Learning* 23 (3): 8–13.

Gasparini, Leonardo, Sebastián Galiani, Guillermo Cruces, and Pablo Acosta. 2011. "Educational Upgrading and Returns to Skills in Latin America: Evidence from a Supply-Demand Framework, 1990–2010." Working Paper 5921, World Bank, Washington, DC.

IBGE (Brazilian Institute of Geography and Statistics). 2007. *National Sample Survey of Households (Pesquisa Nacional por Amostra de Domicílio, PNAD).* Rio de Janeiro: IBGE.

INEP (National Institute of Educational Studies and Research Anísio Teixeira). 2013. *Censo Escolar da Educação Básica 2013: Resumo Técnico.* Annual report, INEP, Brasilia.

King, K., and R. Palmer. 2010. *Planning for Technical and Vocational Skills Development.* Paris: UNESCO (United Nations Educational, Scientific and Cultural Organization) International Institute for Educational Planning.

KRIVET (Korea Research Institute for Vocational Education and Training). 2015. PowerPoint presentation at the Inter-American Development Bank and Inter-American Investment Corporation's "Knowledge Sharing Forum on Development Experiences: Comparative Experiences of Korea and LAC." Washington, DC, March 26.

Marra, Karla, Jociany Luz, Joana Silva, and Renata Gukovas. 2015. "Mapping of the Current Network of Active Labor Market Programs (ALMPs)." Policy report—background paper for this report, World Bank, Washington, DC.

Menezes-Filho, Naércio. 2012. "Apagão de Mão de Obra Qualificada? As Profissões e o Mercado de Trabalho Brasileiro entre 2000 e 2010." Policy Paper 4, Centro de Políticas Públicas do INSPER e University of São Paulo.

Mok, K. H. 2010. "Innovation and Higher Education: A Comparative Study of Five Asian Societies." Background paper prepared for World Bank 2011, Hong Kong Institute of Education, Hong Kong.

Neri, Marcelo. 2010. *A Educação Profissional e Você no Mercado de Trabalho.* [Vocational Education and You in the Labor Market.] Research report, FGV/CPS, Rio de Janeiro.

OECD (Organisation for Economic Co-operation and Development). 2011 and 2012. "Education GPS: The World of Education at Your Fingers." OECD Education GPS website, http://gpseducation.oecd.org.

Reis, Mauricio. 2015. "Vocational Training and Labor Market Outcomes in Brazil." *The B.E. Journal of Economic Analysis & Policy* 15 (1): 377–405.

Rodríguez, Alberto, Carl J. Dahlman, and Jamil Salmi. 2008. *Knowledge and Innovation for Competitiveness in Brazil*. WBI Development Studies. Washington, DC: World Bank.

Schwartzman, Simon. 2014. "O Centro Paula Souza e a Educacao Profissional no Brasil." [Paula Souza Center and Vocational Education in Brazil.] In *Basic Education in São Paulo: Progress and Challenges*, edited by B. Negri, H. de Gama Torres, and M. H. Guimarães de Castro, 187–216. São Paulo: Fundação SEADE.

Schwartzman, Simon, and Claudio de Moura Castro. 2013. *Estudo e Trabalho da Juventude Brasileira*. [Study and Work of Brazilian Youth.] Research report, Institute for Labor and Society (IETS), Rio de Janeiro.

Severini, E., and V. Orellano. 2010. "O Efeito do Ensino Profissionalizante sobre a Probabilidade de Inserção no Mercado de Trabalho e sobre a Renda no Período Pré-PLANFOR." [The Effect of Vocational Training on the Inclusion Probability in the Labor Market and on Income in the Pre-Period PLANFOR.] *Economics* 11 (1): 155–74.

Silva, Joana, Renata Gukovas, and Luiz Caruso. 2015. "The Wage Returns and Employability of Vocational Training in Brazil: Evidence from Matched Provider-Employer Administrative Data." Research paper—background paper for this report, World Bank, Washington, DC.

Vasconcellos, L., F. C. Lima, J. G. Fernandes, and N. A. Menezes-Filho. 2010. "Avaliação Econômica do Ensino Médio Profissional." [Economic Assessment of Secondary Vocational Education.] Assessment Report 14, Economic Evaluation of Social Projects Program, Itaú Social Foundation.

World Bank. 2013. "SABER (Systems Approach for Better Education Results): Strengthening Education Systems to Achieve Learning for All." Database, World Bank, Washington, DC. http://saber.worldbank.org/index.cfm.

Labor Regulation Reform to Support Firm Productivity While Also Protecting Workers

Introduction

Brazil has a rich set of labor market regulations and institutions, including mature systems of support to the unemployed, minimum-wage policy, and labor courts. Consolidated by the 1988 Constitution, current labor regulations and institutions are well established in Brazil, and adjustments since 1988 have been mostly parametric. The 1988 Constitution was the result of a participatory process, and it has set the principles of universality, nondiscrimination, and workers' rights. The latter include worker protection against dismissals and the provision of income support in case of dismissal without just cause (in the forms of unemployment insurance [UI] and severance pay).[1] It also introduced specific labor-related laws (for instance, regarding indexation between social benefits and the minimum wage) that imply that changes in labor regulations have many spillovers to other policies. In addition, it defined a set of mandated nonwage labor costs (such as contributions to social insurance and labor-related taxes) applicable to formal workers, defined as "workers with carteira" (a signed employment card) (Oviedo 2015).

Reviewing and adjusting labor regulations could be valuable for moving workers' and firms' incentives toward longer tenures, more hiring, and ultimately higher labor productivity. For example, job turnover in Brazil is remarkably high by international standards. Short worker tenure can decrease firms' incentives to invest in training. However, high turnover is a feature of both formal and informal labor markets (where workers are not entitled to UI) and is usually motivated by workers' reallocation to higher-paying jobs (in 57 percent of cases in 2013) (Zylberstajn and Silva 2015). Still, the design of UI has an influence on separations from formal jobs, because they are more likely to happen around the minimum thresholds of employment duration required for UI eligibility (Gerard and Gonzaga 2012). As highlighted in chapter 1, Brazil is also an outlier when it comes to nonwage labor costs such as social insurance expenditures and labor-related taxes. In the formal sector, these costs represent 33 percent of the cost of labor (versus an average of about 20 percent in Organisation for Economic Co-operation and Development [OECD] countries) (ILO 2014). Moreover several additional mandated costs specific to Brazil increase further the cost of formal employment. The country's high nonwage labor costs may present a constraint to formal employment and firm growth. Under stagnant labor productivity and an increasing minimum wage, such costs can erode competitiveness and thus hurt firms' investment in innovation and training as well as prospects for job creation. Finally, the increasingly heavy caseloads in labor courts (more than 3 million cases in 2013, higher than OECD rates [Oviedo 2015]) can slow decision making, affecting firms' incentives to hire new workers.

Labor regulation is one of the more difficult social policy areas, offering perhaps the fewest clear answers, and yet it is an issue of growing importance. As part of a broader social contract between the state and its citizens, labor regulations and institutions occupy a policy area where reforms must preserve protections and incentives for individuals. However, the agenda of labor productivity growth calls for efficient, agile workforce reallocations among skills and firms. Hence, an important question moving forward is: *How can labor regulations more effectively support firm productivity while best balancing protections and incentives for individuals?* This report highlights some agenda items based on their potential to shift workers' and firms' incentives toward longer tenures, more hiring, and ultimately higher labor productivity:

- *Integrating job-search requirements into UI eligibility* to encourage the unemployed to more actively seek work
- *Analyzing mandated nonwage nonlabor costs* to understand the effects of each (social security contributions, unemployment funds, labor-related taxes) and considering whether selected fine-tuning could more effectively support the desired social contract of worker protections and growth of formal sector employment and wages—part of a broader discussion on the adequacy and sustainability of the social security (pension) system
- *Reducing incentives for unnecessary labor disputes while streamlining dispute resolution* by creating automatic mechanisms for some types of labor disputes, revising and strengthening the mediation and negotiation mechanisms, and simplifying labor codes to reduce the scope for ambiguity and therefore litigation

In addition to these reforms, it is important to recognize that although labor productivity affects the *path* of the minimum wage through the annual adjustment formula, that path also affects labor productivity. Brazil's minimum wage has almost doubled in real terms since 2002, which has helped to reduce poverty and inequality. This growth has been faster than in most Latin American and Caribbean countries, but its current level (as measured by the share of gross national income [GNI] per worker) is in line with international comparators. The minimum-wage automatic adjustment rule in Brazil establishes that each year's increase be equal to the GDP growth rate of two years prior, which maintains a link to labor productivity. In view of slower GDP growth and tighter labor markets, achieving simultaneous minimum-wage expansion, high employment of low-skilled workers, and strong firm performance and competitiveness will require a focus on increasing labor productivity (Goal 1).

Existing Labor Regulations and Institutions

Legislative and Constitutional History

During the first half of the 20th century, Brazil built the foundation of its current labor regulations and institutions (including UI, severance pay [the Severance Indemnity Fund, FGTS], mandated nonwage labor costs, and the minimum wage).[2] The Lei Elóy Chaves of 1923 set the legal framework of the contributory social security system, introducing old-age, disability, and survivor pensions. The Consolidation of the Labor Laws (CLT) of 1943 established the ground rules for labor relations between employers and workers. It also instituted the use of the carteira assinada (formal contract) where a worker's entire "formal" employment history is recorded. The CLT included a large body of laws that determine the individual and collective rights of workers, employers, and unions. For workers, these include the maximum hours of work per week; the maximum overtime hours per week; the extent of paid leave; the duration of paid maternity leave; the minimum working conditions (for example, night shifts); the minimum notice period for dismissal; and so on. It also determines who is a formal worker and who is not, through the obligation to use the carteira assinada. As a result, studies of informality in Brazil are remarkably consistent in their definition of informal workers as those who (currently) work without a carteira (Gill 2002).[3] These laws remained in place largely unmodified until the Federal Constitution of 1988 established the current system of social protection and labor legislation (Oviedo 2015).

Overview of Employment Protection Mechanisms

The first of two unemployed-support mechanisms is UI. A government-funded UI program covers all workers with a carteira who lose their jobs. Put in place in 1986 and expanded by the 1988 Constitution, UI is financed through a 0.65 percent tax on firms' total sales or by a higher percentage on the firm's value added (depending on the economic sector), and its annual expenditure equals 2.5 percent of total eligible payroll (Gerard and Gonzaga 2013). All involuntarily dismissed workers (from a formal job in the private sector, after at least six months of tenure) are eligible for three to five monthly payments (the maximum benefit duration based on the accumulated tenure over the three years prior to layoff). Benefit levels are based on the average wage in the three months before layoff, at replacement rates of 60–100 percent. Workers must apply in person for benefits in the first month only; after the first month, benefits are available through the government-owned bank, Caixa Econômica Federal, for the entire duration of the benefit, as long as the worker's name does not appear in the new-hires database (Brazil, Ministry of Labor and Employment 2014). Spending on UI in Brazil tripled in the 2000s despite record low unemployment due to higher wages and increased share of formal jobs in total employment (Zylberstajn and Silva 2015).

The second support mechanism is a severance fund. The Severance Indemnity Fund (FGTS) was established in 1966 as the main instrument to protect workers from financial hardship in the event of dismissal. The FGTS was created to reform the firing protection rules established in the CLT, in particular to relax the prohibition on dismissing workers with 10 or more years of tenure. Its main goal is to guarantee that workers who are dismissed for reasons other than just cause (causa justa) get some form of compensation (Ferrer and Riddell 2011).[4] The design of FGTS is more akin to a severance payment than to a UI savings account. In contrast with UI, the same amount of severance pay is paid regardless of the duration of the unemployment spell. Employers have to deposit 8 percent of monthly wages into an individual account in the worker's name. The account is managed by a public bank (Caixa Econômica Federal), guaranteeing an annual return of 3 percent plus the reference rate ("taxa de referencia," currently about 0.8 percent), which often results in a negative annual return below inflation (FGTS 2012).[5] Workers can access these funds only if they (a) are dismissed for causes other than just cause; (b) have retired; (c) suffer a severe illness (such as human immunodeficiency virus [HIV] or cancer); or (d) are purchasing their first home.[6] The difference between benefits in case of dismissal for just cause and dismissal for causes other than just cause (which often include economic dismissals) is the origin of many litigation processes. If a worker is to be dismissed for causes other than just cause, the employer must give the worker advance notice and time to search for another job (in practice, amounting to additional pay for 30–90 days, depending on the worker's tenure).[7] In addition, the employer must pay a fine to the worker, equivalent to 40 percent of the total FGTS balance, plus a 10 percent fine to the government. A worker who quits receives only his or her share, not the firm's.

In Brazil, labor disputes are adjudicated by a special branch of the judiciary: labor courts. Under Brazilian law, contracts that do not fulfill all the provisions of the law are considered void, and workers (with or without carteira) may sue their employers for breach of law. Employers carry the legal burden of proof and must provide evidence that labor regulations were fulfilled. The worker, on the other hand, needs to prove that the labor relationship existed (one eyewitness is considered sufficient). A statute of limitations allows workers to sue their former employers for violations up to five years after the contract termination. Usually parties are directed to a mediated negotiation first, and they appear before the judge only if negotiations fail. If declared guilty, the employer may be fined and ordered to pay compensation to the worker, even if the parties had reached different previous agreements.

Minimum-Wage Level and the Role of Legislation

Since 2002, Brazil's minimum wage has almost doubled in real terms, and its growth rate has been higher than in most other Latin American and Caribbean countries, as shown in figure 3.1, panel a (World Bank 2014). However, on two reference indicators, the minimum wage in Brazil is currently in line with international comparators: First, the ratio of Brazil's minimum wage to GNI per

Figure 3.1 Minimum-Wage Growth and Ratio to GNI per Worker, Selected Economies

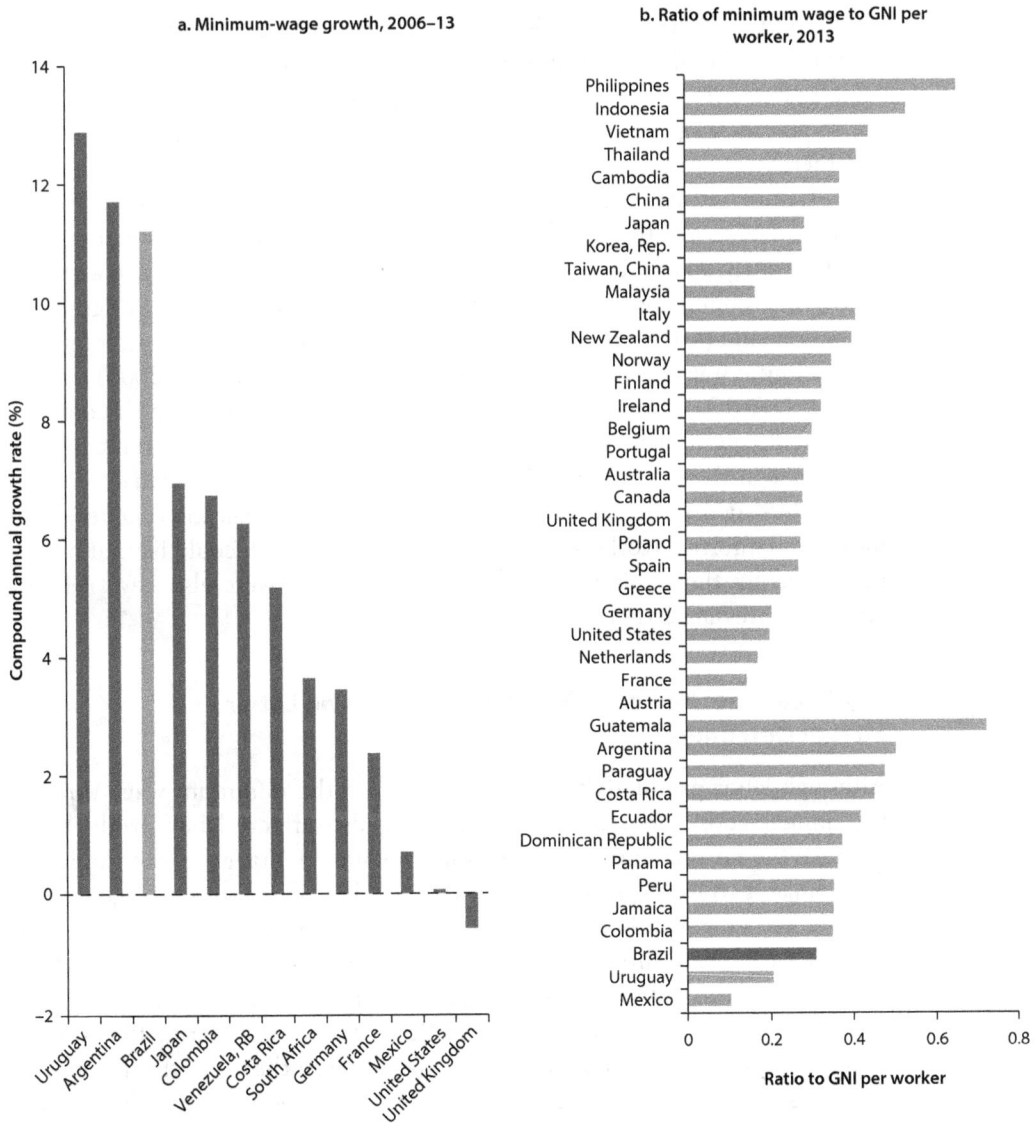

a. Minimum-wage growth, 2006–13

b. Ratio of minimum wage to GNI per worker, 2013

Source: World Bank 2014.
Note: Calculations are in real terms and minimum-wage per month in local currency units.

Source: Kuddo, Robalino, and Weber, forthcoming.
Note: GNI = gross national income.

worker (a proxy for value added per worker, a measure of labor productivity) was 0.31 in 2013 (figure 3.1, panel b) (World Bank 2014).[8] That result is on par with the average ratio of 0.3 among other upper-middle-income economies, slightly above the OECD average (0.27), and below the Latin American and East Asian regional averages of 0.38 and 0.37, respectively (Kuddo, Robalino, and Weber, forthcoming). Second, relative to median wage, Brazil's minimum wage also performs relatively well: it was about 70 percent of the median wage and 42 percent of the mean wage in 2011 (ILO 2013a). In high-income countries, minimum wages fluctuate between 37 percent and 60 percent of the median wage, with most countries clustering around 40 percent (ILO 2013a).

During the 1980s and 1990s, the minimum wage reduced formal employment (and even informal employment, in some cases) and did not significantly reduce poverty rates (Gill 2002). In contrast, in the 2000s, both the existence of the minimum wage and its levels helped to decrease labor earnings inequality and thereby income inequality and poverty, ultimately helping to make labor markets more pro-poor.[9] During this decade, the wage distribution became more compressed around the minimum wage in the formal and informal sectors, mostly through an increase in the wages of the lowest-paid workers and a smaller mass of the population at or below the minimum wage, as shown in figure 3.2. A considerable (and increasing) proportion of low-paid workers currently earn the minimum wage (23 percent as of 2012, up from 18 percent in 2005) (Lemos 2009; ILO 2013a), now similar to the 25 percent average among peer countries (Kuddo, Robalino, and Weber, forthcoming). However, it is important to note that although the minimum wage contributed significantly to inequality reduction, factors such as the decrease in wage gaps between urban and rural residents, formal and informal workers, and men and women (which could have also been influenced by the minimum wage policy indirectly) were also key (Ferreira, Firpo, and Messina 2014).

Key Challenge: Avoiding Detrimental Effects on Labor Market Outcomes

Although labor productivity affects the *path* of the minimum wage through the annual adjustment formula, that path also affects labor productivity. Because the current formula for setting the annual change in the minimum wage links it to GDP growth two years ago, current minimum-wage growth may exceed current labor productivity growth for a large share of firms. This could affect their ability to accumulate capital and invest in training, particularly among firms with high percentages of workers earning close to the minimum wage. It also reduces firms' competitiveness, thus hindering the creation of higher-quality jobs. Evidence shows that in more than one-third of manufacturing firms, value added per worker increased less than minimum-wage growth in 2012–13 (Maciente, Silva, and Gukovas 2015). Changes in rent sharing between wages and investment can help avoid immediate employment adjustments, but these changes are easier to sustain in the context of a

Figure 3.2 Comparison of Wage Distribution and Minimum Wage in Brazil, by Worker Type, 2002 and 2013

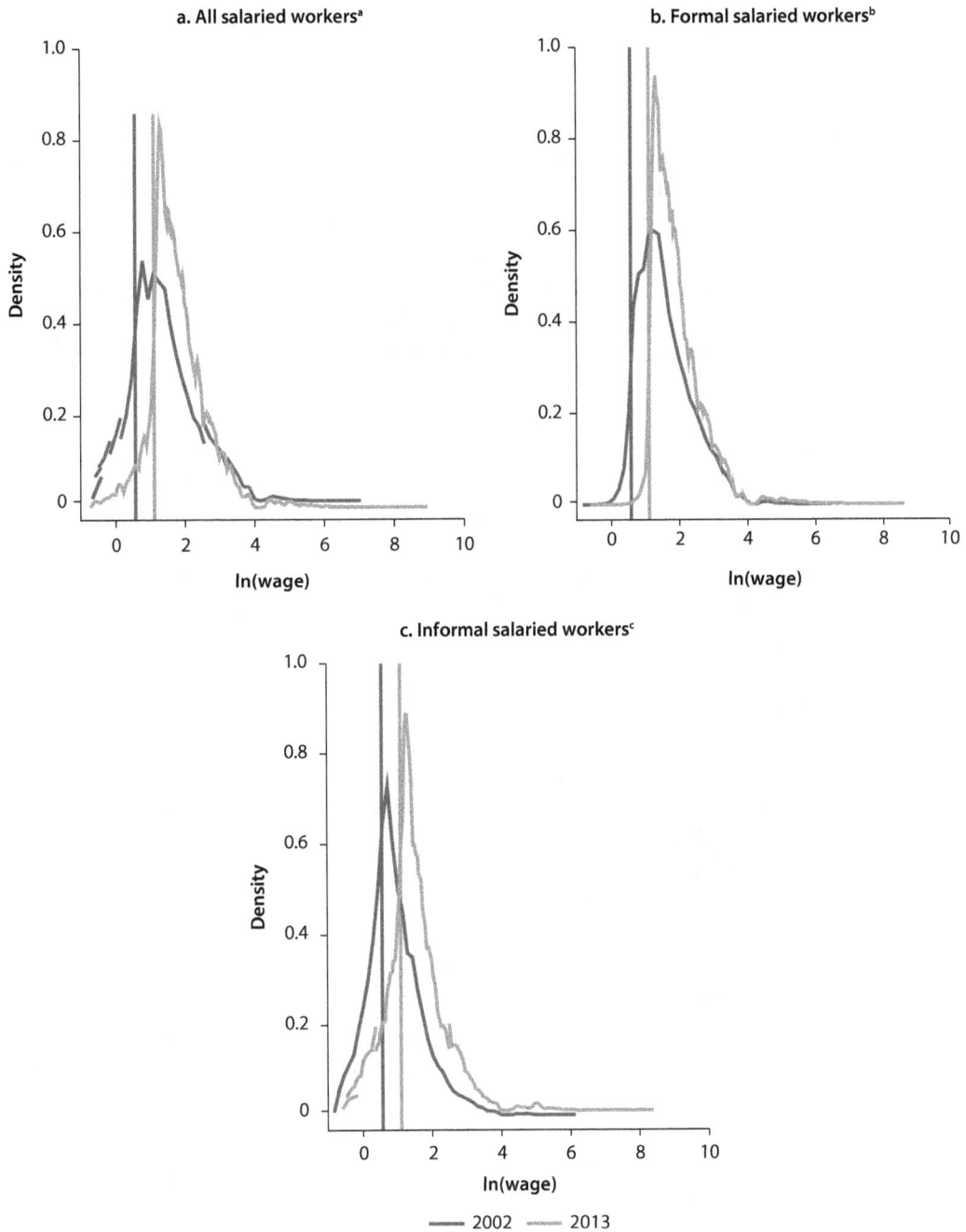

a. All salaried workers[a]

b. Formal salaried workers[b]

c. Informal salaried workers[c]

2002   2013

Source: Based on the National Household Survey (Pesquisa Nacional por Amostra de Domicilio, PNAD), Brazilian Institute of Geography and Statistics, Rio de Janeiro.
Note: Graphs depict kernel density estimates for the wage distribution for full-time workers in Brazil.
a. kernel = epanechnikov, bandwidth = 0.6665.
b. kernel = epanechnikov, bandwidth = 0.0739.
c. kernel = epanechnikov, bandwidth = 0.0726.

positive demand shock (see chapter 1). Furthermore, the firms' response to higher labor costs from minimum-wage increases can affect labor productivity, for example, through (a) decreased demand of unskilled labor and substitution of higher-skilled for less-skilled labor; or (b) decreased investment in training, new technologies, or better management techniques. Firms might also decide to substitute formal workers for informal ones or even to decrease compliance with the minimum-wage law, especially in geographic areas with lower enforcement. Notably, evidence from self-reported earnings in Brazil shows that the share of workers (both formal and informal) earning less than the minimum wage was higher in 2013 than in 2002, a possible unintended consequence of high minimum-wage increases in recent years (Ferreira, Firpo, and Messina 2014). In addition, because many social benefits (such as the social pension) are indexed to the minimum wage, fast minimum wage growth can have important fiscal impacts, further affecting productivity.

Another constraint on labor productivity is Brazil's traditionally high rate of job turnover, which can decrease firms' incentives to invest in training. Job turnover in Brazil is remarkably high by international standards and has been gradually increasing since the early 2000s, with as many as 55 percent of the Brazilian formal sector employees changing jobs in 2012 (figure 3.3, panel a). This high turnover translates into significantly shorter job tenures than in most OECD countries (figure 3.3, panel b). Low tenure is not an undesirable outcome per se, but it can signal an inefficient reallocation of labor, leading to underinvestment in human capital, large transaction costs for firms and workers (created by the search and litigation processes), and large productivity losses (Corseuil et al. 2012). In the context of Brazil's low rate of labor productivity growth in the 2000s, it is crucial to reduce distortions that hinder firms' investment in worker training. In addition, among workers who leave formal jobs to work informally while seeking new formal jobs, there is a potential implicit cost: their formal reemployment rates tend to be low (below 20 percent) (Amadeo, Gill, and Neri 2000; Gonzaga 2003; Gerard and Gonzaga 2013).

A branch of the literature argues that UI and FGTS design could be behind the high job turnover, showing a concentration of firings just below the minimum job-tenure thresholds for UI entitlement (Gerard and Gonzaga 2012). However, Zylberstajn and Silva (2015) find that high job turnover is a feature of both formal and informal labor markets (where workers are not entitled to UI) and is usually motivated by workers' reallocation to higher-paying jobs (57 percent in 2013). Although there is no single solution to increase job attachment without creating disincentives for productivity, the recent government proposal of increasing the minimum employment duration for UI eligibility can reduce spending on UI (which has tripled since 2002 despite record low unemployment linked to higher formal employment and wages). Nonetheless, it is essential to assess the proposal's effect on UI coverage—particularly among the low-skilled, who tend to have shorter employment spells.[10]

Figure 3.3 Employee Turnover Trends and Tenure in Brazil and Selected OECD Countries

| a. Turnover rate, formal employees in Brazil, 2003–12 | b. Average employee tenure, selected OECD countries, 2009 |

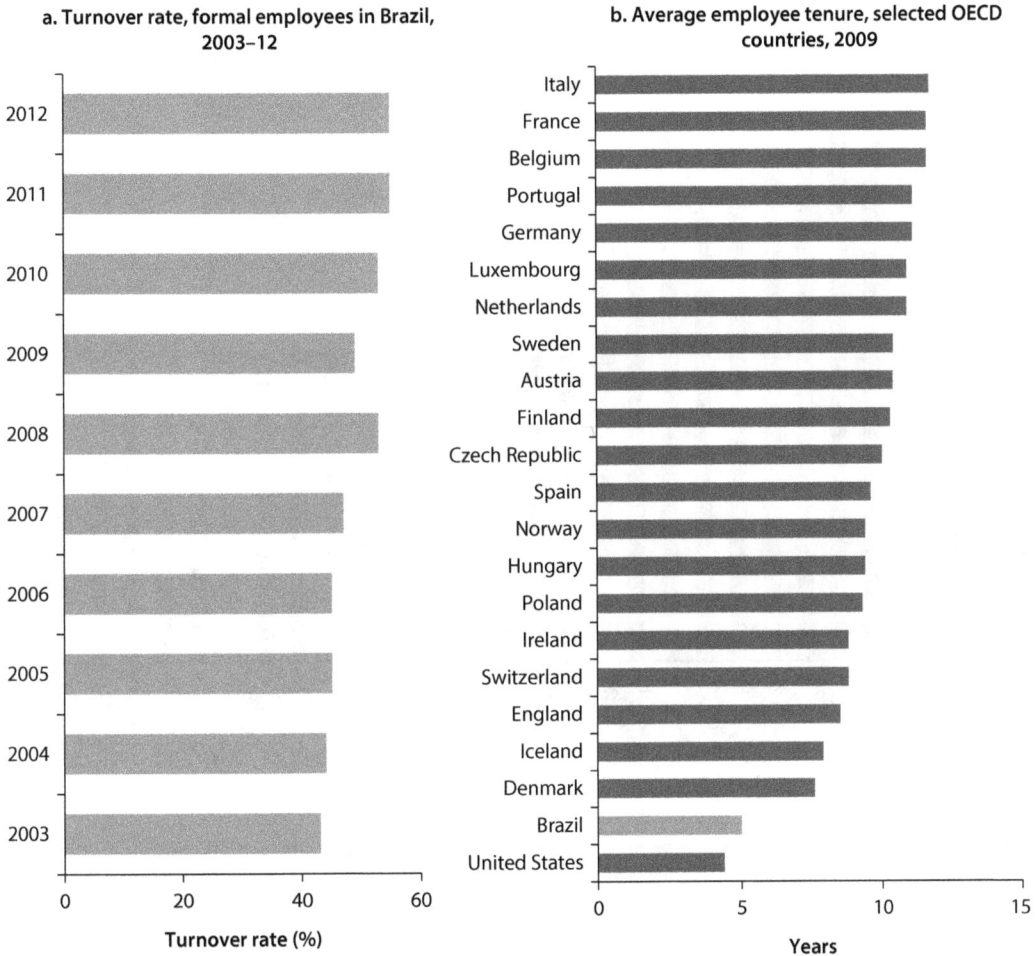

Source: Zylberstajn and Silva 2015.
Note: OECD = Organisation for Economic Co-operation and Development.

Source: DIEESE 2011.

In addition, Brazil's high nonwage labor costs can hurt firms' investment in innovation and training and promote firm exit, further hurting labor productivity. In the formal sector, mandated nonwage costs such as social insurance and labor-related taxes represent 33 percent of all labor costs, far exceeding the OECD average of about 20 percent (figure 3.4). These costs pose potential unintended consequences for formalization, firm growth, and ultimately competitiveness through the high cost of doing business. Importantly, several additional mandated costs make labor expenditures soar even higher for formal employers in Brazil.[11] This high cost burden calls for a detailed analysis of financing of each component of these items, the trade-offs involved in reducing (workers' and firms')

Figure 3.4 Share of Mandated Nonwage Labor Costs in Total Hourly Compensation in Selected Economies, 2012

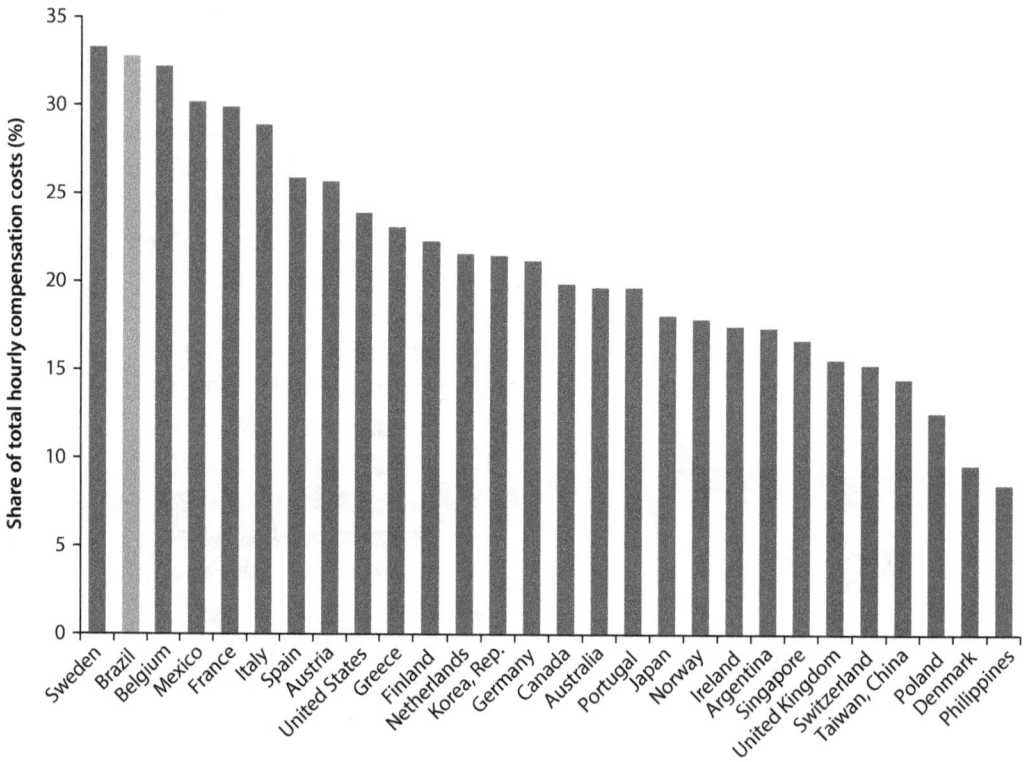

Source: ILO 2014.
Note: Mandated nonwage labor costs represent employers' expenditure on benefits other than wages granted to their employees as compensation for an hour of labor in the manufacturing sector.

contributions, and the linked benefit's role in the social contract between the state and citizens.

Simulations suggest that reducing the nonwage costs of formal jobs could decrease informality without increasing unemployment. Using two-sector matching models calibrated to the Brazilian labor market of the early to mid-2000s, Ulyssea and Cortez Reis (2006) and Ulyssea (2010) find that the costs of formal job creation, captured by the nonwage costs, are a crucial factor affecting the shares of formal and informal workers in the labor force as well as the wage gap between them. For example, a 70 percent reduction in the costs of creating a formal job (relative to an informal one) is estimated to reduce informality by about 8 percentage points and unemployment by 4.8 percentage points.

Finally, ineffective labor dispute resolution mechanisms can create considerable uncertainty for employers and employees and economic insecurity for households. The labor laws' objective of protecting against sudden income loss will not be fulfilled if dispute resolution is too prolonged. Moreover, extended litigation affects both firing and hiring decisions because firms may be reluctant to hire new workers if they anticipate that future dismissals are likely to lead to lengthy dispute processes (Kugler and Pica 2008). This can hamper the job real-location dynamics and therefore productivity (Messina and Vallanti 2007; Martin and Scarpetta 2012). Brazil already has sound judicial foundations to deal with labor disputes efficiently and fairly. However, some features of this system might cause an increasingly high number of disputes to reach labor courts every year (3 million cases in 2013 alone; see Oviedo 2015). The burden of litigation can increase both administrative costs and waiting times while also discouraging employers from entering into labor contracts.

The Way Forward: A Policy Agenda

How can labor regulations and institutions better support firm productivity while also protecting individual worker safeguards and incentives? There is no single answer to this question. Hence, we highlight four adjustment paths that could move workers' and firms' incentives toward longer tenures, more hiring, and ultimately higher labor productivity: ensuring that minimum wage gains are accompanied by labor productivity growth, integrating job-search requirements into UI eligibility, assessing potential reduction of mandated nonwage labor costs, and reforming labor dispute resolution. We also discuss how other countries have designed and implemented these reform paths.

Ensuring that Minimum Wage Gains Are Accompanied by Labor Productivity Growth

First, it is important to keep Brazil's minimum wage in line with international standards and ensure that gains are accompanied by labor productivity growth. The previous section discussed how important the minimum wage has been to the reduction of poverty and inequality. Although its growth has been high, the current level is not out of line with international standards. The current rule that links annual minimum-wage growth to GDP growth will determine growth at lower rates in the next few years. Sustaining the minimum-wage increases will depend on Brazil's capacity to raise its labor productivity to compete.

Integrating Job-Search Requirements into UI Eligibility

Second, Brazil needs to integrate job-search requirements into UI eligibility to encourage job seekers to become more active in seeking work and improving their employability. The tension between protecting workers' income during periods of unemployment and providing the right incentives to work is always present when designing unemployment protection policies and programs. Indeed, traditional UI programs may tend to prolong unemployment periods, increase reservation wages, and discourage active job searches (Card and Levine 2000). Over the years, several innovations have adjusted UI programs to address this problem. In one important trend that could be relevant to Brazil, many OECD countries have created mechanisms to enforce or reward active job searches and reentry into the labor market (box 3.1). The OECD experience indicates that strengthening requirements for UI recipients to actively look for work, take up suitable job offers, or participate in active labor market programs (ALMPs)—or else risk benefit sanctions—can help to offset the negative impact of generous unemployment benefits on employment incentives while increasing the sustainability of UI programs (Vodopivec 2004; Venn 2012; OECD 2013). Broadly, rather than significantly adjusting the entitlement

Box 3.1 The OECD Experience in Integrating Job-Search Requirements into Unemployment Insurance Eligibility

Requirements for independent job searching vary widely among OECD countries (Venn 2012). A few countries (such as Greece, Spain, and Turkey) had no formal requirements at the time of the most comprehensive survey in 2007, but most OECD countries now require claimants to either provide proof of job-search activity or keep a record of their job searches and applications, which they must provide upon request to the employment centers. The most-rigorous requirements are found in countries such as Australia and the United Kingdom, where claimants must take a specified number of job-seeking steps every two weeks and provide relevant evidence to their employment adviser. Monthly job-search reporting is more common—for example, in France, Japan, the Republic of Korea, and Switzerland. Table B3.1.1 shows the frequency and number of job applications or actions that are expected in a range of countries with such requirements.

Table B3.1.1 Job-Search Requirements for UI Eligibility in Selected OECD Countries

Country	Required job-search reporting (frequency)	Actions to be reported per month (number)
Australia	Every 2 weeks	8–20
Canada	Variable requirements	"Reasonable" efforts expected
Czech Republic	Every 2 weeks	Unspecified
Denmark	At least once every 3 months	Variable requirements (depending on IAP)
Finland	From 1 week to 1 month	Variable (depending on IAP)
France	Once a month (after 4th month)	Variable
Japan	Once every 4 weeks	2
Korea, Rep.	Variable, from weekly to every 4 weeks	2
Netherlands	Every 4 weeks	4
New Zealand	Every 6 weeks	Variable (depending on IAP)
Norway	Every 3 months	Unspecified
Switzerland	Once a month	4–10
United Kingdom	Every 2 weeks	10
United States	Every 2 weeks	10

Source: Based on Venn 2012.
Note: UI = unemployment insurance. IAP = Individual Action Plan.

conditions (such as employment or contribution requirements to gain access to benefits and sanctions for voluntary unemployment), OECD countries have prioritized the following:

- *Strengthening job-search requirements* for access to UI payments (including availability for interviews and other contacts during unemployment)
- *Instituting worker incentives* such as bonuses for faster job reentry and longer employment tenure
- *Monitoring job-search efforts* and imposing sanctions for refusing job offers

Strengthening job-search requirements, monitoring, and benefit incentives or sanctions increase the job-finding rate of benefit recipients. Evidence suggests that stricter job-search requirements and reporting reduced the average duration of unemployment by 1 percent relative to no reporting requirements in the United States (Klepinger et al. 1997). An experiment that increased the required number of weekly employer contacts from two to four reduced the average duration of benefit payments by two to four weeks; moreover, informing claimants that reported contacts would be verified with the employers magnified this impact (Martin and Grubb 2001; Vodopiv̆ec 2004). Similarly, Fredriksson and Holmlund (2003) show that imposing sanctions, giving warnings, and enforcing compliance with job-search requirements have strong effects on the outflow rate from unemployment.

To avoid an association of fast reemployment with wage losses, some countries have coupled increased job-search requirements with stronger activation policies, including reform of employment services to improve job-search assistance, expansion of access to training, or provision of subsidized jobs after an unsuccessful job-search period. Evidence from Germany suggests that such reforms reduce the reservation wages of the unemployed, encouraging people to return to work. However, those who remain unemployed can be worse off, and reentry can be hard and can become associated with wage losses (Mortensen and Pissarides 1994; Detragiache, Engbom, and Raei, forthcoming). To address this issue, the German reforms were coupled with a strong activation policy (for example, through intermediation services) and incentives to invest in productivity enhancement (such as worker training). These measures were seen as more-intensive forms of job-search support that were made available only if less-intensive support (such as self-service or assisted job searches) had not worked (that is, after a period of unsuccessful job searching and guided by the principle of "mutual obligations" so that job seekers do not perceive the additional help as a penalty but rather as an opportunity).

Assessing Reduction of Mandated Nonwage Labor Costs

Third, it is important to analyze various mandated nonwage labor costs for potential reductions. A constructive analysis would assess how to best avoid distortions in formal employment or unemployment while ensuring the desired social contract, as part of a broader discussion on the adequacy and sustainability of the social security (pension) system. Making formal labor more affordable relative to informal labor could increase the pace of formal job creation. The analysis would consider the distortion caused by mandated nonwage labor costs. Using this information, the government could prioritize the reduction of some costs, taking into account its view of the desired social contract.

Reforming Labor Dispute Resolution

Fourth, Brazil needs to reduce incentives for unnecessary labor disputes while streamlining dispute resolution. A more effective labor dispute resolution mechanism in Brazil could entail reforms in two fronts. First, simplifying the regulatory language, including the definition of dismissal for causes other than just cause, to reduce the scope for ambiguity and thus for litigation could reduce the margin for unnecessary labor disputes (box 3.2). Second, strengthening (a) automatic mechanisms for some types of labor disputes and (b) stronger mediation and negotiation mechanisms could cut litigation expenditures and speed up decision making. (For results of such reforms in South Africa, see box 3.3.) A worker who claims that his employment has been unjustifiably terminated should be entitled to appeal that termination to an impartial body; however, some processes could

---

Box 3.2 Italy's Simplified Labor Law Code

Italy has simplified its labor regulations into a short code. This process, launched around 2008–09, published the first edition of a "simplified" code in November 2009 that replaced 100 old statutes with 70 short sections. Following revisions, the Simplified Labor Law Code (SLLC) was announced in the preamble of the Poletti Decree in May 2014. A group of senators, labor lawyers, and other stakeholders reviewed the Italian labor code, listed the key principles of the legislation, and mapped under those principles all the pertinent laws that Italy has enacted, starting with the SLLC. They simplified the language (to be easily readable by anyone and easily translatable into English) and prepared a new text of a limited number of provisions (see a sample summary in table B3.2.1).

Table B3.2.1 Summary of Italy's Simplified Labor Code for Part-Time Work

Old law	Simplified code
13 articles, 3,803 words	1 statute, 3 paragraphs, 117 words
The following was (over-)regulated:	The following is regulated:
• Form and content of contract	• Written form
• Maximum overtime every week and every year	• Nondiscrimination and proportional change in standards
• Reasons for overtime	• Reduced time schedule
• Reduced time schedule	
• "Flexible" and "elastic" clauses	
• Convertibility of elastic clauses	
• Related penalties	

Source: Adapted from the site http://www.pietroichino.it.

Box 3.3 Flexible, Tailored Labor Dispute Resolution Services: Evidence from South Africa

South Africa codified and simplified a body of labor jurisprudence into a Labor Relations Act (enacted in 1995). Before the reform, the extremely high caseload (mainly dismissal disputes) caused major backlogs in the courts. The act, among other things, reworked the law of dismissal "for causes other than just cause" to reduce the time and cost of resolving dismissal disputes.

The new act also established the Commission for Conciliation, Mediation and Arbitration (CCMA), which is responsible for dispute resolution (apart from formal litigation) in certain labor dispute categories by implementing conciliation to reduce the incidence of court action and litigation. Its mandate includes (a) the provision of accessible, expeditious conciliation in "rights" disputes (mostly, claims of dismissal for causes other than just cause) (around 100,000 cases were addressed by CCMA through conciliation in 2012); and (b) mediation of unresolved collective bargaining disputes. Despite its high caseload, CCMA has managed to quickly resolve a high percentage of cases—particularly dismissal cases—through conciliation and arbitration, significantly decreasing the percentage of dismissal disputes requiring court action. Several key factors have contributed to CCMA's effective operation:

- *Use of technology.* For instance, CCMA developed and tailored an electronic case management system and uses text messages to notify parties of hearings.
- *Early intervention.* CCMA offers to facilitate collective bargaining at an early stage in key disputes to prevent them from spiraling into disruption and violence.
- *New services that improve labor relations.* CCMA's workplace mediation services or conciliation services, for instance, frame negotiations and discussions between representatives of employers, employees, and unions in a way that facilitates mutually acceptable agreements.

Source: Benjamin 2013.

involve an arbitration committee or arbitrators (Noord, Hwang, and Bugeja 2011; ILO 2013b; Teague 2013). Ex post audits of dismissals could be enabled by law or collective agreement to ensure that the workers' rights have not been compromised.

Notes

1. In 2012, the share of dismissals without just cause was close to 60 percent in Brazil, which is above the Organisation for Economic Co-operation and Development (OECD) average (Oviedo 2015).

2. For a detailed review of Brazil's labor market regulations and institutions, see Oviedo (2015).

3. Where used, the shorthand term, carteira, refers in this report to the carteira assinada, also formally called the Carteira de Trabalho e Previdência Social (Work and Social Security Card).

4. Dismissals for just cause (causa justa) comprise, for example, firings for misbehavior or if the job ceases to exist. If just cause does not legally define why a worker is fired, the firing will be classified as being for other reasons, which has implications for the worker's entitlement to UI and FGTS. Many litigation processes in the labor courts hinge on the establishment of just cause as the reason for firing.

5. Brazil's benchmark interest rate, the rate underlying trading in all other debt in the market, is 10.75 percent (Hong and Wirz 2014). With an inflation rate of around 6 percent per year, the real return of the FGTS is still slightly below the lowest possible market return.

6. In 2012, 90.6 percent of FGTS withdrawals corresponded to either dismissal without just cause (63.3 percent), retirement (14.2 percent), or home purchase (13.1 percent) (FGTS 2012).

7. For workers with one year of tenure or less, the notice period is 60 days. For workers who have been with the same firm beyond one year, the notice period increases by 3 days per year of tenure, limited to 30 days, with a possible total of 90 days (Law No. 12.506) (Oviedo 2015).

8. Using the World Bank's *Doing Business* methodology, the minimum-wage level is expressed as a share of average gross national income (GNI) per worker, used as a proxy for average earnings (World Bank 2014). However, the data should be interpreted with care in cross-country comparisons, particularly because countries differ in the proportion of the population that is employed.

9. Regarding the period until 2004, see Lemos (2009). Regarding 2004–12, see Bosch and Gonzalez-Velosa (2014) and Ferreira, Firpo, and Messina (2014).

10. Although the report focuses mainly on de facto regulations, it acknowledges the large gap between the law and its implementation, and the latter is what ultimately affects economic incentives and firm performance. Most of the recent empirical work (for example, Almeida and Carneiro 2009, 2012) has shown that the enforcement of labor regulations affected labor outcomes and job quality. In particular, stricter enforcement of the benefits had a clear, positive impact on overall employment quality, measured by the compliance with these mandated benefits. However, when enforcement increases, employers try to offset the cost of increased mandated-benefit provision by adjusting nominal wages or reducing some voluntary benefits to contain total labor costs. For some better-paid workers, the imposition of state-mandated benefit packages comes at the cost of wages or other benefits (such as private health insurance) that they might value more (see Almeida, Carneiro, and Narita 2013).

11. Firms' costs for formal employees include the 13th month salary (8.33 percent). (As in most Latin American countries, employees are entitled to an additional "13th month" salary, payable by the employer each year in December.) Employers also pay transportation costs (around 1 percent, up to 6 percent); social security charges (National Institute of Social Security [INSS]/FGTS) on the 13th-month salary (2.98 percent); a vacation bonus (2.78 percent, or one-third of one month's salary when the employee takes vacations); and social security charges (INSS/FGTS) on the vacation bonus (1 percent). In addition, firms have to pay the FGTS penalty of 40 percent (4.5 percent) when dismissing an employee. Finally, depending on the sector, additional payments are required for food staples and health insurance. Hence, nonwage costs can total up to 70 percent of total compensation (James 2011).

References

Almeida, Rita, and Pedro Carneiro. 2009. "Enforcement of Labor Regulation and Firm Size." *Journal of Comparative Economics* 37 (1): 28–46.

———. 2012. "Enforcement of Labor Regulation and Informality." *American Economic Journal: Applied Economics* 4 (3): 64–89.

Almeida, Rita, Pedro Carneiro, and Renata Narita. 2013. "Producing Higher Quality Jobs: Enforcement of Mandated Benefits across Brazilian Cities between 1996–2007." Working Paper 2013–22, Department of Economics, University of São Paulo (FEA-USP).

Amadeo, Edward Joaquim, Indermit S. Gill, and Marcelo Cortes Neri. 2000. "Brazil: The Pressure Points in Labor Legislation." Economics Working Paper 395, Graduate School of Economics, Getulio Vargas Foundation, Rio de Janeiro.

Benjamin, P. 2013. "Assesing South Africa's Commission for Conciliation, Mediation and Arbitration (CCMA)." DIALOGUE Working Paper 47, ILO, Geneva.

Bosch, Mariano, and Carolina Gonzalez-Velosa. 2014. "Minimum Wages, Inequality, and the Returns to Schooling in Brazil." Unpublished manuscript, Inter-American Development Bank, Washington, DC.

Brazil, Ministry of Labor and Employment. 2014. "Plano de Emprego no Brasil." Ministry of Labor and Employment, Brasilia.

Card, David, and Phillip B. Levine. 2000. "Extended Benefits and the Duration of UI Spells: Evidence from the New Jersey Extended Benefit Program." *Journal of Public Economics* 78 (1): 107–38.

Corseuil, Carlos Henrique L., Miguel Nathan Foguel, Gustavo Gonzaga, and Eduardo Pontual Ribeiro. 2012. "The Effects of a Youth Training Program on Youth Turnover in Brazil." Working Paper 042, Network of Applied Economics (Rede de Economia Aplicada, REAP), São Paulo.

Detragiache, E., N. Engbom, and F. Raei. Forthcoming. "The Effect of German Labor Market Reforms on Employment and Wages." Unpublished manuscript, International Monetary Fund, Washington, DC.

DIEESE (Inter-Union Department of Statistics and Socio-Economic Studies). 2011. *Rotatividade e flexibilidade no mercado de trabalho.* [Turnover and Flexibility in the Labor Market.] São Paulo: DIEESE.

Ferreira, Francisco H. G., Sergio P. Firpo, and Julian Messina. 2014. "A More Level Playing Field? Explaining the Decline in Earnings Inequality in Brazil, 1995–2012." IRIBA (International Research Initiative on Brazil and Africa) Working Paper 12, University of Manchester, United Kingdom.

Ferrer, Ana M., and W. Craig Riddell. 2011. "Unemployment Insurance Savings Accounts in Latin America: Overview and Assessment." Discussion Paper 5577, Institute for the Study of Labor (IZA), Bonn.

FGTS (Severance Indemnity Fund). 2012. *Relatório de Administração, Exercício.* Annual management report, Ministry of Labor and Employment, Brasilia.

Fredriksson, P., and B. Holmlund. 2003. "Improving Incentives in Unemployment Insurance: A Review of Recent Research." Working Paper 922, Center for Economic Studies and the IFO Institute, Munich.

Gerard, François, and Gustavo Gonzaga. 2012. "Social Insurance under Imperfect Monitoring: Labor Market and Welfare Impacts of the Brazilian UI program." Working Paper 039, Network of Applied Economics (REAP).

————. 2013. "Informal Labor and the Cost of Social Programs: Evidence from 15 Years of Unemployment Insurance in Brazil." Discussion Paper 608, Department of Economics, Pontifical Catholic University of Rio de Janeiro (PUC-Rio).

Gill, Indermit. 2002. *Brazil Jobs Report*. Report 24408-BR, World Bank, Washington, DC; Institute for Applied Economic Research, Brasilia.

Gonzaga, Gustavo. 2003. "Labor Turnover and Labor Legislation in Brazil." *Economia* 4 (1): 165–222.

Hong, Nicole, and Matt Wirz. 2014. "Brazilian Bonds Make a Comeback." *Wall Street Journal* (March 25).

ILO (International Labour Organization). 2013a. *Key Indicators of the Labour Market 2012*. 7th ed. Geneva: ILO.

————. 2013b. *Labour Dispute Systems: Guidelines for Improved Performance*. Geneva: ILO.

————. 2014. *Key Indicators of the Labour Market*. 8th ed. Geneva: ILO.

James, Gary. 2011. "Business Basics in Brazil: Big Opportunities, Challenges Go Hand in Hand." *Journal of Accountancy* (November): 34. http://journalofaccountancy.com /issues/2011/nov/20114143.html.

Klepinger, Daniel, Terry R. Johnson, Jutta Joesch, and Jacob M. Benus. 1997. *Evaluation of the Maryland Unemployment Insurance Work Search Demonstration*. Final report, Maryland Department of Labor, Licensing and Regulation, Office of Unemployment Insurance, Baltimore.

Kuddo, A., D. Robalino, and M. Weber. Forthcoming. "Manual on Labor Regulations." Unpublished manuscript, World Bank, Washington, DC.

Kugler, A., and G. Pica. 2008. "Effects of Employment Protection on Worker and Job Flows: Evidence from the 1990 Italian Reform." *Labour Economics* 15 (1): 78–95.

Lemos, S. 2009. "Minimum Wage Effects in a Developing Country." *Labour Economics* 16 (2): 224–37.

Maciente, Aguinaldo, Joana Silva, and Renata Gukovas. 2015. "Employment Creation, Labor Productivity, and Firms' Dynamics." Research paper—background paper for this report, World Bank, Washington, DC.

Martin, J., and D. Grubb. 2001. "What Works and for Whom: A Review of OECD Countries' Experiences with Active Labour Market Policies." Working paper 20001/14, Institute for Labour Market Policy Evaluation, Uppsala, Sweden.

Martin, J. P., and S. Scarpetta. 2012. "Setting It Right: Employment Protection, Labour Reallocation and Productivity." *De Economist* 160 (2): 89–116.

Messina, J., and G. Vallanti. 2007. "Job Flow Dynamics and Firing Restrictions: Evidence from Europe." *The Economic Journal* 117 (521): F279–F301.

Mortensen, T., and A. Pissarides. 1994. "Job Creation and Job Destruction in the Theory of Unemployment." *The Review of Economic Studies* 61 (3): 397–415.

Noord, Hugo van, Hans S. Hwang, and Kate Bugeja. 2011. "Cambodia's Arbitration Council: Institution Building in a Developing Country." DIALOGUE Working Paper 24, International Labour Organization, Geneva.

OECD (Organisation for Economic Co-operation and Development). 2013. *OECD Employment Outlook 2013*. Paris: OECD.

Oviedo, Ana Maria. 2015. "Labor Market Regulations and Institutions in Brazil." Policy paper—background paper for this report, World Bank, Washington, DC.

Teague, P. 2013. "Resolving Workplace Disputes in Ireland: The Role of the Labor Relations Commission." DIALOGUE Working Paper 48, International Labour Organization, Geneva.

Ulyssea, Gabriel. 2010. "Regulation of Entry, Labor Market Institutions and the Informal Sector." *Journal of Development Economics* 91 (1): 87–99.

Ulyssea, Gabriel, and Mauricio Cortez Reis. 2006. "Imposto Sobre Trabalho e Seu Impacto nos Setores Formal e Informal." [Tax Work and Its Impact on Formal and Informal Sectors.] Discussion Paper 1218, Institute for Applied Economic Research (IPEA), Brasilia.

Venn, Danielle. 2012. "Eligibility Criteria for Unemployment Benefits: Quantitative Indicators for OECD and EU Countries." Working paper, OECD, Paris.

Vodopivec, Milan. 2004. *Income Support for the Unemployed: Issues and Options.* World Bank Regional and Sectoral Studies. Washington, DC: World Bank.

World Bank. 2014. *Doing Business Report 2015: Going Beyond Efficiency.* Washington, DC: World Bank.

Zylberstajn, Eduardo, and Joana Silva. 2015. "Earnings Consequences of Labor Turnover: The Case of Brazil." Research paper—background paper for this report, World Bank, Washington, DC.

CHAPTER 4

Labor Market Programs to Strengthen the Workforce and Policies to Raise Small-Business Productivity

Introduction

Brazil has an opportunity to leverage its labor market programs and policies to promote more effective job matches, address skill gaps, and promote entrepreneurship. Like most other middle-income countries, Brazil has a range of active labor market programs (ALMPs) that aim to help with job searching and matching, improve employability, and connect people to more productive employment. Other programs and policies promote self-employment and the growth of micro and small enterprises.[1] An important ALMP (discussed in detail in chapter 2) is Brazil's National Program for Access to Technical Education and Employment (PRONATEC).[2] Aside from PRONATEC, the main ALMPs in Brazil include labor intermediation services through the National Employment System (SINE); programs that specifically support unemployed and vulnerable youth; and other training programs, such as professional training for unemployment-benefit recipients (Bolsa Formação). Brazil also promotes entrepreneurship and development of micro and small enterprises through several financial and nonfinancial support programs and services.[3] Finally, Brazil has pioneered the Economía Solidaria (solidarity economy) principle. In all of these areas, Brazil has invested in programs and policies that address the key challenges identified in this report (Marra et al. 2015).

However, improvements to several areas could help achieve better outcomes. Although government spending on labor market policies has increased, it primarily finances passive policies such as low-wage supplements (Abono Salarial) and unemployment insurance (UI).[4] As a result, Brazil's federal ALMP spending continues to lag behind the Organisation for Economic Co-operation and Development (OECD) average. Several OECD and Latin American countries

Sustaining Employment and Wage Gains in Brazil • http://dx.doi.org/10.1596/978-1-4648-0644-5   111

implemented major reforms to public employment services to focus them more on the job placement rates of their clients. Such a reform could improve SINE's results in Brazil. Similarly, youth programs could be further strengthened by adding "soft skills" (personal skills) and on-the-job components (in the workplace) to training. Entrepreneurship programs, in turn, could be better coordinated to avoid fragmentation and better linked to programs and complementary services to maximize their impact. Overall, given the wealth of available information and the innovative nature of active labor market policies (including Economía Solidaria programs that support urban and rural cooperatives), strengthening of monitoring and evaluation systems for regular follow-up on uptake and results of the various programs could be a powerful tool for their improvement.

It is necessary to adapt and refocus existing ALMP and entrepreneurship support policies around their key objectives and strengthen monitoring and evaluation. Specifically, *more-efficient public employment services* could support better, faster job searches and produce better job matches. *Higher-quality youth programs and policies* could better equip unemployed youth for jobs and provide firms with better-prepared workers. *More coordinated, more effective entrepreneurship programs* could promote earnings growth and increase small-business productivity, thus increasing microentrepreneurs' earnings. *Stronger monitoring and evaluation (M&E) of SINE and other ALMPs* could improve efficiency and sustainability of the overall system. Achieving these goals will require commitment to several key priorities:

- *Adopting a placement-focused management approach in SINE* by (a) introducing client profiling and placement-focused case management; (b) strengthening services for businesses that seek low-skilled workers; (c) outsourcing of certain SINE functions to private sector providers; and (d) using results-based reimbursements
- *Adding both on-the-job and "soft-skills" components to youth-targeted ALMPs* to better equip unemployed youth for jobs, including links between training and apprenticeships (for example, by redesigning the "Apprentice Law")
- *Improving the coordination among various entrepreneurship support programs* by (a) establishing more effective links between financial and nonfinancial support programs, as well as links with other labor market programs and services, to promote small-business productivity; and (b) reviewing and consolidating fragmented programs to improve efficiency
- *Ensuring that M&E systems provide adequate data* on SINE's placement rates, youth programs' results on beneficiaries' earnings and employability, and entrepreneurship support's effects on business survival, for evidence-based program expansion and design adjustment.

Although all of these reforms are critical, SINE reform emerges as the top priority to improve the overall ALMP system's performance. A reformed SINE can play an integrative role across different programs and services. International experience shows that PES are the lowest-cost ALMP interventions and can be particularly effective in increasing placements among the poor (also referring them to other needed services, not just training). A new approach whereby the service to be provided by SINE is *placement* (instead of just registering firms' job vacancies and job searchers' profiles)—referring a person to training only if *not* placed in a job—can significantly improve the overall system's efficiency.

As highlighted in chapter 1, ALMPs (by improving job matches and better equipping youth for jobs) could help reduce frictional unemployment for a given level of aggregate demand while also increasing the labor productivity and growth of small businesses (Goal 1). This chapter focuses on reforms toward that goal. In the domain of labor programs, chapter 5 focuses on adaptations of SINE and other ALMPs to better serve the poor, ultimately helping to better connect the poor to more productive jobs (Goal 2).

Existing Active Labor Market Programs

In Brazil, a wide range of ALMPs aim to address labor demand and supply needs and to improve labor market functioning. This chapter discusses the three main types of ALMPs in Brazil: (a) *public employment services (SINE)* that facilitate job search and matching; (b) *professional training programs* other than PRONATEC (discussed in chapter 2); and (c) *youth programs and policies* that seek to improve young people's labor market outcomes by enhancing their skills and employability and connecting them to jobs. Various support programs for self-employment and micro, small, and medium-size enterprises are discussed separately as well as efforts to promote the Economía Solidaria even though, in practice, these programs overlap significantly in their objectives and target groups. Unlike most OECD countries, where the unemployed are usually the largest target group for ALMPs, Brazil aims to reach a wider group of ALMP beneficiaries, including the self-employed in need of access to credit or entrepreneurship training, vulnerable populations, communities that need technical assistance and assets to start productive employment, and others. Under each category, different federal and subnational programs target various groups, including the unemployed, young job seekers, the self-employed, and micro and small enterprises (table 4.1).[5]

The range and spending of federal ALMPs has expanded significantly in recent years, but passive policies such as UI and Abono Salarial continue to absorb most of the labor program budget. This is in stark contrast with countries such as Argentina and Chile, where passive policies claim only 10 percent and 40 percent, respectively, of labor program spending (World Bank, forthcoming). Given that both active and passive policies are financed out of the same source (the Worker Protection Fund, or FAT), the overall budget envelope for ALMPs remains limited in light of growing expenditures on passive policies such as UI (figure 4.1, panel a) and Abono Salarial.[6] Under good labor market conditions with low long-term unemployment, ALMPs focus on improving matching efficiency, potentially decreasing frictional unemployment. In these cases, spending on ALMPs may be lower, but as the labor market worsens, more ALMP spending may be warranted to ensure that those who are

Table 4.1 Primary Labor Market Programs in Brazil, 2015

	Type of programs	Objective	Programs in Brazil
ALMPs	Labor intermediation services	Provide intermediation service for workers in search of a job and for firms in the hiring process	National Employment System (SINE)
	Professional training	Increase skills of the unemployed through short-term training	PRONATEC FIC, PRONATEC Bolsa Formação Seguro Desemprego, short-term qualification (Bolsa de Qualificação)
	Youth-targeted programs and policies	Increase employability of vulnerable youth and connect youth to jobs	Vocational training for youth (ProJovem Trabalhador), Apprentice Law (Lei do Aprendiz)
Support to MSEs	Access to finance[a]	Increase access to finance for micro and small enterprises	Targeted microcredit (PNMPO), preferential loans to MSEs (PROGER)
	Nonfinancial support of entrepreneurship	Promote entrepreneurship, micro and small enterprises, and formalization	SEBRAE nonfinancial support services, Individual Microentrepreneur (MEI) microcredit program
	Support of Economía Solidaria	Support development of cooperatives and other forms of collective enterprises	Solidarity economy (Economía Solidaria)
	Passive labor market policies	Provide financial support to the unemployed and income support to low-earning formal employees	Unemployment insurance, low-wage supplement (Abono Salarial)

Note: ALMPs = active labor market programs; MSEs = micro and small enterprises; PNMPO = National Program for Targeted Productive Microcredit; PROGER = Employment and Income Generation Program; PRONATEC = National Program of Access to Technical Education and Employment; SINE = National Employment System; SEBRAE = Brazilian Micro and Small Business Support Service; MEI = Individual Microentrepreneur. Economía Solidaria (solidarity economy) refers to programs that support urban and rural cooperatives.
a. Includes only programs under the auspices of the Brazilian Ministry of Labor and Employment.

laid off can quickly find jobs—acknowledging that, in a downturn, the effectiveness of such measures is likely to be diminished and they might need to be complemented by other policies.

Brazil's National Employment System, SINE, was established in 1975 and currently has 1,620 offices around the country. Relative to the OECD countries, however, Brazil's spending on intermediation services is quite low. Brazil spent less than 2 percent of overall federal ALMP spending on SINE in recent years (figure 4.1, panel a). In contrast, OECD countries spend, on average, 10 percent of their ALMP budgets on placement and related services, resulting in much higher spending as a share of gross national product (figure 4.1, panel b). It is important to note, however, that this figure for Brazil is a lower bound as it covers federal spending only, excluding state-level spending.

Brazil's ALMP portfolio differs somewhat from that of the OECD countries, with more focus on training. ALMPs in Brazil include training, such as short-term vocational training courses (PRONATEC), training for UI beneficiaries (Bolsa Formação Seguro Desemprego, also known as PRONATEC-MTE), and youth training (ProJovem Trabalhador). Smaller programs include professional qualification opportunities for current employees such as Bolsa Qualificação, which allows formal sector workers to take short-duration qualification courses while on unpaid leave from their jobs for two to five months (in case their firms face temporary downfalls).

Figure 4.1 Labor Market Program Spending in Brazil and Other Selected Countries

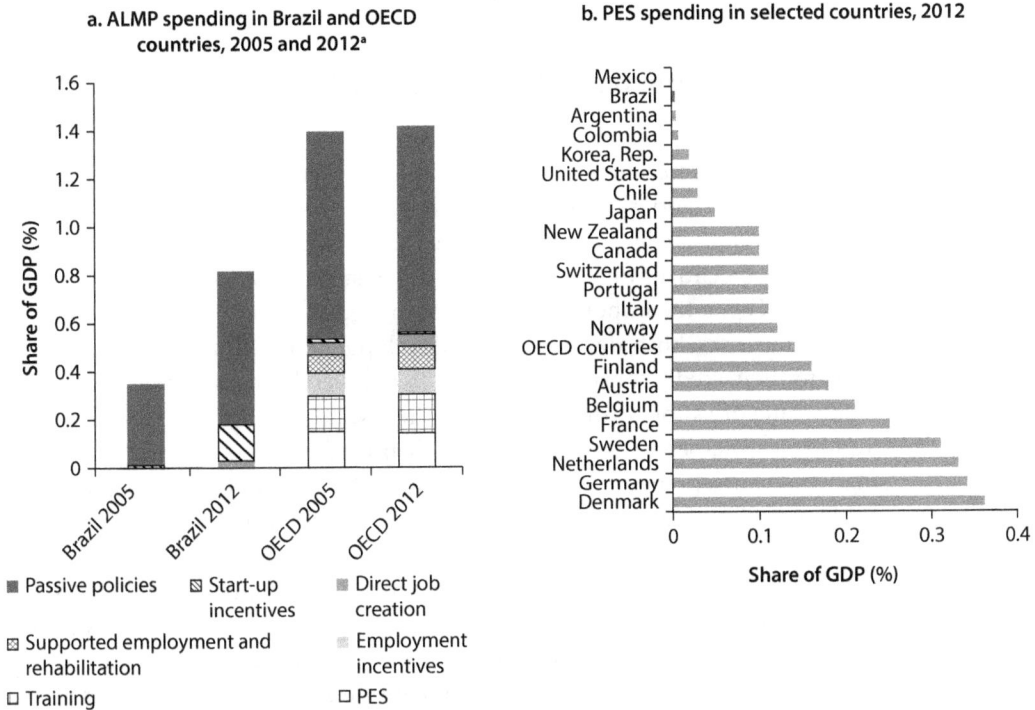

a. ALMP spending in Brazil and OECD countries, 2005 and 2012[a]

b. PES spending in selected countries, 2012

■ Passive policies   ⊠ Start-up incentives   ■ Direct job creation
⊠ Supported employment and rehabilitation   ▨ Employment incentives
□ Training   □ PES

Sources: Brazil, Ministry of Labor and Employment 2014c; Marra et al. 2015; OECD 2013.
Note: ALMP = active labor market program; OECD = Organisation for Economic Co-operation and Development; PES = public employment service. Figure covers federal spending only (lower bound).
a. "Passive policies" include unemployment insurance only and exclude Abono Salarial. "Active policies" include the National Employment System (SINE), PRONATEC Initial and Continuing Training Programs (FIC), Bolsa Qualificação (allowing formal workers to take short-duration qualification courses during unpaid leave), the Sustainable Fisheries Resources Program, the National Program for Targeted Productive Microcredit (PNMPO), and Economía Solidaria, but does not include the Employment and Income Generation Program (PROGER) or Brazilian Micro and Small Business Support Service (SEBRAE) services.

Given low skills among the poor and the employability barriers facing many young people in the labor market, improvements in vocational training and connecting young people to jobs were key focuses of the employment policy. As chapter 2 describes in detail, expansion of vocational training aims to fill the skills gaps in the working-age population, including youth. Youth-targeted ALMPs and policies aim largely to connect young people with jobs. The Apprentice Law (Lei do Aprendiz), introduced in 2000, requires medium-size and large firms to employ 5 percent of their workforces as apprentices (Marra et al. 2015), further discussed in box 4.4. More recently, PRONATEC Apprentice (PRONATEC Aprendiz) aims to improve programs to fulfill the Apprentice Law by offering subsidized training to apprentices, as under this law they must be enrolled in training courses provided by Sistema S or other institutions recognized by the Ministry of Labor and Employment while working. This program provides federal funding to micro and small firms to take on apprentices, despite not contributing into the professional education system (that is, the Sistema S network of course providers).

Existing Support for the Self-Employed and Entrepreneurship

Brazil also offers many services and programs to the self-employed and to micro, small, and medium-size enterprises. These services and programs largely fall into two categories: programs to improve access to finance as well as non-financial services such as (a) entrepreneurial orientation; (b) managerial training; and (c) incentives for formalization, d) consulting services, and e) technical assistance. Given the importance of access to credit for the growth of micro and small enterprises, both developed and developing countries have programs to alleviate their credit constraints. Brazil offers several programs tailored to different categories of firms, including the National Program for Targeted Productive Microcredit (PNMPO), which provides access to microcredit for small-scale entrepreneurs, and a national line of credit under the Employment and Income Generation Program (PROGER), which provides subsidized loans to a range of firms, both large and small.

Nonfinancial services also exist to address constraints beyond access to credit. Small-scale entrepreneurs face not only a possible lack of skills (basic, technical, business, financial, or noncognitive) but also a lack of social capital. Other constraints may involve the general business environment, limited access to markets, and so forth (Cho, Robalino, and Watson 2014). Brazil has a long history of supporting micro and small businesses through the Brazilian Micro and Small Business Support Service (SEBRAE). Created in 1972 as a public institution, SEBRAE became a private nonprofit organization in 1990, with the mission of promoting the sustainable and competitive development of small businesses.[7]

Existing Economía Solidaria (Solidarity Economy) Approaches

Brazil's Economía Solidaria is of increasing interest to other countries as a potential model to promote productivity and inclusion, especially among the poor and vulnerable populations. This approach promotes productive employment by encouraging and supporting associations, cooperatives, and informal groups to form collective enterprises based on principles of solidarity (collective ownership, equality, and collective decision making). Economía Solidaria is not a new concept, but in the past decade it has received much more support from the state and local governments. Nationally, the federal government created the National Secretariat for Solidarity Economy in 2003, which implements the Program of Development of Solidarity Economy to promote, strengthen, and expand Economía Solidaria through integrated policies for generating employment and fostering inclusion in both rural and urban areas. In Brazil, 30,000 solidarity-based enterprises now exist, employing about 2.3 million people (World Bank 2013).[8] Economía Solidaria support aims to increase the capacity and income-generating opportunities of the poor through multisectoral approaches built around four main modalities:

- *Information and communication* campaigns and support
- *Training and technical assistance* (including training of trainers, incubation projects, and technical support)
- *Investments, loans, and solidarity finance* (such as productive microcredit and community development banks)
- *Marketing and market access support* (assistance with certifications and accreditations for fair trade standards, trade centers, assistance with applying for public procurement bids, and other support)

The Way Forward: A Policy Agenda

To what extent do existing labor market policies achieve their objectives, and how can Brazil improve them to increase their impact? This section explores several high-priority reforms that could help to meet this overarching challenge: (a) strengthening PES to facilitate job searches and matches, (b) strengthening and expanding youth programs to improve labor market outcomes for youth, (c) coordinating entrepreneurship programs to improve individual prospects and business productivity, and (d) refocusing M&E systems on tracking and evaluating results.

Strengthening Public Employment Services to Facilitate Job Searches and Matches

Stronger focus on job placement is a necessary avenue to improve SINE's effectiveness in connecting job seekers to jobs. OECD experience shows that well-functioning PES can be cost-efficient at facilitating job searches and matches (Betcherman, Olivas, and Dar 2004).[9] In Brazil, however, SINE plays a relatively small role: only a minority of job seekers use its services, and the placement rates for registered job seekers remain relatively low by international standards: 12 percent in Brazil, compared with 36 percent in Mexico and 48 percent in the United States.[10] In 2012, although the number of SINE-registered unemployed had increased, only 23 percent of SINE's vacancies were filled, and fewer than 11 percent of those referred to jobs were placed (figure 4.2). These results call for SINE to focus on *placement* as a service to be provided, rather than on *registrations* as outcomes.

Brazil's PES could play a bigger role in facilitating job searches and matches. Brazil improved SINE's functions significantly by introducing the Mais Emprego (More Jobs) integrated information service portal (box 4.1). It also started an important reform of setting placement targets (Marra et al. 2015). However, SINE can be further strengthened through policies that emphasize a placement-focused management approach, including the following strategies:

- Introducing client profiling and placement-focused case management
- Strengthening services for businesses that seek low-skilled workers

- Outsourcing of certain SINE functions to private sector providers
- Using results-based disbursement, including for outsourced services

Introducing Client Profiling and Placement-Focused Case Management

Given SINE's potentially integrative role in Brazil's skills and jobs policies, the highest-priority reforms are to target its services more efficiently by profiling clients and to adopt a placement-focused management approach. PES in Brazil do not currently pay sufficient attention to placement as the ultimate outcome. Through client profiling (which many OECD countries use to tailor services to the unemployed), SINE could develop individual action plans (IAPs)

Figure 4.2 SINE Registration, Vacancy, and Job Placement Trends, 2003–13

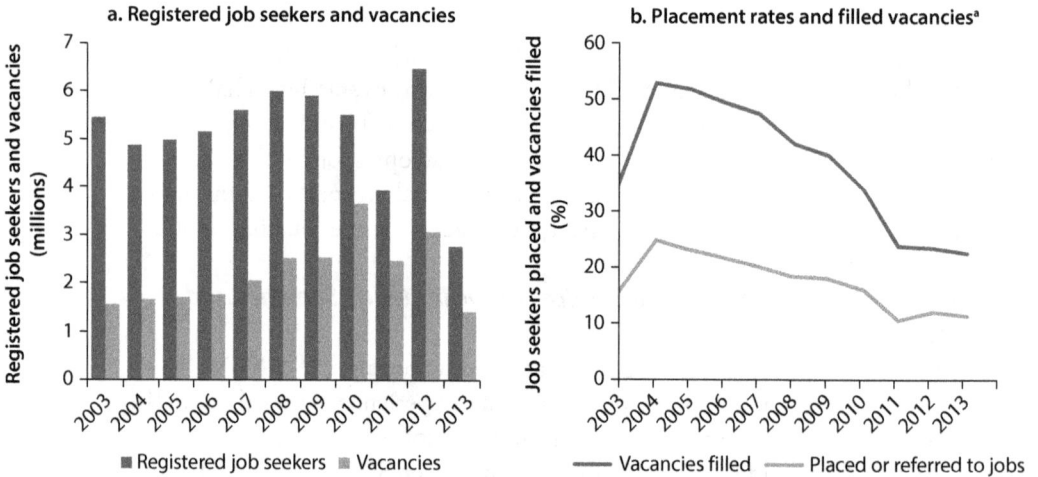

Source: SINE annual statistics, Brazil Ministry of Labor and Employment, Brasilia (accessed January 30, 2015), http://portal.mte.gov.br/sine /relatorio-anual.htm.
Note: SINE = National Employment System.
a. The placement rate is the percentage of job seekers whom SINE referred to employers and who were placed into jobs.

Box 4.1 The "More Jobs" System (Sistema Mais Emprego)

Mais Emprego was created in 2010 to make Brazil's National Employment System (SINE) more efficient. Through the new system, all available positions and all applicants are visible to all decentralized units of the Ministry of Labor and Employment that are involved in labor intermediation.

In 2012, the Mais Emprego system referred more than 8 million workers to more than 3 million positions. Of those, almost 6.5 million workers were sent to job interviews, and more than 700,000 were placed.

Source: Brazil, Ministry of Labor and Employment 2014a.

that could improve job-search effectiveness and better tailor ALMP referrals.[11] (Box 4.2 describes a profiling tool recently introduced in Sweden.) The current system, which routes most job seekers into training, might not be the most cost-efficient approach, whereas profiling and other placement-focused tools can increase cost-effectiveness in several ways:

- *Categorizing job seekers.* Profiling can differentiate between those likely to easily find a job and those likely to have more difficulties. By prioritizing the latter (and adding caseworker incentives to work more with the harder-to-place clients), SINE can better manage its caseload.
- *Leveraging extensive existing information systems.* Integration of profiles with other existing data can help caseworkers more efficiently tailor ALMP interventions to job seekers (who do not all need training equally). This information could help SINE to regularly assess the characteristics of the long-term unemployed or other disadvantaged job seekers to identify and better address their barriers in the labor market.
- *Enabling better alignment of placements with market demand.* By developing analytical tools based on existing management systems to generate high-quality, up-to-date information on local labor market supply and demand, SINE could aptly respond to changing market conditions and trends, potentially improving both placement and efficiency.

Box 4.2 Statistical Profiling Supports Early Interventions for High-Risk Job Seekers in Sweden

In 2011, Sweden created an information technology–based system called the Assessment Support Tool (AST) that allows PES counselors to identify high-risk job seekers early to assign more-intensive support to those at high risk of long-term unemployment (LTU). The tool was conceived as an add-on information stream to caseworkers, recognizing that labor market success depends on variables such as social networks, ambition, and mental and physical strength that statistical data do not easily capture.

The AST establishes a mechanism enabling caseworkers to override regular procedures and to fast-track high-risk job seekers toward early interventions. The normal wait time for ALMP activation can be overridden if the AST establishes a job seeker to be at high risk of LTU. The AST calculates a risk score that segments job seekers under four categories: (a) very good employment prospects, (b) good employment prospects, (c) weak employment prospects, and (d) high LTU risk. The AST signals caseworkers to consider early interventions for clients within the latter category by overriding regular wait times and standard protocols. In-depth assessment is conducted earlier than for other clients and it involves more frequent meetings.[a] Other measures, including vocational training, work experience, occupational rehabilitation, or other employment preparatory activities can also be activated early on (figure B4.2.1).

box continues next page

Box 4.2 Statistical Profiling Supports Early Interventions for High-Risk Job Seekers in Sweden
(continued)

Figure B4.2.1 Profiling and Early Intervention Process for High-Risk Job Seekers in Sweden

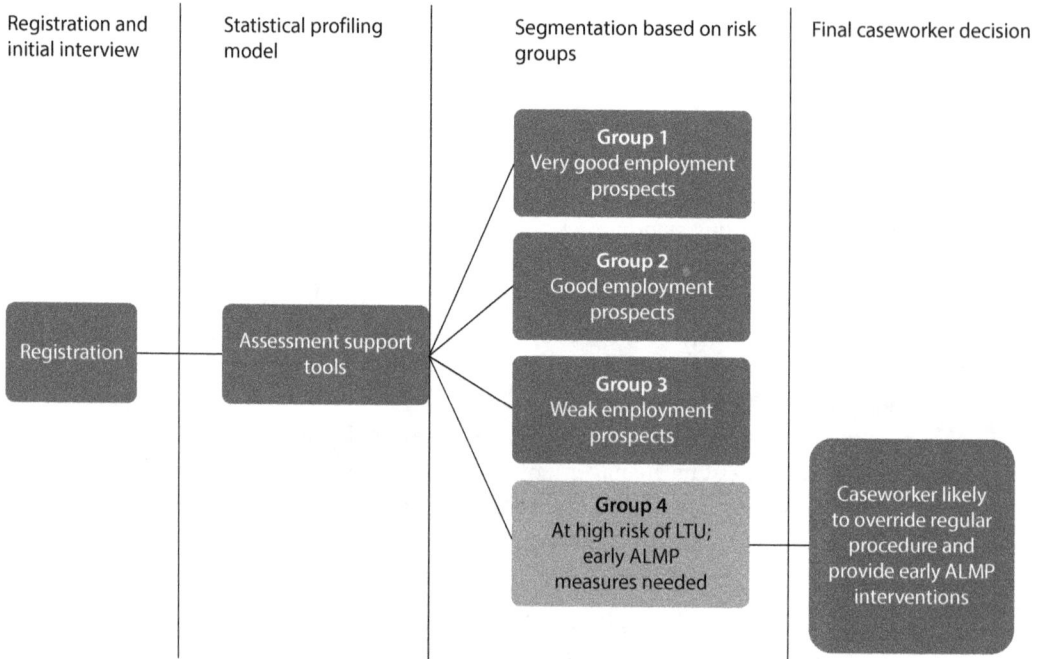

Source: © World Bank. Reproduced with permission from Loxha and Morgandi 2014; further permission required for reuse.
Note: LTU = long-term employment; ALMP = active labor market program.

Source: Loxha and Morgandi 2014.

a. Source information received during a World Bank study tour in Stockholm, Sweden, to the Swedish PES during October 15–16, 2013. Source also based on tailored written information shared directly by Swedish PES with the authors of Loxha and Morgandi (2014).

Client-oriented case management that tailors support based on employability could improve services for the poor and hard-to-serve. Brazil can strengthen SINE by better targeting those categories of the unemployed that usually require more intensive case management than "market-ready" job seekers do. The targeted case management may include additional support to obtain training or professional qualifications in demand on the labor market. Countries such as Germany and the United Kingdom have introduced case management models based on the job seekers' employability and chances of labor market success: in short, the harder-to-place individuals get more intensive support. For such a system to work, PES job counselors (or private providers) must have financial or other incentives to work with the disadvantaged.

Strengthening Services for Businesses that Seek Low-Skilled Workers

In OECD countries, employment services do extensive outreach to employers to increase the extent of their vacancy listings as well as to place hard-to-serve individuals. In Brazil, SINE could play a more proactive role, especially when it comes to strengthening services for businesses that demand low-skilled workers. This effort would entail active outreach to, and maintenance of relationships with, large employers that hire low-skilled labor in particular.

Using Results-Based Performance Management, Including Outsourcing

Brazil can further improve both outcomes and efficiency by introducing results-based performance management, including outsourcing of certain SINE functions to private sector providers. In several European countries, contractual arrangements with private providers improved outcomes for particular groups, brought innovation to service delivery, and induced competition, as box 4.3 discusses further (Marra et al. 2015). The degree of outsourcing has varied from full contracting to private and not-for-profit providers (under the Job Services Australia model, for example) to outsourcing only certain PES functions such as training, orientation, vocational rehabilitation, or community-based work placement (as in Germany, Italy, and Spain). In Germany, for instance, unemployment-benefit recipients are eligible for a placement voucher for job-search assistance from private providers. Robust performance management can improve the effectiveness of both public and private PES providers (Nunn 2012).

Implementation of SINE Management Reforms

Successful improvement of SINE's placement rates and efficiency depends on the setup of overall management processes and targets that integrate the interventions outlined above. SINE management can ensure that the focus remains on efficiency and effectiveness by incorporating several important dimensions:

- *Establish indicators and targets* that focus on ultimate results (placements into jobs, job sustainability, and so on)
- *Define roles and responsibilities*, and establish results-based annual evaluations
- *Establish the legal framework for outsourcing* of certain labor intermediation services to private providers
- *Make supervisory methods explicit*, including how results will support the next year's activity planning and budget transfers
- *Establish coordination mechanisms* (similar to those that implement Bolsa Família programs) between the Federation and municipalities and technical assistance programs to build municipalities' supervision and implementation capacity (such as technical assistance to strengthen procurement capacity)
- *Establish performance-based payments* based on increased employability, earnings, and beneficiary satisfaction—making this information publicly available to help potential job seekers become more informed

Box 4.3 International Experience with Private and Nongovernmental Employment Service Providers

Public employment services (PES) are complemented by partnerships with private and nongovernmental institutions in many countries, such as Australia, the United Kingdom, and the United States. These countries' experiences show that operating in partnership with private providers is complex, but it can lead to improved results with lower costs. These countries have three main types of employment service providers, each with their respective functions, strengths, and weaknesses:

Government agencies (PES) typically perform initial client registration, provide basic job matching and job-search assistance, monitor job-search responsibilities to receive unemployment insurance, and provide information about various services. Evaluations show that PES can be cost-effective, but given their high caseloads and wide range of administrative duties, they may have limited ability to work with the hard-to-place candidates.

Nonprofit agencies are usually community-based and generally are better at dealing with more difficult cases (such as people with disabilities or people addicted to drugs or alcohol) that require an integral, more personal approach and community support. These agencies tend to have better knowledge about the job-seeking difficulties of the most vulnerable people, and they are better equipped to support them. On the other hand, their technical and managerial capacity can be lacking, and their information technology (IT) systems tend to be less developed.

Private agencies have the capacity to scale up quickly and can work with large numbers of beneficiaries; they tend to have better technical knowledge and IT systems and can respond to changes in the market faster. However, contract design can have significant impact on their performance and cost-effectiveness. For instance, in the absence of explicit requirements and incentives for working with the hard-to-place, private agencies are likely to engage in "creaming" (working only with those who are easy to place).

Australia and the United Kingdom adopted a "black box" approach to employment services contracting, meaning that the government focuses more on the final outcomes—job placement, quality, and sustainability of jobs—than on *how* the providers achieve these results. This approach is more flexible and allows innovation and experimentation, but it also requires the government to carefully design incentives for providers. In the United Kingdom, for example, payments are higher for more difficult-to-place workers. Moreover, the payment structure incentivizes not only job placement but also job sustainability. The government pays a small fee when a service provider starts working with an unemployed worker, but it pays for a job placement only after six months on the job. Payments for sustained job placements continue for up to two years (figure B4.3.1).

box continues next page

Box 4.3 International Experience with Private and Nongovernmental Employment Service Providers *(continued)*

Figure B4.3.1 United Kingdom Payment Scheme for Employment Service Providers

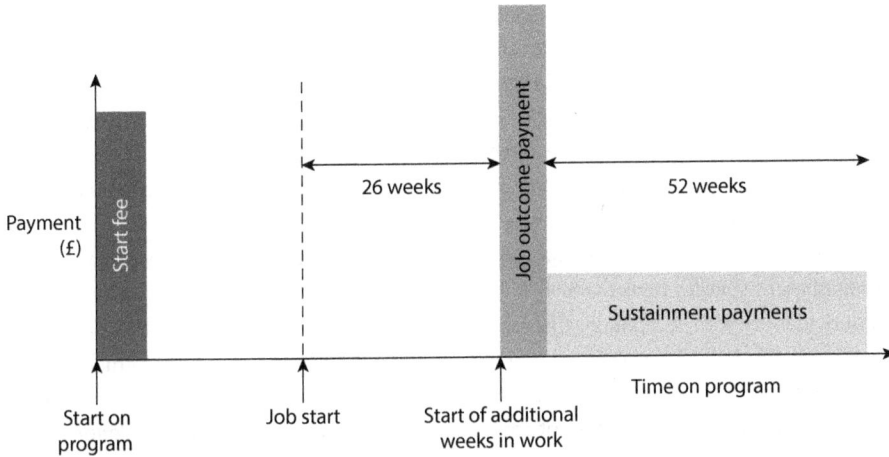

Source: United Kingdom Department for Work & Pensions 2012. Reproduced, with permission under UK Open Government Licence v3.0.
Note: £ = pounds sterling.

Source: Based on Marra et al. 2015.

Strengthening and Expanding Youth Programs to Improve Labor Market Outcomes for Youth

The Apprentice Law currently does not provide firms with sufficient incentives to hire apprentices, limiting the law's impact. Launched in 2000, the Apprentice Law (Lei do Aprendiz) calls for medium-size and large firms to hire enough apprentices (14–24 years old) to maintain a minimum 5 percent apprentice-to-workforce ratio (box 4.4). However, compliance has been low: in 2013, firms hired 335,800 apprentices, whereas full compliance could have added as many as 1.24 million (Marra et al. 2015). Hence, only 23 percent of potential apprentice slots have been filled. The key to increasing the law's effectiveness is a better understanding of firms' business needs, the existing candidate pool, and information on the benefits to the youth served. Addressing the underlying causes of low compliance and increasing flexibility across sectors or types of firms according to technology could give firms better incentives to recruit more apprentices. Introducing additional financial incentives to hire apprentices may also be considered.[12]

International evidence strongly suggests that dual apprenticeship systems (which combine classroom training with on-the-job training and experience, as in Austria, Denmark, Germany, and Switzerland) allow for smoother transitions from school to work (Quintini and Manfredi 2009; Quintini, Martin, and Martin 2007). In Brazil, however, the number of apprenticeships remains low: in 2012,

---

Box 4.4 Brazil's Apprentice Law (Lei do Aprendiz)

The Apprentice Law was enacted in 2000 to facilitate the inclusion of youth in the labor market. It requires all medium-size and large companies to hire youth between the ages 14 and 24 years while they undergo technical and professional training in the occupations for which they were hired. This is done under a special employment contract of up to two years. While working, the apprentices must also be enrolled in training courses provided by Sistema S or other institutions recognized by the Ministry of Labor and Employment (MTE). The law aimed to provide youth with specific skills demanded by the labor market along with experience that could help them start their professional careers.

Under the law, apprentices are to make up 5–15 percent of the workforce. The establishment-specific percentage is calculated based on the total number of employees excluding those with occupations that require more education. MTE monitors firms' compliance through (a) the Annual Social Information Report (RAIS), the national registry of formal employment that has information of all workers in the formal sector; and (b) the data provided by training providers, which includes student enrollment, attendance, dropout, and completion rates.

In return, firms receive a payroll subsidy in the form of a lower deposit to the apprentices' Service Indemnity Fund (FGTS) account (2 percent of the basic wage) than the standard rate required for other employees (8 percent).

Apprentices' training courses must be at least 400 hours long and the daily workload, including the technical training, should be under 6 hours when the apprentice is still in the secondary school, and 8 hours if he or she has already finished it.

Partially low compliance could be explained by the difficulties firms may have in finding adequate technical courses, which may be now alleviated by PRONATEC. There is also evidence that apprentices are mainly hired for administrative work. Furthermore, impacts on employability remain moderate: until 2012, only about 50 percent were hired by their employers into more permanent jobs.

Source: Based on Marra et al. 2015.

---

only 1 percent of the eligible youth (ages 15–24 years) were working as apprentices (OECD 2014). Better enforcement of the Apprentice Law—along with additional incentives to hire apprentices—can increase the opportunities for young people to gain on-the-job experience and improve their labor market outcomes. The introduction of PRONATEC apprenticeships (offering state-subsidized training to apprentices) is an important step in this direction. However, it might only partly meet the need given the current low number of apprentices in small and medium-size firms.

The small scale of most other youth-targeted labor market programs limits their potential impact. For instance, ProJovem Worker (ProJovem Trabalhador) was created in 2008 under the Integrated National Program for Youth Inclusion (ProJovem Integrado). It provides professional training for vulnerable youth (ages 18–29 years). In 2012, only 4,000 vulnerable young people were qualified through this program. Training programs' success depends largely on the strength of their content, the relevance of the skills provided, and how well those skills serve the local labor demand. In Brazil, however, youth programs also tend to focus on classroom training and often lack on-the-job training components. Even Brazil's most employment-oriented youth program, ProJovem Worker, has no work-based component. In contrast, most other Latin American countries offer youth-targeted ALMPs with strong on-the-job training components—for example, Jóvenes por Más y Mejor Trabajo in Argentina (OECD 2014).

Research suggests that combining technical and life-skills classes with on-the-job training such as internships or apprenticeships may be more effective than providing vocational training classes alone (Honorati and McArdle 2013). Such comprehensive youth training programs in several Latin American countries have proven effective in promoting employability. Training programs can enhance their impact by introducing a component on socioemotional "soft skills" (such as teamwork, leadership, self-confidence, and perseverance) to increase the employability of disadvantaged youth.[13] A growing number of youth programs around the world have incorporated such components; moreover, soft-skills training can also be useful to older job seekers from disadvantaged backgrounds. Examples include the Entra 21 program in 18 Latin American countries, the Jordan NOW program, and the Juventud y Empleo program in the Dominican Republic (McKenzie 2014). Other mechanisms that could decrease dropouts, attract interest, and stimulate participation in training programs (especially in slums and other vulnerable environments) include providing informational resources on access to child care and elder care and ensuring that safe transportation and nocturnal courses (with security) are available.

In summary, the following reforms could increase the impact of youth-targeted programs and better equip unemployed youth for jobs:

- *Evaluate and redesign the Apprentice Law* by setting more realistic requirements for firms and introducing an incentive package that could increase take-up
- *Introduce both on-the-job and "soft skills" components* into other youth-targeted ALMPs while better linking training to apprenticeships

Coordinating Entrepreneurship Programs to Improve Individual Prospects and Business Productivity

Brazil has a rich range of entrepreneurship programs, consisting of both financial and nonfinancial support, but they are not always targeted at micro and small businesses. Brazil spends a non-negligible amount on programs supporting entrepreneurship, both by subsidizing preferential rates for lending and microcredits and by offering additional (or alternative) nonfinancial support. For instance, SEBRAE has one of the largest budgets relative to similar organizations in several other countries (figure 4.3, panel a). Although SEBRAE assists only micro and small businesses, not all entrepreneurship support programs focus exclusively on small enterprises. For example, the government created PROGER in 1994 to stimulate job creation by enabling access to credit for micro and small

Figure 4.3 Small-Business Agency and Program Budgets in Brazil and Other Selected Countries, 2014

a. Small-business agency budgets, selected countries

b. PROGER execution, by segment

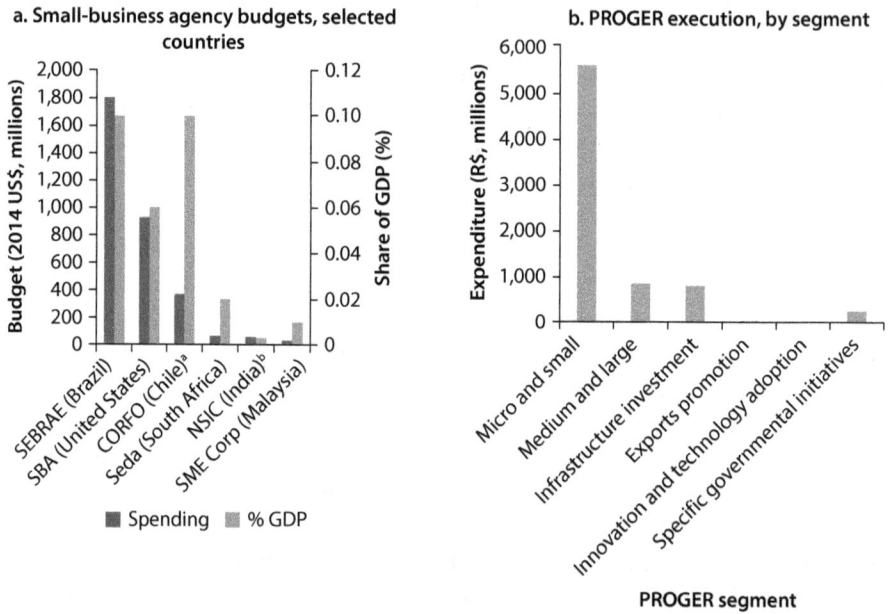

Source: Timm 2014.
Note: SEBRAE = Brazilian Micro and Small Business Support Service; SBA = Small Business Administration; CORFO = Chilean Economic Development Agency; Seda = Small Enterprise Development Agency; NSIC = National Small Industries Corporation; SME Corp = Small and Medium Enterprise Corporation.
a. 2013 budget.
b. 2012–13 gross income.

Source: Brazil, Ministry of Labor and Employment 2014b.
Note: PROGER = Employment and Income Generation Program. Innovation and technology segment has not been executed since 2013. R$ = reais.

enterprises and associations of small rural producers. As the program evolved, however, it expanded its scope and started financing larger companies in specific sectors such as infrastructure, exporting manufacturers, and tourism. Although most PROGER lending still goes to micro and small firms, significant resources are channeled to other firms (figure 4.3, panel b). This has led to some concerns about impacts of the policy on increasing small-business productivity as well as potential crowding out of the private financing institutions that could otherwise serve the larger firms.

Entrepreneurship support programs could be better coordinated and better linked with complementary programs and services to increase their impact. Although SEBRAE does not offer financial products, it can refer its clients to such services and provide financial education, assistance with business plans, and other nonfinancial support. On the other hand, the subsidized credit lines offered through PROGER are offered through large banks including the Brazilian Development Bank (BNDES), Banco do Brasil, and Caixa Econômica Federal. The process of receiving credit is hence delinked from other services that may be essential for a beginning entrepreneur to be able to use credit properly, and potential synergies are not fully exploited. Brazil can increase the impact of these entrepreneurship support programs through better coordination and cross-referencing, including to labor market programs that could also benefit entrepreneurs and small businesses (such as technical training, which can raise worker productivity). Notably, the majority of entrepreneurship programs in other countries that aim to improve earnings opportunities for self-employed workers provide a combination of multiple services, such as training, access to finance, advisory and mentoring services, and networking (Cho, Robalino, and Watson 2014).

International evidence on entrepreneurship promotion programs is mixed, suggesting that take-up is often low, costs are high, and positive results are concentrated among the older, more qualified, more motivated participants. Given the great variety of programs offered and the lack of sufficient evidence on their impacts, a review of the existing programs in Brazil is urgently needed to determine whether they are improving income-earning opportunities for the poorest. Following such a review, overlapping programs can be consolidated (for instance, PROGER offers more than a dozen different credit lines) and ineffective ones phased out to make space for more-effective, more-efficient programs.

In summary, to strengthen Brazil's entrepreneurship support programs, the following priorities emerge:

- *Improve coordination to increase small-business productivity* by linking financial and nonfinancial support programs more effectively and by linking all of those programs with other labor market programs and services
- *Review and consolidate fragmented programs* to improve their overall efficiency

Refocusing M&E Systems on Tracking and Evaluating Results

Strengthening M&E systems is essential to improve the performance of both SINE and the labor market programs and policies to support entrepreneurship and Economía Solidaria. Existing M&E systems focus mainly on inputs and sometimes on outputs, but not on outcomes such as placements, earnings increases, sales, and so on. In some cases, M&E is quite weak or even nonexistent, and it needs to be extended to better inform policies.

It is difficult to make evidence-based improvements to labor programs without a comprehensive M&E system focused on tracking outcomes such as employability. Such a system can enhance policy development, program management, and ultimately employment outcomes for the targeted populations. Several of Brazil's monitoring systems—such as the world-renowned Annual Social Information Report (RAIS), the General Register of Employed and Unemployed Individuals (CAGED), and SINE's More Jobs (Mais Emprego) databases—already produce rich administrative data that can be used to track inputs and outputs of various policies. Merging these various databases on a regular basis with standardized procedures allows program evaluations to be made, albeit not without limitations. Countries with similar administrative systems, such as Australia and Sweden, have started conducting regular impact evaluations of their ALMPs (see box 4.5

Box 4.5 M&E Systems That Improve Employment Services Delivery: International Experience

Traditionally, monitoring and evaluation (M&E) of public employment services focused on inputs, measuring expenditures, and tracking employment centers' activities (such as number of beneficiaries being registered and counseled). But countries such as Argentina and the United States have achieved better employment results by modernizing their M&E systems to put more emphasis on final results such as number of beneficiaries who find jobs and the quality of these jobs (wages and duration). This shift in M&E systems—from inputs to results—leads to better information on what works and what does not in employment services, which leads to better service delivery. To implement a modern M&E system, one has to define the indicators, gather data to calculate the indicators, and use the indicators to improve services.

The four main types of indicators used in modern M&E systems are (a) the number of beneficiaries; (b) the employment rate of beneficiaries (proportion of people who received employment services at time t and are employed at time $t+1$); (c) job retention (number of beneficiaries employed in time $t+1$ who are still employed at time $t+2$ and $t+3$); and (d) expenditure by beneficiary. Australia also emphasizes an indicator of beneficiary satisfaction, assessed through surveys. For training programs, countries also use the average increase in beneficiaries' wages and the adequate job rate (number of beneficiaries who received training at time t and had jobs in time $t+1$ in a sector or occupation to which the training was relevant).

After the indicators are defined, the data must be gathered to calculate those indicators. There are three main ways to collect data for M&E of employment services:

Surveying beneficiaries through telephone calls, text messages, the Internet, or a combination of these methods

Merging the administrative data of the employment services with that of official employment and wages databases

Directing data collection through interviews at employment services, contracted services providers, or employers

With the indicators defined and calculated, a government can use this information to improve service delivery. A common way of doing that is by setting goals for employment services providers and giving incentives to good performers, then scaling up successful providers and scaling down unsuccessful ones. However, when checking performance against goals, evaluators have to be careful. A naïve approach can stimulate undesirable activities, such as job centers focusing on people who are easier to employ. Evaluators also should take into account local economic conditions when setting goals, so that job centers in regions where labor markets are worse have more-flexible goals.

In Brazil, the State of Pernambuco has set up a comprehensive M&E system for its vocation training programs using these indicators with important results.

Source: Based on Marra et al. 2015.

---

regarding international M&E best practices). M&E systems in these countries require that every government program be evaluated every three to five years (Angel-Urdinola and Leon-Solano 2013). Implementing robust approaches to tracking the program participants' employability is a key to learning what works best in different settings (Almeida, Behrman, and Robalino 2012). Through this effort, consolidated data on program quality and efficiency, beneficiaries' employability, and client satisfaction will become routinely available—enabling analyses not only of program-level efficiency and performance but also of participant-level outcomes and how they relate to gender, educational level, location, and so forth.

In summary, to bring Brazil's M&E systems to that next level requires the following improvements:

- *Introducing indicators of employment outcomes* in addition to inputs and outputs, developing a results-based M&E framework
- *Conducting periodic evaluations* to inform the design and improve the cost-effectiveness of all programs
- *Developing rigorous impact evaluations* of strategic programs and using the results to guide program scale-up
- *Introducing M&E systems where they are weak or do not exist*, such as for Economía Solidaria programs

Notes

1. This chapter discusses only programs under the purview of the Ministry of Labor and Employment.

2. A large part of Brazil's ALMP policies involve the short-term qualification courses offered through PRONATEC's Initial and Continuing Training (FIC) programs. However, given the specificities of these programs, they are discussed in detail in chapter 2.

3. In Brazil, microenterprises (microempresa) are those with gross annual revenue up to R$240,000 (US$81,600) per year; small businesses (empresa de pequeno porte) have gross annual revenue between R$240,000 and R$2,400,000 per year (General Law of Micro and Small Enterprises, December 14, 2006).

4. Abono Salarial (Salary Bonus) provides a tax benefit equivalent to one minimum wage for those formal sector workers who receive fewer than two minimum wages per month on average in a given year.

5. The analysis in this report is focused on the federal programs under the auspices of the Ministry of Labor and Employment. Vocational training programs are not discussed here because chapter 2 covers PRONATEC FIC in detail, while chapter 5 further discusses PRONATEC-MDS (which coordinates training with social assistance through the Ministry of Social Development and Fight against Hunger) and other productive inclusion programs aimed at the vulnerable.

6. Given recent increases in the minimum wage, spending on Abono Salarial increased exponentially, from 0.25 percent of gross domestic product (GDP) in 2011 to 1.15 percent in 2012 (SINE annual statistics, Ministry of Labor and Employment

[accessed January 30, 2015], http://portal.mte.gov.br/fat/relatorio-de-gestao-do
-fat.htm). Because only formal sector workers with a history of contributions are
eligible for Abono Salarial, that program does not benefit the most-vulnerable
workers.

7. SEBRAE is funded by a monthly social contribution paid by employers. Its network
of almost 700 on-site service centers throughout the country, more than 5,000
small-business experts, and a large pool of external consultants work toward trans-
ferring knowledge and know-how to those who own or intend to start a business.
SEBRAE serves more than 1.5 million companies each year through entrepreneurship education (in areas including management, human resources, market access,
and access to financial services); formalization support under the Individual
Microentrepreneur (MEI) program; support to agribusiness firms (guidance, information, training, and consultancy to small farmers and ranchers, business associations, cooperatives, and small-scale agro-industries); and support to firms in other
sectors. For more information, see the SEBRAE website at http://www.sebrae.com
.br/sites/PortalSebrae/canais_adicionais/sebrae_english.

8. For more information about Brazil's Economía Solidaria initiatives, see World Bank
(2013).

9. A review of ALMP impact evaluations worldwide concluded that "employment services are generally the most cost-effective intervention: employment and earnings
impacts are usually positive and, compared to other ALMPs, employment services are
inexpensive" (Betcherman, Olivas, and Dar 2004).

10. Brazil job placement data are from the Ministry of Labor and Employment, Brasilia
(accessed January 30, 2015), http://portal.mte.gov.br/sine/relatorio-anual.htm.
Mexico job placement data are from the National Employment Service, Secretariat of
Labor and Social Welfare, Mexico City (accessed January 30, 2015), http://www.stps
.gob.mx/bp/secciones/conoce/areas_atencion/areas_atencion/servicio_empleo
/resultados_programas.html. U.S. job placement data are from Barnow (2012).

11. Development of individual action plans (IAPs) that lay out programs and services to
promote an individual's employability is a common practice in many OECD countries. For example, in Germany, the Netherlands, and the United Kingdom, public
employment offices that adopt this approach can identify major employment constraints early in the process (Almeida, Behrman, and Robalino 2012).

12. The current government incentive for firms to provide apprenticeships is a lower firm
contribution to the Severance Indemnity Fund (FGTS). In contrast, other countries
have combined social security rebates, lower minimum wages, and direct subsidies to
encourage firms to hire apprentices. For examples see OECD (2014).

13. The Brazilian labor program that currently includes soft-skills training is
ProJovem Worker. The program includes 100 hours of social training on topics
such as information and communication technology, ethics, citizenship, personal
hygiene, rights at work, occupational health and safety at work, and entrepreneurship (OECD 2014).

References

Almeida, Rita, Jere Behrman, and David Robalino, eds. 2012. *The Right Skills for the Job?
Rethinking Training Policies for Workers*. Human Development Perspectives Series.
Washington, DC: World Bank.

Angel-Urdinola, Diego, and Rene Leon-Solano. 2013. "A Reform Agenda for Improving the Delivery of ALMPs in the MENA Region." *IZA Journal of Labor Policy* 2 (1): 1–25.

Barnow, Burt S. 2012. "Employment Services in the United States." Presentation for World Bank Webinar on Workforce Development in the United States, Washington, DC, July 17.

Betcherman, Gordon, Karina Olivas, and Amit Dar. 2004. "Impacts of Active Labor Market Programs: New Evidence from Evaluations with Particular Attention to Developing and Transition Countries." Social Protection Discussion Paper 402, World Bank, Washington, DC.

Brazil, Ministry of Labor and Employment. 2014a. "Employment Plan 2014—Brazil." Ministry of Labor and Employment, Brasilia.

———. 2014b. *Informe: Informações Gerenciais do Programa de Geração de Emprego e Renda.* [Report: Employment and Income Generation Program.] Ministry of Labor and Employment, Brasilia.

———. 2014c. "Sumário Executivo DES CODEFAT SMA PSD." [Executive Summary Deliberative Council of the Worker Support Fund, Monitoring and Evaluation System, Unemployment Insurance Program.] Ministry of Labor and Employment, Brasilia.

Cho, Yoonyoung, David Robalino, and Samantha Watson. 2014. "Supporting Self-Employment and Small-Scale Entrepreneurship: Potential Programs to Improve Livelihoods for Vulnerable Workers." Working Paper 92629, World Bank, Washington, DC.

Honorati, Maddalena, and Thomas P. McArdle. 2013. "The Nuts and Bolts of Designing and Implementing Training Programs in Developing Countries." Social Protection & Labor Discussion Paper 1304, World Bank, Washington, DC.

Loxha, Artan, and Matteo Morgandi. 2014. "Profiling the Unemployed: A Review of OECD Experiences and Implications for Emerging Economies." Discussion Paper 1424, World Bank, Washington, DC.

Marra, Karla, Jociany Luz, Joana Silva, and Renata Gukovas. 2015. *Mapping of the Current Network of Active Labor Market Programs (ALMPs).* Policy report—background paper for this report, World Bank, Washington, DC.

McKenzie, David. 2014. "Hard Measurement of Soft Skills." *Development Impact* (blog), June 2, World Bank, Washington, DC. http://blogs.worldbank.org/impactevaluations /hard-measurement-soft-skills.

Nunn, Alex. 2012. "Performance Management in Public Employment Services." Analytical paper, European Commission Mutual Learning Programme for Public Employment Services, DG Employment, Social Affairs and Inclusion, Brussels.

OECD (Organisation for Economic Co-operation and Development). 2013. "Labour market Programmes: Expenditure and Participants." OECD Employment and Labour Market Statistics database (accessed March 22, 2015), doi: http://dx.doi.org/10.1787 /data-00312-en.

———. 2014. *Investing in Youth: Brazil.* Paris, France: OECD Publishing. http://dx.doi .org/10.1787/9789264208988-en.

Quintini, Glenda, and Thomas Manfredi. 2009. "Going Separate Ways? School-to-Work Transitions in the United States and Europe." OECD Social, Employment and Migration Working Paper 90, OECD, Paris.

Quintini, Glenda, John P. Martin, and Sébastien Martin. 2007. "The Changing Nature of the School-to-Work Transition Process in OECD Countries." Discussion Paper 2582, Institute for the Study of Labor (IZA), Bonn.

Timm, Stephen. 2014. "Why We Can Learn More from Brazil's SEBRAE." *Small Business Insight* (blog), August 14. http://www.smallbusinessinsight.org/blog/why-we-can-learn-more-from-brazils-sebrae.

United Kingdom Department for Work & Pensions. 2012. "The Work Programme." Brochure, UK Department for Work & Pensions, London.

World Bank. 2013. "Solidarity-Based Economy Provides Employment and Income to 2 Million Brazilians." *World Bank News*, July 25. http://www.worldbank.org/en/news/feature/2013/07/25/cooperatives-solidarity-economy-in-Brazil.

———. Forthcoming. "Latin America and the Caribbean Social Protection Database." World Bank, Washington, DC.

Productive Inclusion Policies to Better Connect the Poor with More Productive Jobs

Introduction

Since the 2000s, social assistance in Brazil has focused on finding the poor, reaching them, and helping their children through the flagship conditional cash transfer program Bolsa Família and a strong Central Social Assistance System (SUAS). As a next step in 2011, the policies also started to focus on connecting the poor to jobs. In this spirit, the government launched the (rural and urban) "productive inclusion" axis of the Brasil Sem Miséria (Brazil Without Extreme Poverty) Plan in 2011 (Brazil, Ministry of Social Development and Fight against Hunger 2013). The other two axes of the plan are (a) the "income support" axis (better coverage by Bolsa Família of the extreme poor through the Busca Ativa [Active Search] strategy to reach poor citizens not yet reached by the program), and (b) the "access to services" axis (improving the same population's access to basic services). The productive inclusion axis fosters the participation and inclusion of the poor in the economic arena (employment or income-generating activities). It thereby helps the poor to improve their own productivity and convert it into sustainable incomes.

Rather than creating new programs, productive inclusion policies focus mainly on expanding the coverage of existing ones to the poor, using the national registry of the poor and vulnerable (Cadastro Único) to target new beneficiaries.[1] These programs range from technical and vocational training to support of self-employment and family agriculture. Urban and rural areas require specific approaches based on the different nature of their economic activities. Urban programs focus on training (by allocating to the poor 40 percent of the slots in PRONATEC, the National Program for Access to Technical Education and Employment, described in detail in chapter 2) and support to microentrepreneurs (through formalization and microcredit support). Rural programs focus on the expansion of integrated interventions for family agriculture by expanding the coverage (and coordination between programs) of existing agricultural and rural development programs to the poor. The rural productive inclusion approach consists of the integrated provision of three types of support: (a) microcredit and matching grants, (b) technical assistance to improve agricultural production, and (c) access to markets through public procurement.

Compared with Brasil Sem Miséria's income support axis (through Bolsa Família), the productive inclusion axis involves a greater range of programs, which need to be coordinated across a wider range of agencies and whose results depend not only on more-complex household behaviors but also on the larger economy. Brazil's innovations in this area have served as examples for other countries—particularly the approach of building productive inclusion around a flagship income support program (Bolsa Família) and using social assistance targeting tools (such as Cadastro Único, or Single Registry) to identify beneficiaries and target the support.

The productive inclusion agenda goes beyond a single ministry or even a whole administration. It is an overarching commitment to meet the long-term challenge of helping the poor to gain and retain better, more productive jobs. As described in chapter 1, most of Brazil's poor are working, but their incomes are low and their upward mobility is limited. Moreover, more difficult economic conditions in the coming years could hinder their further inclusion in labor markets and complicate efforts to translate skills into sustainable incomes. Although policies that increase labor productivity for all will help to expand overall opportunities, the poor will need not only high employment and productivity gains but also better, more productive jobs if they are to continue improving their livelihoods. As chapter 1 also discussed, the income gaps between the poor and middle class remain large, reflecting persistent differences in labor market outcomes. The rural poor are primarily engaged in low-productivity agriculture (with no or very low earnings) while the urban poor are a heterogeneous group, some of whom are unemployed and most of whom are working poor (either as wage earners or self-employed).

Brazil has a large set of programs, covering many needs and target groups. This report argues that the path forward on productive inclusion will be to address next-level challenges on familiar terrain, not new frontiers. What are these challenges? To make existing programs more efficient and sustainable by refocusing on their objectives and diversifying support to assist the poor on several fronts:

- *Soft-skills development, apprenticeships, and placement services that better address the employability barriers of the poor.* As highlighted in chapter 1, to raise labor productivity and earning, the poor need not only traditional skills development but also a comprehensive integration of those programs with added "soft skills" training (including communication, perseverance, and conflict resolution skills), apprenticeships/hands-on training, placement services, and entrepreneurship support that better serve their needs.

In short, the goal is to better link social assistance programs not only to training (PRONATEC) but also to the active labor market programs (ALMPs) including intermediation services provided by the National Employment System (SINE) and entrepreneurship support provided by the Brazilian Micro and Small Business Support Service (SEBRAE) and the Ministry of Labor and Employment.

- *Closing the remaining gaps in access to child care, other social services or psychosocial support.* Brazil has programs in all these areas, but it is worth considering whether they are present in the right balance and quality, and importantly, whether for each client they are adequately integrated and sequenced.

- *Increasing the quality and efficiency of the current assistance model of expanding the coverage of existing agricultural and other rural development programs for the poor,* acknowledging that workers in family agriculture are a diverse group in terms of their experience (in terms of the different types of agricultural activities), and the impact of the support is likely to depend on these aspects.

- *Diversified support for transitions to nonagricultural jobs.* Although rural productive inclusion policies have focused on improving the productivity of those in family agriculture, upward mobility for many might mean shifting to nonagricultural jobs, which requires assistance such as hands-on, community-based training; skills certification; and vocational and technical training tailored for rural areas.

- *Implementation of monitoring and evaluation (M&E) systems.* Brazil could use more results-based mechanisms to better manage program supply and refocus on the key outcomes in productive inclusion programs. Better evidence of results might be obtained by leveraging Brazil's sophisticated set of administrative records between the Ministries of Labor and Employment, Education, Agriculture (and other ministries' rural development programs), and Social Assistance—including the Annual Social Information Report (RAIS), the General Register of Employed and Unemployed Individuals (CAGED), Cadastro Único, and administrative records of the Food Acquisition Program (PAA).

How could Brazil strengthen both urban and rural productive inclusion policies to better connect the poor to more productive, higher-earning jobs? In urban areas, one important strategic direction would be to focus more on increasing employability and labor earnings, thus converting support into sustainable income. Most such support is in the form of training, but insufficient soft-skills development, inefficient job-search mechanisms, and inadequate support services may limit the impact of training on labor market outcomes among the poor. The following approaches could better focus urban productive inclusion policies on increasing labor market participation and earnings:

- *Adapt public employment services (SINE) and other ALMPs to better serve the poor* (such as through better alignment of services with beneficiary profiles and local labor markets), and *diversify urban productive inclusion beyond PRONATEC* through synergies with these adapted programs
- *Expand support to address employment barriers beyond technical skills* by adding soft-skills and more hands-on components to PRONATEC while increasing students' or trainees' accessibility to child and elder care, transportation subsidies, night courses, and other support for the poor
- *Strengthen M&E systems* to provide adequate data on the job placement rates of trainees who completed the courses and on earnings or wage increases associated with program participation, thus enabling evidence-based program expansion and design adjustment

In rural areas, productive inclusion involves increasing earnings opportunities and productivity in family agriculture, but that key focus needs to be complemented by investment in people's skills and productivity, not just their businesses. Because rural employment is concentrated in low-productivity (family) agriculture, maximizing the earnings potential of these businesses is critical. However, although these programs promote incomes for many, upward mobility for others will mean moving to the nonagriculture sector. In this context, adapting training and entrepreneurship programs to the skills and experience of the rural poor would be helpful. Although the existing rural productive inclusion model is comprehensive, it lacks M&E systems to trace success in increasing earnings of beneficiaries and business survival. This information could play a key role in enhancing the cost-effectiveness and impact of these interventions. In this context, the following approaches could strengthen and diversify rural productive inclusion programs:

- *Establishing M&E systems* to measure programs' results on beneficiaries' earnings and business survival and adopting management approaches and results-based reimbursements using this information
- *Introducing profiling of family farmers* (including their experience in the different types of agricultural activities) and using the results to decide how to best allocate different support
- *Continuing to encourage use of Cadastro Único* to target expansion of coverage of rural development and agriculture programs among the poor
- *Diversifying support aimed at enhancing access to markets* for the goods produced by poor farmers beyond the quotas for public procurement (for instance, through other market access services such as those offered by SEBRAE)
- *Promoting private sector partnerships,* including with the financial system, to improve access to credit and technology

- *Adapting and improving access to rural entrepreneurship* (microenterprise) programs and *expanding access to hands-on, community-based training and skills certification* to enhance people's productivity

Existing Productive Inclusion Policies

Urban Productive Inclusion

To promote productive inclusion in urban areas, the government has focused on training. Under Brasil Sem Miséria, vocational training for the poor expanded quickly and dramatically through PRONATEC.[2] The establishment of PRONATEC in 2011 represented a major policy shift, as chapter 2 discusses in detail. In the past, most technical vocational education and training (TVET) beneficiaries were from better-off backgrounds. Today, 40 percent of all PRONATEC training slots target the poor; in 2014, 1.28 million PRONATEC enrollees were Cadastro Único registrants. This expansion was largely anchored in the government's Gratuity Agreement with the Sistema S course providers. Under that agreement, the providers use two-thirds of the net revenue—financed by a 1 percent tax on firms—to offer subsidized (free) training to low-income individuals, up from half of net revenue in 2009.[3]

In addition to training, the government created formalization and microcredit programs, but they remain modest in size and scope. The Crescer (Grow) national microcredit program provided 3.6 million loans from 2011 to 2013. The Individual Microentrepreneur (MEI) program creates incentives for formalization of microfirms (box 5.1). It was expanded to support Bolsa Família

---

Box 5.1 Program to Support Individual Microentrepreneurship

The Individual Microentrepreneur (MEI) program was designed to facilitate formalization of small businesses and to reduce the bureaucracy involved in opening and sustaining a formal small business by reducing taxes and contributions and making the process easier and faster. Another MEI goal is to increase social protection coverage of small and microentrepreneurs, focusing on their potential contribution toward the continued expansion of formal job creation.

According to the Secretariat of the Federal Revenue of Brazil, 1 million entrepreneurs join the program annually: by the end of 2013, 3.6 million small businesses formalized through the program. An econometric analysis (specifically, transition probability analysis) using microdata from the Monthly Employment Survey of the Brazilian Institute of Geography and Statistics finds that the MEI program has considerably increased the formalization probability of both small businesses and the self-employed, an occupational group that historically has had high rates of informality (Corseuil, Neri, and Ulyssea 2013). Using the National Household Survey, the analysis also finds a statistical association between the MEI program and increased social protection coverage among small businesses. However, only 10 percent of MEI participants are Bolsa Família beneficiaries, and low uptake and low firm survival rates combine to limit this program's success.

Source: Brazil, Ministry of Labor and Employment 2014.

---

beneficiaries who are entrepreneurs (406,000 in 2014) (Brazil, Ministry of Social Development and Fight against Hunger 2014).

Rural Productive Inclusion

Brazil has a long history of rural development and agricultural programs that focus mainly on the Northeast region. The approach of this program varies from support to individual small farmers to community-driven development (CDD) programs. Some programs finance small-scale investments in basic infrastructure to improve access to water and electricity. Others make landownership possible for landless rural families by opening access to credit and investment capital through matching grants. The guiding principles underlying CDD programs are more decentralization of decision making, direct transfer of funds, and involvement of local authorities and community-based organizations of family farmers (World Bank 2010). The existing agricultural and rural development programs have been integral to the rural productive inclusion axis of Brasil Sem Miséria: rather than creating new programs, the coverage of existing ones has been expanded to the poor, using the national registry of the poor and vulnerable (Cadastro Único) to target new beneficiaries.

At all levels, the government has invested heavily in integrated interventions to improve the productivity of family agriculture and overall rural productive inclusion, but some needs remain unmet. The current model of assistance is based on expanding coverage of existing agricultural and rural development programs to the poor, anchored on partnerships between the Ministry of Social Development with the Ministries of Rural Development and Agriculture. Through this model, the government expanded integrated interventions for family agriculture along the following dimensions: (a) microcredit and matching grants through the Development Fund program; (b) technical assistance to promote rural production; and (c) market access through public procurement (figure 5.1).[4] These efforts were complemented by access to key inputs such as water and electricity through the Água para Todos (Water for Everyone) and Luz para Todos (Electricity for Everyone) programs. Specifically, 750,500 water reservoirs were built with the support of Agua para Todos (Brazil, Ministry of Social Development and Fight against Hunger 2013).

The Way Forward: A Policy Agenda

Expanding but Also Adapting Existing Training and ALMPs to the Needs of the Poor

Most urban productive inclusion support comes in the form of training (PRONATEC), discussed in chapter 2, but helping the poor to move to more productive jobs often takes more than training. Diversifying support could be valuable for three primary reasons:

- *During economic slowdowns, training effects may be modest* (particularly for youth), and on-the-job experience and soft-skills components are key (Almeida, Behrman, and Robalino 2012).

Figure 5.1 Primary Types of Support Programs for Rural Productive Inclusion in Brazil

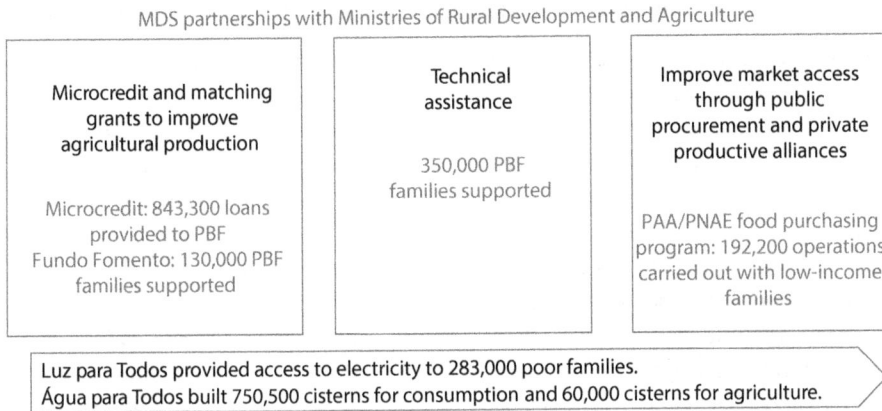

MDS partnerships with Ministries of Rural Development and Agriculture

| Microcredit and matching grants to improve agricultural production

Microcredit: 843,300 loans provided to PBF
Fundo Fomento: 130,000 PBF families supported | Technical assistance

350,000 PBF families supported | Improve market access through public procurement and private productive alliances

PAA/PNAE food purchasing program: 192,200 operations carried out with low-income families |

Luz para Todos provided access to electricity to 283,000 poor families.
Água para Todos built 750,500 cisterns for consumption and 60,000 cisterns for agriculture.

Source: Based on Brazil, Ministry of Social Development and Fight against Hunger 2013.
Note: MDS = Ministry of Social Development; PBF = Bolsa Família Program; PAA/PNAE = Food Acquisition Program. "Fundo Fomento" is a development fund. "Luz para Todos" is the Electricity for Everyone program. "Água para Todos" is the Water for Everyone program.

- *Training is one of the most expensive ALMPs*, thus many countries first use job intermediation (public employment services, or PES) and turn to training only if intermediation does not work (OECD 2007).
- *The poor face numerous, mutually reinforcing disadvantages that reduce their employability* relative to nonpoor trainees and job seekers. Many lack the skills and experience to obtain high-paying, high-productivity jobs. Other important constraints (as highlighted in chapter 1) include ineffective job-search mechanisms (mostly informal networks); difficulties in retaining jobs; and limited access to child care, psychosocial counseling, and other support services.

Brazil has programs in all these areas (training, job intermediation, and social support), but the challenge lies in whether they offer the right balance and quality of services and, importantly, whether they are focused on the poor and adequately integrated and sequenced for each client. Coordinating and tailoring the existing services to the poor has its own set of challenges (box 5.2). To diversify labor market support to the poor beyond training, better coordination (referral and counterreferral) could be key—not just between social assistance and PRONATEC (or other training) programs but also with all the various ALMPs. Although the coordination between social assistance and training was successfully implemented under PRONATEC-MDS, improving integration between social assistance and the ALMPs including job intermediation (through SINE) remains an increasingly urgent challenge.[5] Skills development and labor programs have many entry points that are often unintelligible for users and call for user interfaces with a "no wrong door policy" and a better interface with social assistance centers. With better integration, social workers who refer the poor to productive inclusion programs in the Program for the Promotion of Access to the Work World (ACESSUAS/WORK) would have a more diverse set of productive

---

Box 5.2 Productive Inclusion in the Slums of Rio de Janeiro: A Qualitative Study

The productive inclusion of urban dwellers in slums is a complex and underinvestigated domain. A qualitative case study developed for this report combined a literature review, stakeholder consultations, and field interviews of participants and officials managing productive inclusion initiatives in three favelas of Rio de Janeiro with a combined population of nearly 75,000. The analysis focuses on the structure and performance of the primary productive inclusion programs offered in three favelas: Manguinhos, Rocinha, and Alemão. These programs are offered by a mix of governmental, nongovernmental organizations, and private sector providers. The case study's main findings are described below.

Program outreach and awareness efforts. The challenge of locating, reaching, and informing potential and past program participants looms large as a key barrier for both program uptake and monitoring and evaluation (M&E). Yet program implementers have deployed a variety of methods to enhance awareness and mobilization, including creative solutions ranging from fairs to social networks.

Program enrollment challenges and successes. The highly mobile, dynamic nature of slum livelihoods makes it challenging to ensure proper documentation for program enrollment. For example, the provision of school certificates (grades 5 or 6) might prove difficult for migrants, hence preventing them from participating in training and other activities. At the same time, programs have shown considerable creativity and flexibility in adapting services to customer needs, such as accommodating work schedules and designing demand-driven vocational or entrepreneurship training.

Formalization efforts. Formalization of microenterprises generates a number of positive spillovers, including enhanced access to credit and economies of scale in purchasing supplies. New legislative provisions notwithstanding, the bureaucratic costs of the formalization process sometimes outweigh its benefits, hence discouraging applications.

Institutional presence and effectiveness. The continuous physical presence of actors on the ground is a key ingredient for success of program implementation. Institutions physically present in the community were perceived as significantly more effective than institutions located remotely or adopting a time-bound approach.

Participant benefits and costs. Evidence on income gains from training is mixed. Anecdotal evidence indicates that new skills can help the poor to save possible expenses (such as for domestic repairs). A central contribution of the training is to improve beneficiaries' motivations for planning work-related activities and projects. At the same time, qualitative benefits such as self-esteem and social integration seem substantial, especially in initiatives where favela and non-favela people participate together.

Limited linkages to labor markets. "What happens after the training?" is a core question of most participants. Programs are currently strengthening the participants' particular (technical) employability needs, but these strengths are tempered by gaps in other areas (for example, verbal skills) and limited intermediation of the involved institutions with potential job opportunities. The programs have taken some steps to address the issue—including coaching programs, guidance counseling, and databases of the best pupils who could serve as role models or mentors. However, ensuring a proper continuum of posttraining interventions remains

box continues next page

Box 5.2 Productive Inclusion in the Slums of Rio de Janeiro: A Qualitative Study *(continued)*

a core, complex area to be strengthened. Another is increasing the traceability of the beneficiaries' trajectories (such as between informal and formal work, in terms of income evolution,
and so on).

*Limited coordination between productive inclusion programs and complementary domains of
social assistance.* Coordination between the complementary domains of social assistance and
productive inclusion could be improved, including (a) the connections between conditional
cash transfers and employment-oriented programs, and (b) the use of a referral and counterreferral system with social assistance programs. A larger intersectoral coordination agenda for
improving service delivery in the slums would include ways to overcome the incompatibility
of various programs' management and information systems, especially for M&E.

Youth training. Finally, increasing the attractiveness of training for the youth is another key
challenge. For youth, courses that used traditional approaches and lacked hands-on components had higher dropout rates. More innovative, cutting-edge approaches need to be developed (including available social media and information technologies) to increase youth's
interest in undertaking and completing training.

Source: di Villarosa 2015.

---

inclusion interventions to choose from, beyond PRONATEC. Another key to
effective coordination is to implement common processes and goals between
training, social assistance, and labor programs.[6]

Strengthening M&E Systems

Strengthening the M&E systems of urban productive inclusion programs would
be valuable to improve the focus on the programs' main objective: connecting
the poor to more and better jobs. Evaluations of training programs' and ALMPs'
impact on labor market insertion and earnings of the poor are lacking, as are
systems to regularly monitor these results and make them available to prospec-
tive beneficiaries. Existing systems focus on tracing the number of PRONATEC
slots, the number of microcredit operations conceded to Bolsa Família beneficiaries, and the number of microfirms belonging to Bolsa Família beneficiaries that
were formalized. Although these indicators are important to monitor operations
(inputs, activities, and outputs), they do not trace the programs' impact on labor
market insertion rates, beneficiaries' earnings, and achievement of targets for
hard-to-reach populations. The Ministry of Social Development and Fight
against Hunger has made substantial progress in strengthening and using education and labor administrative datasets to analyze the formal labor market insertion and map the educational trajectories of Bolsa Família beneficiaries. In
addition, the ministry added a productive inclusion module to the 2014 National
Sample Survey of Households (PNAD) and started a poverty panel survey in the
Northeast and South regions (interviewing the same families nine times over
three years to trace poverty over time). These powerful new tools could yield

additional evidence on outcomes. Evidence on programs' ultimate results can be used to guide program expansion. Given the complexities of productive inclusion interventions, it is key to have constant feedback and adjustment loops, based on M&E of final outcomes.

Adapting PRONATEC Content, Pedagogies, and Services

In spite of lower socioeconomic backgrounds, subsidized PRONATEC graduates who complete vocational training and find formal jobs have the same or better earnings increases than nonsubsidized students, but the share who find formal jobs is lower, calling for a stronger connection between PRONATEC and SINE. A background paper for this report compares subsidized PRONATEC trainees who found formal jobs with other "similar" formal workers (in terms of observable characteristics) who had not had subsidized training in a difference-in-differences estimation (Silva, Gukovas, and Caruso 2015).[7] The paper investigates the impact of vocational training (through the Sistema S network's National Service for Industrial Training [SENAI], which provides 80 percent of all PRONATEC's short-duration courses) on the wages of graduates and assesses heterogeneity across course modalities.[8] It also evaluates whether beneficiaries of subsidized PRONATEC training have lower returns and insertion in formal jobs than other students.

Using data from the Annual Social Information Report (RAIS) merged with trainee-level SENAI records, the paper finds that subsidized PRONATEC students who find formal jobs have higher earnings returns from training than do similar students whose training is not subsidized. In both cases, the returns vary by training modality—the difference between returns of subsidized and nonsubsidized students being greatest (about 3 percentage points) among those taking qualification courses (figure 5.2, panel a).[9] However, the paper also finds that, all other observable factors being equal (including gender, race, educational background, course duration, and modality), subsidized PRONATEC students have a lower probability of formal employment at three and six months after course completion (figure 5.2, panel b).

The large expansion of PRONATEC made it possible for a more vulnerable population to attend the courses, but that population generally has less work experience or formal education than the traditional young, skilled, or semiskilled TVET students (Silva, Gukovas, and Caruso 2015). Therefore, some PRONATEC courses need to be simplified or adapted. In particular, the design of course offerings and modalities needs to take trainee profiles into account. Specifically, soft-skills training can also be useful to older job seekers from disadvantaged backgrounds (see, for example, the Entra 21 program in 18 Latin American countries, the Jordan NOW program, and the Juventud y Empleo program in the Dominican Republic [McKenzie 2014]). In addition, the contents and course loads (hours required) of certain technical education modalities may need to be adjusted to accommodate the trainees' varying educational levels and life situations. Similarly, vocational training can be better adapted to trainees with low levels of schooling and

Figure 5.2 Vocational Training Effects on Subsidized/PRONATEC Graduates vs. Nonsubsidized Graduates in Brazil, 2007–12

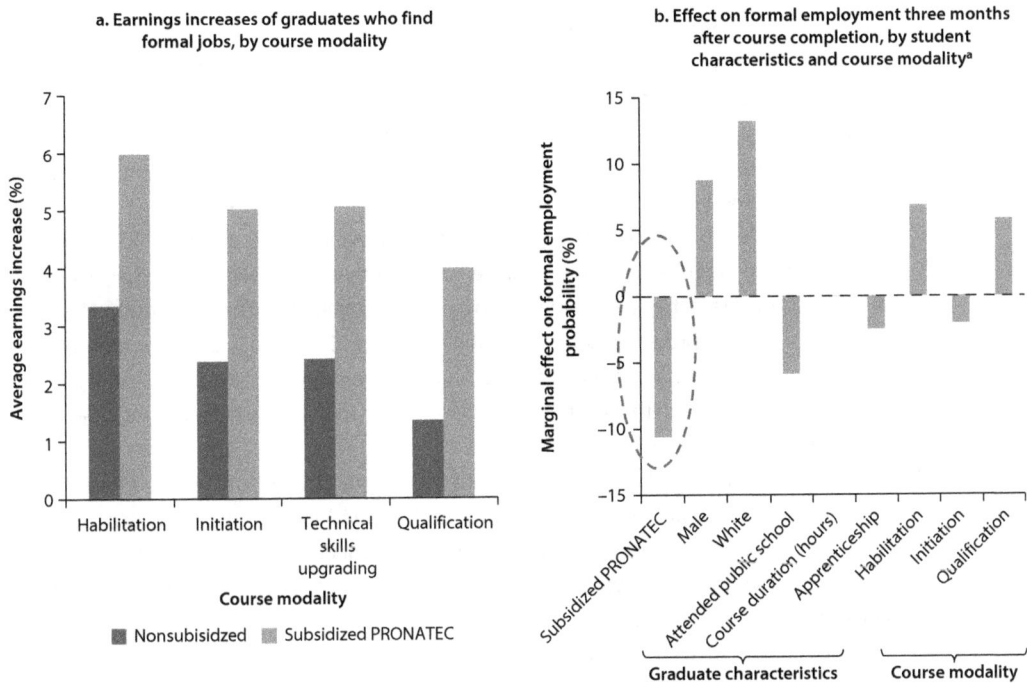

a. Earnings increases of graduates who find formal jobs, by course modality

b. Effect on formal employment three months after course completion, by student characteristics and course modality[a]

Source: Silva, Gukovas, and Caruso 2015.

Note: PRONATEC = National Program for Access to Technical Education and Employment. Estimates are derived from comparisons of subsidized PRONATEC trainees who found formal jobs with other comparable formal workers that had not had this type of training in a difference-in-differences estimation. Data from the Annual Social Information Report (RAIS) were merged with trainee-level records of the National Service for Industrial Training (SENAI). The results compare earnings and employment returns from training courses in four modalities: (a) habilitation (longer courses, averaging 1,200 hours, for current high school students or recent graduates); (b) qualification (shorter courses, averaging 200 hours, for workers and directed at building skills for particular jobs); (c) technical upgrading (for workers aimed at upgrading skills for a particular job); and (d) initiation (to prepare for low-complexity functions).

a. Figure shows the marginal effect of student characteristics and course modalities on the average probability of finding a formal job three months after course completion. The calculation assesses the probability associated with different characteristics of graduates in a regression context, including whether the trainee is a subsidized PRONATEC graduate or nonsubsidized. Course duration refers to the number of hours of training that students have to devote to complete the training.

scheduled to ensure an adequate supply of night courses. Dropout rates can be decreased and attendance improved by addressing nonclassroom barriers (such as lack of child care or transportation). Addressing the particular needs of women, youth, and other disadvantaged groups is also key and often involves expanding support to address employment barriers beyond technical skills (box 5.3).

Finally, Brazil can further improve PRONATEC's geographic equity by guiding its expansion into underserved areas with high poverty rates. A redistribution of PRONATEC training slots across municipalities and course subjects to correspond with low-skilled labor market supply and demand would better serve the urban poor. This could be achieved, first, by identifying the municipalities with large working-age populations registered in

Box 5.3 Adapting Training Programs to Vulnerable Urban Youth

Several Latin American and Caribbean countries have created a set of alternative training programs, typically targeted for vulnerable youth, commonly referred to as Jóvenes programs. Their key feature is a comprehensive package of training that goes beyond traditional technical and vocational training by including "soft skills" and life skills components as well as workplace experience. These programs are implemented by nongovernmental organizations and the private sector under government supervision.

Impact evaluations of Jóvenes-type programs in Argentina, Chile, the Dominican Republic, Peru, and Uruguay have produced positive results in terms of beneficiaries' chances of job placement as well as job quality as measured by salary, benefits, and formal contracts. However, the success of these programs depends on their design and the quality of the targeting mechanisms. Strong links between the programs and employers are central to ensuring that training remains relevant and that on-the-job experience through internships is an integral part of the training (Cunningham et al. 2008).

In Kenya, the Technical and Vocational Vouchers Program offered training vouchers to beneficiaries (UNESCO 2006). This program was implemented in 2008 with the recruitment of approximately 2,160 out-of-school youth (ages 18–30 years). The program evaluation showed that offering young adults vouchers that cover training costs does encourage enrollment (74 percent of participants who received vouchers enrolled in some type of vocational training, compared with less than 4 percent of those in the control group). Participation rates were higher among those who received unrestricted vouchers (79 percent versus 64 percent), which could be used for both public and private providers, and dropout rates among those who received restricted vouchers (only to be used with public providers) were higher (by 16 percentage points) (Hamory Hicks et al. 2011).

In Uganda, the Youth Opportunities Program (YOP) had a key successful feature: group-based support of entrepreneurship. Targeting poor unemployed or underemployed youth (ages 15–35 years), YOP offers a highly decentralized, community- and district-driven system of youth vocational training. It provides up to US$10,000 in grants to youth groups that submit proposals in which they identify a vocational skill of interest and a vocational training institute. Grants are used to enroll in the vocational training institute, purchase training materials, and equip graduates with the tools and start-up costs for practicing the trade after graduation. The program also includes components addressing conflict resolution. A randomized trial showed that groups that received community grants were almost four times more likely to participate in vocational training and twice as likely to be engaged in skilled work, improved their profits by 50 percent, and increased their savings by 20 percent compared with the control group. They were also more likely to engage in civic activities and less likely to engage in aggressive activities (especially men) (Blattman, Fiala, and Martinez 2011).

Sources: Cunningham et al. 2008; Blattman, Fiala, and Martinez 2011; Hamory Hicks et al. 2011.

Cadastro Único who need skills development but are not PRONATEC enrollees. Second, incentives must be created for PRONATEC expansion into those municipalities. Third, administrative data on the qualifications and experience of the Cadastro Único populations, by municipality, can help to identify the course subjects that would best increase the trainees' employability and earnings in specific municipalities.

Adapting SINE and Other ALMPs

As described in chapter 3, ALMPs include a diverse set of programs. In urban areas, their potential clients are a diverse group with varying labor market difficulties and therefore varying needs for support. As shown in the labor market profiles in chapter 1 (annex table 1A.1), most of the poor in the urban labor force are working, but their incomes are low: 25.8 percent of the urban workers are low-earning employees, and 16.8 percent are low-earning self-employed, and up to 7.2 percent are unemployed (based on IBGE 2013).[10] The heterogeneity of this segment implies that connecting the urban poor to better, more productive jobs requires diverse elements. Better results could therefore be achieved by tailoring ALMP services to the profiles of the poorest and aligning those services with the needs of local labor markets (including the favelas). By directly promoting labor market insertion, such policies could also be a stepping-stone for the success of all other skills and jobs programs, including PRONATEC.

The most disconnected or "hard-to-serve" individuals may need multidimensional support to improve employment outcomes, and other countries provide models for such support. As OECD experience has shown (box 5.4), public employment services and other ALMPs can better match poor job seekers with

---

Box 5.4 Adapting Employment Services to Beneficiaries' Needs through Profiling: Experience from Germany and the United Kingdom

Workers seek employment services for different reasons, and employment services show better results when they adapt their services to each beneficiary's needs and potential. The first step is to learn more about the beneficiary's job-relevant characteristics—a step called profiling. There are two main types of profiling: one based on beneficiary information gathered upon the first request for employment services, and the other based on self-selection through the length of the unemployment spell.

Germany

In Germany, customers are first profiled based on the intake interview when they request employment services. The interviewer assesses the customer's motivation to find a job; technical and social competencies; job aspirations; and any barriers to work such as housing, transportation, or family difficulties. Based on this interview and any relevant administrative data,

box continues next page

Box 5.4 Adapting Employment Services to Beneficiaries' Needs through Profiling: Experience from Germany and the United Kingdom *(continued)*

the customer is classified into one of four groups: activation customers, counseling customers, market customers, or support customers. Different groups receive different services:

- *Support customers*, for example, are motivated to work but lack technical skills, so they are referred to training centers.
- *Activation customers* have low training needs but need to increase their motivation or commitment.
- *Market customers*, being both highly motivated and highly skilled, can be covered by for-profit employment service providers.
- *Counseling customers*, on the other hand, have both high activation and high training needs and thus are referred for further profiling to better assess the support they should receive.

United Kingdom

In the United Kingdom, profiling also takes the length of the unemployment spell into account. The main idea is to offer progressively more intense employment services to customers who need them more—determining who needs them more according to the time they spend looking for a job. After being profiled, a customer is then referred to one of three types of support:

- *Self-services.* Self-services have two modalities: Internet searches and supported self-services at the job centers (local public employment services with advisors and employment counselors), which include individual job-seeking advice, training on résumé writing, and participation in job clubs.
- *Personal services.* Personal services at the local employment offices have three modalities: (a) employment counseling, including interviews, action plans, referrals to other ALMPs, and access to about 1,800 employment counselors and specialized counselors for youth and immigrants; (b) vocational rehabilitation for disabled people, provided by special employment counselors and psychologists; and (c) career guidance by psychologists.
- *Individual counseling.* Finally, some beneficiaries are referred to individual multiprofessional counseling at the labor service centers by psychologists and employment counselors who cooperate with the municipal social and health care specialists. Since the beginning of the client's interaction with PES, the client is seen as someone to whom the service to be provided is job placement; that is the focus, not just registering him or her.

Source: Marra et al. 2015.

labor market demands while providing them with more-complete services through the following approaches:

- *Profiling.* Job seekers' interaction with PES (in Brazil, SINE) begins with multidimensional profiling and subsequent direction to services depending on their individual profiles and labor market challenges.
- *Tailored case management.* Individual case management approaches focus on the "hard-to-serve."

- *Caseworker targets and incentives.* Employability and earnings-increase targets can be set as the basis for caseworker incentives to place the hard-to-serve and additional incentives for placements remaining active for at least three or six months.
- *Tailored training and support components.* Poor job seekers benefit from the introduction of new types of support: soft-skills training (such as résumé preparation), on-the-job training or internships, and information on social services for dependents (such as child care).

Adapting Agriculture and Rural Development Programs to the Needs of the Poor

Rural employment is concentrated in low-productivity (family) agriculture, as chapter 1 discussed in detail. Hence, the rural productive inclusion model's current strategic focus on maximizing the earnings potential of family agriculture businesses is the right one, reaching many of the rural poor. Moreover, because the vast majority of workers in family agriculture are poor, improving the productivity of jobs in this sector is a pro-poor policy. Finally, rural areas face climatic, environmental, and other constraints that are not present in urban areas, that limit the possible expansion of rural labor markets, and that make rural workers' earnings more seasonal and volatile. Hence, rural areas need productive inclusion efforts that differ from those in urban areas.

A related question is whether rural productive inclusion programs that focus on family agriculture are effective. To answer this question, it is critical to have M&E systems that track the postprogram returns to beneficiaries' earnings increases and business survival. Therefore, the lack of M&E systems for rural productive inclusion programs poses an important constraint on program expansion and quality improvement. This is particularly important for productive inclusion—a program area that Brazil has pioneered.

International experience shows that some agriculture and rural development programs work better than others for the poor. Particularly, interventions that seek to improve yields or farm income by addressing market-linkage failures, easing access to technologically enhanced inputs, and promoting farmer knowledge through advisory services have the highest share of positive impacts (IEG 2011). In contrast, interventions that seek to enhance land quality—focusing mostly on improving soil conditions—tend to have the lowest reported rate of success. Although microfinance interventions exhibited mixed results on their own, credit was an important complement to the success of interventions or components in value-chain and input-access interventions (IEG 2011). However, evidence is lacking concerning which types of support are most effective for the targeted population (for example, benchmarking technical assistance versus other types of interventions) or which interventions work better in each setting or for each type of beneficiary profile.

Establishing M&E Systems

Expansion of rural productive inclusion programs has not been accompanied by establishment of corresponding M&E systems to track the programs' quality and efficiency and thus to ensure their relevance to the evolving needs of the poor. Currently, each individual agricultural and rural development program whose coverage was expanded under the Brasil Sem Miséria Plan's rural productive inclusion axis has a registry of beneficiaries (poor and nonpoor), and information is collected for each of the various institutions; no integrated system exists. Beyond maintaining the program registry, monitoring for each individual program is limited. Information is available on the number of families supported, including the share of Bolsa Família beneficiaries. However, performance indicators focus on inputs and processes rather than on labor market outcomes—such as the programs' effects on beneficiaries' earnings and survival rates of the supported businesses—or on disaggregation of beneficiaries by gender, age, and experience.

An integrated M&E system for rural productive inclusion programs could be instrumental in the government's efforts to promote an integrated strategy, avoid program overlaps, foster coordination between programs, and increase labor market outcomes among poor beneficiaries. Moving forward, expanding rural productive inclusion programs will require trade-offs—for example, a choice between (a) expanding all three types of support (microcredit, technical assistance, and improved access to markets) to current beneficiary families, or (b) increasing coverage of one or more types of support to more families. Information on which type of support is more effective in each context could improve the programs' efficiency by informing program expansion.

This type of evidence-based expansion of programs and design adjustment can substantially increase their effectiveness, and the success of these efforts depends on establishing a strong M&E system to evaluate their results. However, such an M&E system needs to take into account that rural productive inclusion programs are locally implemented and that the capacity of rural municipalities can be quite limited. Hence, the system should also be as streamlined as possible and, importantly, geared toward supporting municipalities in the M&E process by including capacity building in its implementation as well as incentives designed for municipalities to incorporate M&E into their day-to-day operations.

Introducing Profiling of Family Farmers and Using the Information to Target and Tailor Support

To increase the efficiency and sustainability of the integrated model of rural development and social assistance, programs can target beneficiaries based on detailed profiles that include farmers' previous experience in the types of activities promoted by the program and their results. Using the profiles to decide how to best allocate support could decrease costs and improve results. This information can also be used to better tailor program support to the profile of the poor.

Continuing to Encourage Use of Cadastro Único to Target Coverage Expansion

The strategic use of the Cadastro Único can more effectively target coverage expansion of rural development and agricultural programs among the poor. By building on the successful coordination of information thus far across the administrative records of agriculture, rural development, and social assistance programs, rural production inclusion programs can now target beneficiaries more extensively by incorporating information from new types of programs. In conjunction, continuing to promote the use of Cadastro Único to target rural development programs is key.

Diversify Support Aimed at Enhancing Access to Markets

Brazil can also increase the productive inclusion model's efficiency and sustainability by enhancing agricultural extension services to orient farmers toward market opportunities and better adapting rural credit programs to farmers' needs. Market access could be supported beyond the calls for public procurement for national feeding programs. These calls need to be announced and detailed with sufficient time for producers to make investment decisions, get required certification, and adapt to fulfill the sanitary standards. Furthermore, the comercialização (commercialization) effort requires reform of extension services to ensure better market orientation and more focus on business skills development, licensing, and so forth, taking into account the challenges faced by small family farmers who are predominantly poor and lacking in education. In this regard, it is important to ensure competitive selection of extension service providers and delivery of business development technical assistance in addition to technologies for increased productivity.

Promote Private Sector Partnerships

A key element in promoting innovation is to further promote private sector partnerships. Such partnerships (including with the financial sector) can improve the rural poor's access to credit, technology, and other productivity-enhancing innovations. Services provided by existing organizations (such as SEBRAE, which provides a range of support to small agribusinesses) could also be better linked under the productive inclusion umbrella.

Adapting and Improving Access to Rural Entrepreneurship and Training Programs to Promote Productivity of Those Moving to Nonagricultural Jobs

Support for family agriculture is fundamental to improve the livelihoods and earnings of many of the rural poor, but escaping poverty for many will mean moving into nonagricultural activities. In light of Brazil's ongoing structural transformation (shifting to nonfarm employment), an essential step toward productive inclusion will be to increase rural residents' labor productivity and skills to better equip them for nonfarm jobs. For such rural residents, employability depends on improving their skills to equip them for better jobs and on the viability of their businesses though entrepreneurship support programs. This new direction for rural productive inclusion would require diversification of support beyond the current integrated model for family agriculture, including adapted and improved access to rural entrepreneurship (microenterprise) programs and expanded access to hands-on, community-based training and skills certification, while improved educational foundations can give the extra push (discussed in detail in chapters 2 and 4).

Training and entrepreneurship programs tailored to the rural poor could increase both agricultural and nonagricultural opportunities and earnings. Expansion to rural areas of hands-on, community-based training and skills certification could incorporate linkages to on- and off-farm work experience programs (such as on demonstration farms or at processing units). Expanding the availability of distance learning networks would also strengthen training opportunities, especially for rural youth. Finally, to support microenterprises, a rural credit market analysis could identify market failures and thus increase rural access to entrepreneurship support programs promoted by the Ministry of Labor and Employment or by the state secretaries.

In this regard, many other countries have implemented various innovative training modalities in both rural and urban areas. Vocational training ideally facilitates transitions into more productive employment. In particular, African countries provide several examples of vocational training for the rural poor, mobilizing communities and youth in innovative ways that Brazil could consider in its own program design and implementation (box 5.5).

Box 5.5 Innovative Training Programs for the Most Vulnerable in Rural Areas

Ethiopia's community-based Poverty Reduction and Capacity Building through Livelihood Skills Training Program (EXPRO) combines literacy, soft-skills, and entrepreneurial skills training. Launched in 2000, the program targets adults and out-of-school youth who never completed their formal education, especially in extremely poor rural areas. A collaboration of the Ministry of Education, regional education bureaus, and local TVET commissions, EXPRO trains about 2,000 people annually. The participants undergo intensive training in a trade (such as tailoring, woodworking, tire repair, food preparation, or animal husbandry) at local community centers or vocational education centers for an average of three months; sometimes the training includes a literacy component. The program has attracted more females than males, and some training centers generate their own funding by selling milk or items such as furniture made by former trainees to schools or offices. Although no data exist to evaluate EXPRO's impact on the trainees' employment, trainees have anecdotally reported improvement in their qualifications and motivation to engage in income-generating activities (Sandhaas 2005).

In Uganda, a nongovernmental organization (Uganda Youth Development Link, UYDEL) implemented the Non-Formal Education and Livelihood Skills Training Program (NFELSTP) from 2004 to 2009, with financial and technical support from the United Nations Educational, Scientific and Cultural Organization (UNESCO). Targeting out-of-school and socioeconomically

box continues next page

Box 5.5 Innovative Training Programs for the Most Vulnerable in Rural Areas *(continued)*

vulnerable youth from marginalized rural and urban slums in the Arua and Kampala districts, respectively, NFELSTP focused on practical skills in specific trades including hairdressing, tailoring, motor mechanics, carpentry, electronics, welding, and cookery. It also offered life skills training, focusing on human immunodeficiency virus and acquired immune deficiency syndrome (HIV/AIDS), reproductive health, nutrition, and drug and alcohol abuse. NFELSTP recruited facilitators for community mobilization, coordination, program monitoring, and recruiting of local skilled practitioners in the vocational trades, who acted as teachers and mentors. The program served 184 youth between 2004 and 2006, most of them female. Program dropouts thought it was not addressing their immediate survival challenges (UNESCO 2006), but those who completed the program found gainful employment and had improved self-perception.

Sources: Sandhaas 2005; UNESCO 2006.

Notes

1. Cadastro Único (Single Registry) is the Brazilian federal government's database that identifies and characterizes low-income households (including income, family composition, location, and other information) to provide data that social programs use to select new beneficiaries.

2. PRONATEC is an umbrella program coordinating a variety of existing and new vocational education and training policies, including courses in two modalities: Technical Education (TEC) and Initial and Continuing Training Programs (FIC). Under this program, the Ministry of Education has established partnerships with several other ministries (including Social Development, Tourism, and Communication) to identify and select potential trainees for technical courses.

3. The National Service for Apprenticeship, more commonly referred to as Sistema S, was created in the 1940s and includes different institutions, managed by industry consortia (in manufacturing, commerce, rural sector, agriculture, transport, and cooperatives), that manage vocational training.

4. Public procurement refers to "compras públicas," consisting of government quotas for public contracts to supply school and prison canteens to promote demand for family farm production.

5. PRONATEC-MDS (Ministry of Social Development) focuses on reaching poor and disadvantaged populations. Under PRONATEC-MDS, 40 percent of all PRONATEC training slots are targeted to the poor.

6. As a first next step, all PRONATEC beneficiaries could be automatically registered in SINE and profiled so they can be referred to any other ALMPs that may better fulfill their needs.

7. The difference-in-differences estimation compiles for the same worker the change in earnings between, before, and after the training and compares it to that of similar worker who did not receive training.

8. PRONATEC's FIC courses are generally for the current workforce, consisting of short-duration vocational training and aiming to improve workers' qualification by upgrading their skills. Its TEC courses are generally considered preemployment technical

education, have longer duration, and offer upward permeability with the education system.

9. PRONATEC courses cover four main training modalities: (a) habilitation (longer courses, averaging 1,200 hours, for current high school students or recent graduates); (b) qualification (shorter courses, averaging 200 hours, for workers and directed at building skills for particular jobs); (c) technical upgrading (for workers aimed at upgrading skills for a particular jobs); and (d) initiation (to prepare for low-complexity functions).

10. "Low-earning" is defined as earnings below the poverty line of R$140 (US$47.60) per month per person.

References

Almeida, Rita, Jere Behrman, and David Robalino, eds. 2012. *The Right Skills for the Job? Rethinking Training Policies for Workers.* Human Development Perspectives Series. Washington, DC: World Bank.

Blattman, Christopher, Nathan Fiala, and Sebastian Martinez. 2011. "Can Employment Programs Reduce Poverty and Social Instability? Experimental Evidence from a Ugandan Aid Program." Social Protection & Labor Discussion Paper, World Bank, Washington, DC.

Brazil, Ministry of Labor and Employment. 2014. "Employment Plan 2014—Brazil." Ministry of Labor and Employment, Brasília. https://g20.org/wp-content /uploads/2014/12/g20_employment_plan_brazil.pdf.

Brazil, Ministry of Social Development and Fight against Hunger (MDS). 2013. *Plano Brasil Sem Miséria/Brazil Without Extreme Poverty Plan: Two Years of Results.* Progress report, MDS, Brasília.

————. 2014. *O Brasil Sem Miséria (Brazil Without Extreme Poverty).* Organized by Tereza Campello, Tiago Falcão, and Patricia Vieira da Costa. Brasília: MDS.

Corseuil, Carlos Henrique L., Marcelo C. Neri, and Gabriel L. Ulyssea. 2013. "Uma análise exploratória dos efeitos da política de formalização dos Microempreendedores Individuais." [An Exploratory Analysis of Formalization Policy Effects of Individual Microentrepreneurs.] *Mercado de trabalho* 18 (54): 31–41.

Cunningham, Wendy, Linda McGinnis, Rodrigo García Verdú, Cornelia Tesliuc, and Dorte Verner. 2008. *Youth at Risk in Latin America and the Caribbean: Understanding the Causes, Realizing the Potential.* Directions in Development Series. Washington, DC: World Bank.

di Villarosa, Francesco. 2015. *Favela Pilot Study on Productive Inclusion.* Policy report— background paper for this report, World Bank, Washington, DC.

Hamory Hicks, Joan, Michael Kremer, Isaac Mbiti, and Edward Miguel. 2011. *Vocational Education Voucher Delivery and Labor Market Returns: A Randomized Evaluation among Kenyan Youth.* Report for Spanish Impact Evaluation Fund (SIEF) Phase II World Bank, Washington, DC.

IBGE (Brazilian Institute of Geography and Statistics). 2013. *National Sample Survey of Households (Pesquisa Nacional por Amostra de Domicílio, PNAD).* Rio de Janeiro: IBGE.

IEG (Independent Evaluation Group). 2011. *Impact Evaluations in Agriculture: An Assessment of the Evidence.* Washington, DC: World Bank.

Marra, Karla, Jociany Luz, Joana Silva, and Renata Gukovas. 2015. *Mapping of the Current Network of Active Labor Market Programs (ALMPs)*. Policy report—background paper for this report, World Bank, Washington, DC.

McKenzie, David. 2014. "Hard Measurement of Soft Skills." *Development Impact* (blog), June 2, World Bank, Washington, DC. http://blogs.worldbank.org/impactevaluations /hard-measurement-soft-skills.

OECD (Organisation for Economic Co-operation and Development). 2007. *OECD Employment Outlook 2007*. Paris: OECD.

Sandhaas, Bernd. 2005. "Poverty Reduction and Capacity Building through Livelihood Skill Training at CSTCs and VTCs: The EXPRO in Ethiopia." DVV International: Addis Ababa, Ethiopia.

Silva, Joana, Renata Gukovas, and Luiz Caruso. 2015. "The Wage Returns and Employability of Vocational Training in Brazil: Evidence from Matched Provider-Employer Administrative Data." Research paper—background paper for this report, World Bank, Washington, DC.

UNESCO (United Nations Educational, Scientific and Cultural Organization). 2006. *Non-Formal Education and Livelihood Skills for Marginalized Street and Slum Youth in Uganda*. Uganda Youth Development Link project report, UNESCO, Kampala, Uganda.

World Bank. 2010. "Moving Out of Poverty in Northeast Brazil." International Bank for Reconstruction and Development (IBRD) Results Brief 91659, World Bank, Washington, DC.

Environmental Benefits Statement

The World Bank Group is committed to reducing its environmental footprint. In support of this commitment, the Publishing and Knowledge Division leverages electronic publishing options and print-on-demand technology, which is located in regional hubs worldwide. Together, these initiatives enable print runs to be lowered and shipping distances decreased, resulting in reduced paper consumption, chemical use, greenhouse gas emissions, and waste.

The Publishing and Knowledge Division follows the recommended standards for paper use set by the Green Press Initiative. Whenever possible, books are printed on 50 percent to 100 percent postconsumer recycled paper, and at least 50 percent of the fiber in our book paper is either unbleached or bleached using Totally Chlorine Free (TCF), Processed Chlorine Free (PCF), or Enhanced Elemental Chlorine Free (EECF) processes.

More information about the Bank's environmental philosophy can be found at http://crinfo.worldbank.org/wbcrinfo/node/4.

green press
INITIATIVE

www.ingramcontent.com/pod-product-compliance
Lightning Source LLC
Chambersburg PA
CBHW080423270326
41929CB00018B/3145

9 781464 806445